A PSYCHOLOGY *of*
BODY, SOUL, & SPIRIT

A PSYCHOLOGY *of* BODY, SOUL, & SPIRIT

Anthroposophy, Psychosophy, & Pneumatosophy

Rudolf Steiner

Twelve Lectures

BERLIN

October 23–27, 1909
November 1–4, 1910
December 12–16, 1911

Translated by Marjorie Spock

& ANTHROPOSOPHIC PRESS

The lectures in this book are a translation of *Anthroposophie, Psychosophie, Pneumatosophie* (GA 115), published by Rudolf Steiner Verlag, Dornach, Switzerland, 1980.

© Copyright Anthroposophic Press, 1999
Introduction © copyright Robert Sardello, 1999

Published in the United States by Anthroposophic Press

Library of Congress Cataloging-in-Publication Data

Steiner, Rudolf, 1861–1925.
    [Anthroposophie, Psychosophie, Pneumatosophie. English]
    A psychology of body, soul & spirit : anthroposophy,
psychosophy & pneumatosophy : twelve lectures given in Berlin,
October 23–27, 1909, November 1–4, 1910, December 12–16,
1911 / Rudolf Steiner.
        p. cm.
    Includes bibliographical references and index.
    ISBN 0-88010-397-3 (paper)
    1. Anthroposophy.   2. Soul.   I. Title.   I. Title: Psychology of
body, soul, and spirit.
    BP595.S894A5913   1999
    299'.935--dc21   99–11939
                                                             CIP

Contents

Introduction by Robert Sardello   vii

I.
"Anthroposophy"
OCTOBER 23–27, 1909

1. The Human Being and the Senses   *3*
2. Supersensible Processes in the Human Senses   *21*
3. The Higher Senses, Inner Forces, and Creative Principles in the Human Organism   *34*
4. Supersensible Currents, Group Soul, and the I in Human Beings and Animals   *54*

II.
"Psychosophy"
NOVEMBER 1–4, 1910

1. Aspects of Soul Life   *77*
2. The Activities of Human Soul Forces   *93*
3. The Senses, Feeling, and Aesthetic Judging   *109*
4. Consciousness and Soul Life   *130*

III.

"Pneumatosophy"

DECEMBER 12–16, 1911

1. Franz Brentano and Aristotle's Doctrine of the Spirit *157*

2. Truth and Error in Light of the Spiritual World *170*

3. *Imagination*–Imagination; *Inspiration*–Self-Fulfillment; *Intuition*–Conscience *188*

4. Nature, the Evolution of Consciousness, and Reincarnation *207*

Further Reading *223*

Index *225*

Introduction

by Robert Sardello

On the Focus of this Introductory Guide

This series of twelve lectures by Rudolf Steiner provides a basis for an entirely new psychology.

The first four lectures (on "Anthroposophy") provide a precise, dynamic understanding of the human soul in relation to the activity of sensing and to the subtle processes that structure and form the human body.

The next four lectures (on "Psychosophy") focus on what we can know of the human soul on the basis of direct observation alone. No theorizing takes place; no special faculties are employed. Steiner was a disciplined clairvoyant but here he seeks to show what can be known of soul life through the immediacy of engaged observation of oneself and others. Therefore he refrains here from using his higher capacities, relying only on unmediated observation to form a picture of the activity of soul life. The particular nature of this kind of unmediated observation is important and will be addressed in this introduction.

Finally, the concluding lectures (on "Pneumatosophy") portray the relationship of soul life to spirit life, particularly with regard to how to awaken individual spirit life and how to distinguish between illusory and genuine spiritual experiences.

Although the content of these lectures ranges far beyond the usual subject matter of ordinary psychology, it is here perhaps more than anywhere else in Rudolf Steiner's work that the foundations of a psychology rooted in anthroposophy may be found. This is especially true of the middle set of lectures on "Psychosophy." These not only exemplify the content that any true psychology must encounter and struggle with when it tries to understand the life of the soul, but also illustrate a specifically *psychological* mode of thinking. Deep study of these lectures will result in ways of understanding soul life that one will not find expressed anywhere else in the whole discipline of psychology. More than that, anyone who works carefully with these lectures will find that the beginning of an increasingly conscious soul life becomes possible.

I suggest that readers start by reading the four "Psychosophy" lectures. This allows one to begin by concentrating on what is most important for psychology—a psychological point of view. One can then move on to the four "Pneumatosophy" lectures to see what might, from this point of view, constitute "a psychology of spirit." Finally, turning to the opening four "Anthroposophy" lectures, one can then read those with a view to discovering what might constitute "a psychology of body." This introductory guide follows that order.

(If you choose to read the text straight through, a different and perhaps equally important imagination develops. First, in the "anthroposophy" lectures, a picture of the whole human being unfolds from an inner standpoint. This leads into a deep consideration of the life of the soul: "psychosophy."And then in the last section, we see how soul life can be employed to perceive specifically spiritual realms: "pneumatosophy." My attempt here, however, will be to try to free the psychology implicit in the text and thereby begin to make explicit at least the foundations of a spiritual psychology. For this purpose, I shall follow the order suggested above.)

The lectures took place over a period of three years, from 1909 to 1911, almost a century ago. One might be tempted to think that whatever they have to say about psychology must be dated, and that if it is relevant to the field of psychology at all, it must be only to its history or early development. It is also tempting to think that, since Rudolf Steiner is not usually regarded as one of the founders of modern psychology, his efforts in this direction must be considered, at most, an interesting aside. But a very good argument can be made that these lectures are, in fact, a wellspring for the true stream of psychology, and that all that presently passes as psychology are but wandering tributaries.

I repeat: these lectures form a new foundation for psychology. I say this because the view of the soul presented here has a wider, fuller, deeper, and higher context than is present in any existing psychology. Steiner presents a context for considering individual soul life that includes the forces that actively form the human body and extends to the interplay of the living body with the surrounding world. These relationships are in turn embraced by the ongoing creative and dynamic activity of the cosmos, which is not here considered in the abstract but as consisting of regions of spirit beings. Furthermore, these realms and their interrelationships are considered in terms of their inner form and activity. This context itself forms the field, the enterprise, of anthroposophy, begun by Rudolf Steiner. Something of the nature and perspective of this context, that is, of "anthroposophy," is presented in the first lecture.

My introduction will not compare what Steiner presents with all or even with several other schools of psychology. To do so would lead us far away from the text instead of into it. I mention Steiner's relation to the field of psychology only to alert readers who approach this work from a background of the psychological disciplines to its contemporary importance. This book is not just another psychology to be put alongside all the others. Rather, it presents a possible future for the discipline as a whole.

Anthroposophy and Psychology

A Psychology of Body, Soul, and Spirit may be read not only by those with an interest in psychology but also by those with an interest in further developing the practice of anthroposophy. If the text is really worked with, the way one reads and studies any of Steiner's other works will be radically transformed. At the same time, the very practice of any aspect of anthroposophy will also develop in new ways. Whether one's field is education, medicine, art, drama, eurythmy, economy, or business—no matter what practical form one's spiritual work assumes—the perspective this book offers has the potential to restore the often missing soul element. Because this element is often lacking in anthroposophical work, much of the good that anthroposophical enterprises could bring into the world is unfortunately undermined by the dysfunctional soul life of those involved. The horror stories of those who have been subjected to the "help" of less than healthy anthroposophists could fill several volumes, and probably should be documented.

The soul element in anthroposophical work is often said to reside in artistic endeavors—painting, music, eurythmy, and so on. This point of view is true, however, only insofar as the artistic work is done from a real, conscious presence to the actual processes involved in soul life and does not merely follow formulas for what a particular color, movement, or tone does in the soul. Soul life is certainly not limited only to artistic work, and formalized soul must be understood as something quite different from living soul.

Attempts to develop a spiritual life without developing a consciousness of the fullness, depth, and *particularity* of soul life—which must be entered into not just as preliminary to something else, but as an ongoing task—typically result in living the abstract ideas of spirituality, not its actuality. The instances of abuse wrought by such ignorance, regardless of the spiritual or religious practices involved, are well known. What makes anthroposophy unique, however, is that Steiner *did not* bypass the soul realm and shoot directly for the spirit. The decided lack of soul knowledge and soul work within anthroposophy cannot be attributed to an oversight by its founder. From this point of view, even though this particular series of lectures occurred fairly early in the corpus of anthroposophy, it may well be the most central work, not only to read, but to take seriously as the foundation for a true renewal of the anthroposophical movement.

When this book is read—deeply read—it is impossible to come away from that encounter without realizing that the modern initiatory path of anthroposophy is a *spiritual-psychological* endeavor. This realization means that the whole of anthroposophy must be studied and practiced in a spiritual-psychological manner. By coupling the terms *spiritual* and *psychological,* I mean to convey the possibility of a spirituality practiced out of a deep, abiding, and very particular, rather than general, awareness of one's soul life.

Spiritual practice carried out without the accompanying presence of soul life results in a spirituality that has no "inside" and no depth. Such a spirituality lacks the mark of having encountered, struggled with, gone through, and deeply loved the qualities of soul life as described by Steiner: mindfulness, deep memory, emotion, feeling, beauty, joy, pleasure, inner conflict and tension, vulnerability, loss of control, and even all the more difficult sidetracks these qualities can lead one into. Such qualities, of course, must also be addressed when speaking of spirituality. Experience shows, however, that if these qualities are approached without a deep sense of soul interiority, the ensuing spiritual practices become manic, carry a huge shadow, tend toward dogmatism, and tend to exclude precisely those who might dare to bring this vital, interior dimension to their spiritual work.

Soul Life as the Subject Matter of Psychology

Soul life, as Steiner shows vividly in the four lectures entitled "Psychosophy" (the "wisdom of the soul"), humbles us, because we do not, and cannot, control it. Could anything restrain us more from controlling others than the realization that our own soul life largely controls us and that we have plenty to do to learn to submit to the wisdom of the soul? And what greater deviation from soul life could there be than to think that, from some imagined superior spiritual position, it is our duty to control others?

Steiner indicates why we are unable to control our own soul life and why, instead of trying to control it, we must come to know and follow its ways. The reasons have to do with the origin of soul life itself, and as well with the ongoing content of soul experience. Steiner describes the origin of soul experience as the life of desire. Wisely, he does not define desire, just as he does not define soul. Rather, he points out that desire does not originate within the soul but within the world. Elsewhere, he refers in passing to a second origin of desire: "Boredom causes desire in the soul. It gives birth to a longing for impressions, and the soul life is surrendered to it, yet there is nothing to satisfy that desire." In another place, he speaks of yet another way of considering desire—as the astral, future-time current flowing into the soul. More will be said of this current.

The flow of desire shows up as the most basic polar continuum of forces within the soul—the dramatic, conflicting forces of love and hate. Desire, we could say, expresses itself as the urge toward unity, sought either through the bridging of differences through love or the annihilation of differences through hate. Such differences exist both within ourselves and in our relationships with others. Desire, which may be understood as the deepest unsatisfied longing imaginable—a longing with no object—and its bifurcation into a tension of the opposites of love and hate, gives the soul its dramatic character, and constitutes a built-in urgency toward development—provided, of course, that one remains present to the tensions of inner life.

Because we are so steeped in the pop culture of psychology, which maintains that anyone at all can understand psychology without undergoing a rigorous inner training, such key words may easily be misunderstood. These key words—*desire, love,* and *hate*—do not have the sense and meaning for psychology that they do for ordinary experience. First, they must be understood within the context of the whole life of the soul as described by Steiner. They have little to do with a subjective senses of desire, love, or hate. The desire, the love, and the hate spoken of here are autonomous, inner, dynamic qualities; they do not refer directly to what our habitual "ego" might desire, love, or hate. Even the word *inner* has to be qualified, for it does not mean "subjective," nor does it mean "personal." *Inner* must be understood in a much more metaphorical way, as the dimension that gives life experiences the quality of intimate engagement rather than of a mere string of events.

A constant confusion, present in the very heart of the discipline of psychology, has to do with the assumption that psychology is concerned with the personality and that when we do psychology we are concerned with what goes on "inside" a person. Before psychology even starts, therefore, "interiority," the necessary *standpoint* for the discipline of psychology, is converted into the idea of literal things going on inside people. In other words, we consider a person's "psychology" without ever having developed a truly psychological mode of thinking about soul life itself. Psychology is usually practiced out of the same mode of consciousness we live in everyday life. However, when Steiner speaks of the soul, of desire, of love and hate, he is not speaking of something going on subjectively in some imaginary "everyone." He is speaking of the soul *from the place of soul*—which is the only true and valid subject matter of psychology. In order to understand this book as a whole, then, it is necessary to realize—and to realize deeply—that what is being discussed as "soul" is not an entity of any type, not even an invisible entity. Nor does what is being discussed have to do with some literal content of a supposed invisible entity. When Steiner speaks of "soul" he is speaking a language of *form*. Let me try to express more fully what I mean by "form."

When Steiner describes the inner quality of soul life as a "love-hate tension," this cannot be understood positivistically, as though, somewhere within us, a subjective experience of a tension occurs, or a constant conflict between wanting to love and wanting to hate someone or something. Such an understanding turns the language of form or process into a language of content or stuff. In the language of form, words are used, in order, through words, *to go beyond words*. The polarity serves to awaken the thought-quality that soul is not some kind of container but rather an inner, dynamic, mobile, developing, regressing, conflictual, flowing, relationship. A relationship with what? The soul is "in relation" with desire, with the body, with the spirit—none of which, incidentally, can themselves be considered to utilize the language of content without degrading what they are about.

A reader might well ask why this text is so difficult to read. It is difficult because it is not presented out of ordinary consciousness. But neither is it presented out of clairvoyant consciousness. Instead, it arises out of *soul-consciousness*. The lectures on soul life are certainly given to us from soul-consciousness, and to do psychology we must be able to enter soul-consciousness. Otherwise, we are really not doing psychology at all, but only talking about psychology from the safety of ordinary consciousness. The text is not presented from the viewpoint of Steiner's ego-personality. In fact, it is impossible to do psychology from the viewpoint of ego-personality, although most psychology tries to do just that. Therefore, nearly all psychology is in fact pathological. It is pathological because its very language prohibits entry to the life of the soul.

A Psychology of Body, Soul, and Spirit does not operate within the popular deception that makes many people go looking for the "archetypes within," their "inner child," their "true self," and all the rest. You must understand that the work you are about to read, in being true to soul, puts a deterrent before us: it cannot be understood simplistically or easily. This deterrent, however, is at the same time a doorway through which we may awaken to soul life. Psychology, as practiced in this text, forms an integral part of the work of initiation. All psychology ought to do the same, but it has sold its soul.

Something else brings home my point about the way to approach this work. This has to do with the second intrinsic aspect of soul life described by Steiner. Steiner calls this quality of soul life "judgment." He also says that his meaning of this term must be understood in a "verb" rather than a "noun" sense—*judging* rather than *judgment*. He then further qualifies the term by saying that he is referring to something like "reflection," "mirroring," "pondering," or "mulling over." Thus, what initially seems to be a kind of content, or cognitive act in its concluding stages, is in fact much more subtle. Here the word *judgment* refers, really, to the momentary, provisional end-points of a qualitative, always, at every moment, ongoing soul process. Only in this latter sense does judgment belong to soul life. The word *judgment* generally carries the notion of something that has already happened, a conclusion that has been reached, but in the context of describing the most basic qualities of ongoing soul life, it would be quite incorrect to understand "judgement" in this sense. Even if we add the qualifiers (reflection, mirroring, pondering, mulling over) we still risk making the error of understanding these terms in the everyday sense as something we *do*. We think about things, ponder them, mull them over. The soul's engagement in such activity connotes something different.

You will notice—at specific places in the text, but really in the book as a whole—that words are used to describe soul life, while at the same time these very words seem to have to be erased. For example, *judgment* connotes one thing: an attempt to reach a final conclusion. But, as soon as you think you understand that concept, the term is reintroduced, but is now said to mean "mulling over." "Mulling over" doesn't really go anywhere, except over the same territory again and again. So, what kind of soul quality is being described? It is a quality that can be imagined as a kind of intensive experiencing—living experience, not having experience. Soul experience is something like the reintensifying of what we encounter in inner and outer ways. Such reintensification

never comes to a conclusion, not in soul life. There are provisional conclusions, and these are what we experience as mental images. The soul
quality described as "judging" can be understood to mean that we
relive our life at the same time as we are living it. And this reliving,
which happens simultaneously with living, consists of the upsurge of
personal and even collective past, of waves of emotion, feeling, attention, memory, desire, even past lives, and many other qualities that
qualify any moment as not something just gone through, but gone
through with multileveled meaning.

Once we understand the term *judging* in this way, it becomes clear
why Steiner says that not all experience is soul experience. We may, for
example, perceive a rose, but that experience is not necessarily a soul
experience. Only when it is relived—not necessarily after the fact, but at
the moment it occurs—is the experience a soul experience. Such reliving, contemporaneous with living, describes a basic function of soul life.
Soul life gives interiority to experience.

Psychology as Psychological Thinking

What is the nature, or method, of observation employed by Steiner to
come to this understanding of soul life? This is an important question to
carry with us while reading and studying this book, particularly the section concerned specifically with soul life. Steiner does not give any
direct indication of his method. He says only that "*psychosophy* is to be
a deliberation on the human soul." He then goes on to tell us what will
be considered. Or, he says, "What is soul life when we contemplate it as
such, within the limits just spoken of?" Not much to go on; we must
consider the text as a whole.

Steiner's presentation of soul life is not just his opinions about the
soul. The language of the text is not didactic or dogmatic. It does not
conform to the style of pronouncements. We may conclude that he
derived a great deal from the work of Franz Brentano, since he considers
Brentano's views and limitations in some detail (lecture one of "Pneumatosophy"). But he surely does not merely repeat Brentano's findings,
though Brentano's phenomenological method certainly forms one
aspect of Steiner's style of observation. Steiner's method attempts to

describe faithfully *the essential qualities* of any experience. The method is not introspection, which is a peculiar kind of observation that "looks" inward. In other words, introspection turns an inner experience into naturalistic observation, converting the "inner" into the "outer." We may also be sure that Steiner's method is not empirical in the usual sense. What he has to say does not derive from conducting a series of inquiries about certain matters and then arriving at conclusions.

How does one observe the life of the soul? If we meditate on this question and consider it in light of Steiner's text, we come to an understanding of the nature of the field of psychology: *before you can do psychology, you must already be able to stand within soul life in a conscious way.* The question of method cannot be approached from the outside, searching through all the possible, known methods to see which one fits. It may therefore be more helpful to rephrase the question by asking not what method is used to do genuine psychology but, "What aspect of me is allowed to do psychology?" We may be sure that it is not the ego-personality or the ordinary self that does psychology. The ego-personality could not produce the text you are about to read; that would be impossible. The ordinary ego-personality could, at best, only preach about the values of soul, or about the values of spirit, or even the values of anthroposophy. There is not a trace of preaching in this text, because it is not *about* soul as viewed from some external perspective. If the text were about soul rather than a speaking *within* soul, we would be presented not with a psychology but with a belief system about psychology.

This question of method is so important, because our answer to it determines how we read this book; and it also determines how, beyond the work of reading and study, we go about doing psychology. The requirement for reading this book is to read or hear the text *as the soul that is spoken of.* The text is spoken from the viewpoint of the soul and is addressed to the soul. There is no other possible way to do psychology. Entering this text requires a complete change, and there is no way to do it but to just do it—to plunge in. There is really no way to prepare; it is not a matter of simple transition or gradually growing toward it by developing and harmoniously expanding the habitual self. The method is really quite simple. Steiner does not talk *about* soul; he speaks *from* soul. That is the entire method. There is, however, an entrance fee for doing psychology. The fee is that you need to leave behind your well-known-to-you self-identity. You must suffer the experience of leaving behind not only what you know, but also what you *think* you know of yourself. This require-ment qualifies psychology as integral to the work of initiation.

Another aspect of method seems worth mentioning. Reading this book, you will necessarily experience a rupture from your ordinary ego-personality, which would like to understand the text by the logical means of everyday thinking. This brings you into a new way of think-ing. It takes a different frame of mind to cross the waters and engage in the psychological work of reading this writing. Thus, just as this book cannot be approached from within our usual self-identity, neither can it be approached out of our usual structures of thought. To do so would completely miss another basic requirement of doing psychology. An intellectual training is required, one not necessarily acquired prior to reading and studying this work, but acquired *through* the intellec-tual effort required to read, study, contemplate, and meditate on it.

This intellectual training, it must be emphasized, is not specialized nor acquired through specialist training. In fact, this training takes the opposite direction. This does not, however, mean sinking more deeply into everyday intellectuality. Specialist intellectuality hones the ability to observe the objects of interest, albeit more closely and finely than in daily life, utilizing what we might call "spectator consciousness." If psy-chology goes in that direction the only conceivable outcome is either trivial nonsense or technologies of behavior control based on technical modes of thought. Assuredly, such a misuse of psychology does occur, even in the work of those who purport to be doing soul psychology; it is not exclusive to behaviorism. On the other hand, working from a non-specialist intellectual stance that can be immediately understood, psy-chology often becomes negligible, inconsequential.

The third alternative presented in this series of lectures is that one conceives of a *psychological mode of thought*—a psychological intel-lectuality, as it were. The "Psychosophy" lectures most exemplify that mode of intellectuality in this book. Psychological thinking extends outward—on one side toward the body and sensing, and on the other toward the life of spirit. Notice the extreme difference between the psychological mode of thinking exemplified by Steiner and the kinds of intellectual categories usually associated with psychology. I mean categories such as myths, symbols, empathy, confessional reporting, biography work, dream interpretation, case histories, theories of the self, trauma, abuse, analysis, visualization. For the present-day soul, such categories are passé, because they have been usurped by ego-personality and, rather than serving the soul, serve narcissism. They are categories that belong to dead thinking: one can no longer catch sight of the soul through them. When used by psychology, these categories, unless they are used *to say what cannot be spoken* and not as literal content, become manipulative tools. Sadly, this is all too often the case because almost no psychologist today understands this art of psychological thinking.

By calling into question the present categories of psychology, I am not saying that abuse is invented or that there is no psychological trauma, or that dream interpretation is not helpful, and so on. But when the therapeutic endeavor lacks the capacity to address soul life, remaining instead on the surface, it can, at best, merely make adjustment and adaptation somewhat easier. Yet in so doing, the soul becomes even further walled in and incapable of the transformations it needs to meet and develop the challenges that karma and destiny set for it. The fact is that when the lazy mind takes the phenomena psychology addresses to be some positive content, the soul is left out of psychological categories. When, for example, the events of a person's life are organized in a well-ordered biography—fixed into time periods that make it look as if the events of life are pat and nailed down—then the soul is abandoned by the very endeavor whose work is to care for soul. The soul cannot shine through these categories of time periods, primarily because the principle mode through which soul can shine through in our time is *thinking*. Not just any kind of thinking, but living, psychological thinking! In other words, lazy thought approaches psychological phenomena with the same attitude of consciousness with which it approaches the phenomena of the sense world, unaware that such naturalistic thinking does not apply. *The soul cannot be perceived.* However, in thinking, and only in thinking, it may be apperceived.

I have tried to demonstrate that Steiner demonstrates a psychological mode of thinking. The literalist, approaching this work from outmoded categories of psychological thought, will argue that if this text is a model of psychological thinking, then psychology is really in trouble. The text is so difficult, so elusive, so hard to get hold of, that this mode of thinking could not possibly be brought to bear in actual situations with other people. Of course, that is literally so. The aim while doing therapy would not be to think *what* Steiner presents here, but to think *as* he thinks here. We need a psychological thinking that evokes rather than nails down. We need ways of thinking that, at any given time, address one aspect of the soul's life, and do so in a way that conveys that the reality being addressed is inexhaustible. We need thinking that surrounds and protects the inner life of soul. At the same time, we need this thinking to be clear and precise, not inflated, emotional, sentimental, and full of mystifications. This text, it is easy to see, serves as a model of psychological thinking.

Soul Time

A Psychology of Body, Soul, and Spirit serves not only as a deep source for the renewal and total re-imagining of the field of psychology; it also proposes including within such re-visioning a dimension of psychology that, as far as I know, has *never* been addressed before. This dimension is brought forth in the "Psychosophy" lectures. It has to do with time and the soul. Steiner carefully describes how the soul lives within an actual current of time, which comes to the soul not only from the past but from the future as well. A consideration of this quality changes the way we view the whole of psychology! Certainly, the whole of therapeutic psychology is changed by this astute observation.

There is a huge bias in psychology which advocates understanding the reasons for our present behavior in terms of what happened to us in the past. The bias takes many different forms. For Freud, it was the personal traumas of the past; for Jung, it was both the personal and the collective past. Each psychology has its own version of the past as determinant. Steiner, too, recognizes this factor of the past as important, but he approaches it in a very different manner. For Steiner, certain aspects of the past exist within soul life as autonomous desires, longings, urges, and memories—aspects that were never satisfied, may not be conscious, have no world to relate to, and, most significantly, have no future. It is not a matter of giving such autonomous factors a future, since they can never have that. Rather, his approach is twofold. First, some way is found to give these factors a world. He suggests, for example the procedure of eliciting associations, which can be healing for all such factors of the past—*except for sexual matters.* More important by far, however, is the strengthening of our sensitization to the time current from the future. But what does this mean?

The time current from the future, which is real and actual, moves in the reverse direction of the time current that moves from the past toward the future. Jung's psychology as well as the existential psychology of Maslow and others all focus on the importance of what we can become rather than what we are due to past circumstances. These theories, however, utilize a teleological imagination of the future. There is an understanding that we are moving *toward* something and not merely being pushed from behind. Steiner has a very different sense of the time current from the future, which he hesitatingly calls the "astral body" of the soul. It is the "not-yet" and it plays an enormous role in our soul life. This future time current has nothing to do with literal clock time—it is not in linear time. One can begin to actually experience such a current by imagining, at the end of each day, the events of the day in reverse order. One could also write one's biography in reverse order or simply perform a certain task in reverse every day. After a while, a new sensibility will dawn. It involves living a sense of possibility, as though we are drawn toward something, or the sense of the "not-yet" as a powerful force. This aspect of soul life reverberates into life as openness, as a constantly creative factor, and as real life movement.

The soul has no means of registering the content of its future time current except as it overlaps the time current from the past. Nonetheless, the effort to make this current conscious is experienced as an expansion of soul life. It is experienced as a capacity to live consciously in "not-knowing." This is the capacity to experience the activity of creating our responses to each moment. Becoming aware of this current radically alters the soul qualities of past events as these continue to influence the life of the soul. The two time currents, past and future, overlap; and feeling the not-yet quality (that sense of "not-knowing"), a conscious and creative "not-knowing," also brings the substantial feeling of the possibilities present within the past that affects us. This is the past not only as determiner but as "possibilizer."

Imagine, for example, rewriting your biography. Usually, we consider our biography to be our life story, a life review. We look at our past in order to see how at each moment that past enters the present. Something very different would result, however, if you wrote your biography while paying attention to the open possibilities that attend each past event. Your biography then is not only what has already happened; it also intimates the coming-to-be that accompanies each event you have lived through. Learning to listen for this aspect of the past creates an imaginal biography, a past that is truly worth paying attention to, because at each place along the way one could get a feeling for the future. Not the literal future, but the ongoing "not-yet" that one is in each of life's events. Neglecting this dimension of soul life, a whole half of psychology and of our understanding of the life of the soul has been neglected.

Toward a Psychology of Spirit

The sections of this book are arranged so that each set of lectures—those on the body and sensing, those on soul life, and those on spirit life—can be read more or less independently. Nevertheless, I wish to present a view of the book that emphasizes soul and the inherent foundation for a new psychology. Thus far, I have touched upon the qualities inherent within soul life. Many other extremely valuable considerations concerning the phenomena that derive from these qualities may also be found in the text. Phenomena such as attention, boredom, emotion, aesthetic feeling, and the dramatic character of soul life are all addressed. These phenomena, too, must not be considered with the understanding of ordinary consciousness. Rather than understood through the static ideas of our habitual intellect, they must be worked with in such a way that the continuous, dynamic quality of soul is *felt*.

In addition to the qualities inherent in soul life, Steiner gives detailed pictures of the relationship of the boundaries of soul life with the body, as well as with the spirit. Body and spirit are both intimately bound up with soul life. Yet, at the same time, they must also be considered on their own terms. The lectures on the senses and the body, and the lectures on spirit, express these dual concerns. In his book *Anthroposophy (A Fragment)*, based on the first set of lectures printed here, Steiner considers in detail the life of sensing and how the currents involved in sensing constitute the formative forces of the human body.[1] The autonomous nature of spirit and the healthy way of developing the soul as an organ for perceiving the spiritual worlds is basic to the work of Steiner. It is the subject of his central book, *How to Know Higher Worlds*. To some extent, these two works, *Anthroposophy (A Fragment)* and *How to Know Higher Worlds*, go into the matters of body and spirit in greater detail than the present work which, however, is most valuable for understanding the soul's relationship to body *and* to spirit. It is this aspect that I wish to emphasize as a ground for re-visioning psychology.

The psychology of spirit inherent in *A Psychology of Body, Soul, and Spirit* may be seen as proceeding in two directions. First, there are the considerations of the spirit as it lives in the life of the soul. These considerations have to do with the quality of soul life that we experience as the sense of the "I." Our capacity to arrive at the realization *"I am"* is not, however, inherent in soul life. And yet, paradoxically, once installed in the soul, experiencing and living "I am" (the judging quality, described above) does belong to soul life in an ongoing way. But originally it must come from *elsewhere*—it is not given. The "I" experience does not enter the soul through our sensory relation with the world. There is nothing in the outer world that could lead to the inner capacity of a first experiencing of the "I." The "I" is not of a sensory nature; we do not learn it from experiencing the world. It is an element that differs equally from the current of mental images from the past and from the current of desires from the future. Rather, it is the element that makes it possible to

---

1. *Anthroposophy (A Fragment)* was the result of Rudolf Steiner's attempt in 1910 to write out what he had tried to convey in "Anthroposophy," the first course of the present lectures. See "Further Reading" for this and other books mentioned.

receive the past in an individual way and face the future in an individual way. The sense of the "I" enters soul life from the spiritual world. Within soul life as such, once "I"-being has awakened, we experience a definite "I"-consciousness.

From the point of view of psychology, the experience of the "I" makes certain soul experiences possible. It makes possible, for instance, the free remembering of something from the past. Memory is also evoked by the presence of something in the physical world that touches off remembrances of past occurrences. Here, we have a soul-body relationship. To remember something from the past freely, however, is different. Yet the capacity to do so is crucial for a healthy soul life. This capacity can be developed by the practice of doing some task in the opposite order than we usually do. In fact, this is the same kind of practice we need to do to become aware of the time current from the future. The two capacities are related. As we tap into the reversed time current, we strengthen the capacity of the "I" to freely remember events of the past.

"I"-consciousness is not a familiar term in psychology. "I"-consciousness is not the same as *ego-personality*, though a relationship exists between them. However, the possibility of developing a more fully conscious soul life depends on "I"-consciousness within soul life, that is, on the spiritual aspect of soul life. When the "I," in effect, reflects only the past—as happens when there is no feeling for the time (or future) current—then we have what psychology generally speaks of as ego-consciousness, and its attendant egotism. As Steiner says: "I"-image, or "I"-awareness, has a certain characteristic. It is taken hold of powerfully by all interests and desires, for they anchor themselves firmly in the "I". Despite the egoism represented by such interests and desires, there is certainly something very unique about this self-perceiving of the "I." Steiner adds that the "I" does not belong to the soul current flowing from the future.

So, whereas ego-consciousness is really the accumulation of past experiences reflected by the "I," and such consciousness is (in more usual psychological terms) the *ego*, the "I" is more than this. The "more" consists of "I"-consciousness reflecting, within soul life, the individual spirit nature.

This individual spirit nature is what Steiner means when he says that there is something unique to the "I." Now the term "I" is used throughout Steiner's texts, and the specific manner in which he uses the term has to be determined by its context. Anthroposophists often fail to make the fine but extremely important distinction between "ego" and "I." Consequently, they often do not differentiate between egotism and individual spirit. Even more often, psychologists fail to make such a distinction, and in depth psychology, for example, there is a bias against the "ego," which is, unwittingly, a bias against spirit (the "I").

Steiner recognizes the unique qualities of the "I" and gives detailed descriptions of the interplay between "I"-consciousness and soul life as a whole. If these factors are taken into account, *all psychology must, in fact, be spiritual psychology. Furthermore, when these factors are taken into account, spiritual psychology assumes a clear, definite, and precise meaning—it becomes a discipline concerned with the whole of soul life, which includes the dimension of spirit.*

I have said that the psychology of spirit, as developed by Steiner in this book, proceeds in two directions. The second direction is developed in the series of four lectures entitled "Pneumatosophy," a term meaning the "wisdom of spirit." If, when reading and studying the "Psychosophy" lectures, there are persistent questions about what is meant by "spirit" and what the basis might be for saying that the "I" relates to the spirit aspect of our being, these concerns can be clarified by studying the "Pneumatosophy" lectures.

The "Pneumatosophy" lectures develop the aspect of the psychology of spirit that deals with developing the soul as the perceiving organ for spiritual realities. This path of soul development is well known in anthroposophy, but not enough attention is usually given to exactly what is meant by it. Let us start at the beginning. The reality of spiritual worlds cannot become known to us in a healthy way unless we work toward those worlds *through the soul.* The method requires the repeated and regular formation of an inner, symbolic image that, as far as the physical world is concerned, is an incorrect—an erroneous—picture. A well-known example involves developing an image-based meditation of the Rose Cross. Steiner gives the details of this particular meditation in *An Outline of Esoteric Science*. There is nothing in the perceptual world that has the nature of a black wooden cross with a circle of roses. In *A Psychology of Body, Soul, and Spirit*, Steiner indicates repeatedly that an absolute requirement for this meditative exercise has to do with certain *moral qualities* of soul. This is the second, crucial aspect of a psychology of spirit. The principle may be stated thus: *The psychological foundation of conscious spiritual experience is the contemplation of images without in any way basing such contemplation on self-interest, curiosity, or a desire to achieve something for oneself—not even a higher state of consciousness.*

An even deeper aspect of the psychology of spirit is contained in the method of concentration and meditation that is necessary for the soul to develop into an organ of spiritual perception. We must ask: What in us allows us to consciously make and concentrate on a symbolic image? And there is another question related to the first: Why does Steiner emphasize the erroneous nature of the images to be contemplated? Indeed, why does he not recommend contemplating a "real" spiritual image, such as the image of an angel?

Steiner's response to these questions is quite startling: error originates in the spiritual world, and our stepping stone to this realm is through this aspect of the spiritual world itself! Thus, our first access to the spiritual world is through error. But we must recognize this error consciously. And, in addition to recognizing it, we must have the inner moral force not to be taken into the error: we must be able to utilize the inherent spiritual forces to bootstrap, as it were—or perhaps better said, "soulstrap"—ourselves into the spiritual world. If one were to contemplate, say, an inner image of an angel, the difficulty would be that it is unlikely we would recognize this image, too, as an error. No inner image of an angel accurately portrays in any way the nature of an angel.

The precise nature of the *moral quality* of soul must also be made clear, for only through this moral quality is it possible to use the soul to perceive into the spiritual worlds without coming to any harm. The moral quality, as described by Steiner and worth much contemplation, can be discovered by imagining first that human beings are presently unable to affirm their true and full nature, and then imagining human beings in the future who have the capacity to attain a higher nature. By carefully practicing such an imagination—not just once, but repeatedly— it becomes possible to use the error of inner images to overcome that error and develop toward new capacities. The implication of this procedure is that the psychology of spirit is a practical tool that is concerned not with the present but with the highest possibilities of human reality in the future. *The psychology of spirit is the psychology of the future human being.*

Certain kinds of psychology and so-called spiritual psychology make use of techniques of imagination. The psychology of spirit developed by Steiner, however, throws a whole new light on the use of such techniques. Visualization practices, active imagination practices, shamanic practices adapted for weekend use by spiritual seekers, the use of altered states of consciousness for healing, guided imagery practices—none of these can be accepted at face value as being helpful. In Steiner's terms, such practices all come under the rubric of spiritually illusory practices. They might take one into spiritual realms, but without exception these would be, in Steiner's terms, "Luciferic" spiritual realms. No judgment is made against these realms by Steiner; in fact, his whole method of the psychology of spirit makes use of these very same realms. Nevertheless, what is brought to bear in the methods he suggests is a clear cognizance of the error involved and the attendant moral soul force that can cancel out the destructive effects of making use of spiritual error.

What kind of harm and destructiveness could Steiner have in mind when he speaks of the dire effects of using soul life to develop spiritual capacities without moral balance? He presents those effects in some detail in *How to Know Higher Worlds* and in other writings and lectures. At the very least, it leads to increased egotism—or increased self-absorption—now placed under the mantle of spirituality. The more dire effects include inflation and depression, even psychosis.

It needs to be strongly emphasized that the possibility of taking up the practices offered by Steiner for becoming present to true imagination rather than illusory fantasy depends completely on an ongoing presence, as consciously as possible, to soul life as I have previously described it. Since the soul becomes the medium through which spiritual experience

becomes possible, it becomes imperative to be able to face even the dark-
est, most shadow sides of our soul life, over and over again, and more
and more deeply. We are never finished with the soul. Any attempts to
engage in spiritual practices, such as those described here by Steiner—
*while bypassing the soul or feeling that one has, after all, already done all
that*—can result only in destructive spiritual practices.

A third aspect of the psychology of spirit developed by Steiner, which
is really a kind of subset of the second aspect—the development of
healthy spirit imagination—concerns the creative imagination. The creative imagination belongs to the domain of phenomena considered by a
psychology of spirit. It is important to emphasize this aspect of the psychology of spirit, because creative imagination is often considered a
function of soul life alone. In Jung's psychology as currently practiced,
for example, creativity is considered in this way. As described by Steiner,
however, the creative imagination consists of currents intruding from
the spiritual worlds into soul life and experienced as autonomous
images. Steiner speaks of such images as genuine creative fantasy, occurring midway between mental picturing and fully conscious spiritual
imagination.[2] Creative imagination, then, is a central phenomenon of
the psychology of spirit. In spite of all of its richness, complexity, and
depth, creativity in itself does not belong to the realm of the soul.

Strictly speaking, the psychology of spirit must be differentiated from
the investigations of spiritual worlds that become possible when we use
the life of the soul to develop spiritual perception. In order to remain
true to the discipline of psychology, true psychology of spirit will always
stay close to the soul realm. Such a psychology is interested above all in
the kinds of border phenomena that occur when spiritual worlds touch
the soul realms. It is interested especially in how these border phenomena occur in daily life—how they are a healthy part of soul life, and how
they give indications of movement toward or away from a healthy spiritual life. In the lectures on "Pneumatosophy," Steiner goes beyond these

---

2. Rudolf Steiner uses the terms *imagination, inspiration,* and *intuition* in an extraordinary sense. Thus, throughout this book, these words are italicized when used in that
way. What we ordinarily call "imagination," might be referred to as "mental picturing"
or "fantasy." See lecture three of "Pneumatosophy."

considerations, but in this introduction we are concerned only with spiritual psychology as such.

Let us consider *imagination* more closely. When working with soul qualities to move toward perception of the spiritual worlds, images are used to enter the world of imagination. *Imagination*, for Steiner, is characterized by a particular quality of experience—the presence of inner images that have a distinctly autonomous life of their own. Psychologically considered, when such images occur in life (and indeed they can occur without the specific practices outlined by Steiner), the spiritual worlds have intruded into soul life. Whether such intrusions are helpful or harmful depends on two factors: the moral sensibility of the person experiencing such images and the degree to which that person has in some manner come to a living understanding of soul life. Often such an understanding can occur without having psychological training.

If autonomous images intrude in forceful ways when moral sensibility of the kind mentioned above is absent or weak, then images that seem intense and significant are really no more than imaginal presentations of one's own deficient moral qualities. If, on the other hand, no real sense of soul life is present, the experience of true *imagination* can become overwhelming. Here, we have one basis for developing therapeutic measures that can help people who are experiencing the presence of the spiritual worlds. In present-day psychology, such awakening of *imagination* is often assumed to belong strictly to the soul realm. Autonomous images are said to be soul experiences, with no recognition of the involvement of spirit. There are also many practices that encourage the awakening of autonomous imagery, either taking it to be a way to stimulate individual creativity or taking all such imagery to be spiritually helpful, without any moral consideration. When this kind of *imagination* occurs in a spontaneous and disturbing way, psychology, as currently practiced, usually assumes that such occurrences indicate psychological imbalance. A psychology of spirit can be of the greatest assistance in understanding what is actually happening and how to work with these experiences in healthy ways. Careful work with this text will give very direct indications about the most helpful ways to work with such experiences.

A second way that the spiritual worlds enter soul life concerns the relationship between emotion and action. Emotions belong to the realm of the soul. Understanding the mysterious way that an emotion, impulse, desire, urge, or feeling transmutes from emotion into action—understanding that transition—also belongs to the psychology of spirit. In this transition, soul gets beyond itself. Steiner's consideration of the relationship between emotion and will reveals the nature of this transition. First of all, emotion touches into the body. This is the only way, in fact, that emotion can act in the world. Saying that the body is involved, however, does not clarify any of the process involved. But, if we could be aware of that process, Steiner indicates that we would, in a soul manner, be aware of *intuition*. We can begin to be aware of *intuition* when we begin to realize that what lives in our consciousness—deeply felt and experienced not only as knowledge but also as bodily feeling—is the activity of something that goes beyond our own soul life. Our will is not completely our own; it is the cooperation of soul life, through embodied emotion, with actual spiritual forces.

In addition to imagination and *intuition*, the psychology of spirit also concerns a third element, *inspiration*. *Inspiration* is closer in content to spiritual *imagination* than it is to spiritual *intuition*. Whereas spiritual *intuition* is related to the soul activity of emotion working into the body as forces of will, spiritual *inspiration* for Steiner has to do with the soul's experience of the autonomous images of spiritual *imagination* as more-than-autonomous inner pictures. Spiritual *inspiration* perceives that these autonomous. images are the spiritual deeds of beings of the spiritual worlds. Spiritual *inspiration* consists of forming the thought that the images are indeed the acts of beings. It is difficult for language to describe precisely the nature of this realm. We might, however, express it thus: *inspiration* is the actively-coming-to-form-thought of the reality of spiritual beings revealing themselves through autonomous imagery.

In spiritual work, it is important to recognize the qualities of *inspiration*. Without such recognition, we may be captivated by the play of all sorts of images. These may fascinate us so that we lack a deep respect and reverence for the realms that have opened. One can easily miss the possibility of giving those worlds their proper meaning. Considered in a more psychological way, on the other hand, when one has no understanding of the nature of the spiritual worlds—and has not gone through the kind of careful movement of soul toward those worlds as described by Steiner—then, when *inspirations* enter, sensing the reality of spiritual beings can be extremely frightening. The usual sense of the word "inspiration" must therefore be put aside. As developed by Steiner, *inspiration* does not necessarily mean that one is able to utilize these experiences in an act of creating something in the world. That may happen, but *inspiration* can just as well be a terribly frightening feeling of being invaded.

In the lectures on "Pneumatosophy," Steiner focuses on the necessary procedures for using soul experience to develop the capacities for experiencing the spiritual worlds. I have tried to emphasize the psychology of spirit implicit in the practices described by Steiner. In order to remain psychological, a psychology of spirit must stay strongly on the side of the soul. The boundary where soul and spirit touch must be described from that point of view. Thus, as I have indicated, a psychology of spirit also involves the careful work of understanding how what occurs at this border may or may not be healthy. This allows one to begin to recognize that there are enormous differences between soul pathologies and soul-spirit pathologies. Ordinary psychology does not recognize these differences, and I have barely touched on them here. However, the sufferings of soul and the sufferings that may accompany arrival at the soul-spirit boundary must be differentiated. Each must be worked with in a different way. A therapeutic psychology based on a clear sense of soul does not proceed in the same way as a therapeutic psychology of soul-spirit. Such concerns go beyond the scope of this text, though hopefully it can open up these differences for research.

Soul and Embodiment

The most difficult lectures in this book are the ones that come first, the four lectures that are entitled "Anthroposophy." These deal primarily with sensing and the body. My reflections on these lecturers will focus on the kinds of experiences and phenomena characteristic of the soul-body boundary. Thus they will begin to outline a "psychology of the body." The four lectures do more, however, than merely develop a "psychology of the body." They differentiate "anthropology" from "anthroposophy" and "anthroposophy" from "theosophy." Steiner alludes in a sketchy outline to the long evolution of the human body. This is done to help us understand that the human physical body is intimately interwoven with the whole cosmos. He then presents a way of understanding the human senses—first in an enumerative way, and then more deeply from the perspective of spiritual science. At the time of these lectures, Steiner described ten senses. Later, he spoke of twelve distinct senses.[3]

Steiner first considers sensing through careful attention and observation of ordinary consciousness. Anyone can repeat his observations. As we do so, we come to realize the complexity of sensing. By the way Steiner arranges his presentation, we realize that each different sense provides a *particular* form of knowledge without the intervention of thought. The first description of the senses, however, does not touch on the soul-body relation, and is thus only a preparation for such a consideration.

The second description of the senses goes deeply into the spiritual question: *What makes sensing possible?* Here, sensing is considered by way of clairvoyant consciousness. Steiner develops dynamic pictures of the interplay between spiritual forces and the etheric and astral bodies, which is different for each of the senses. We take a very large leap from the first to this second description of sensing. By carefully following through this spiritual understanding of sensing, we begin to dissolve our notion of the human body as a physical organism that happens to be formed in such a way that it contains a number of sense organs. Even if we do not fully understand the meaning of *Atma, Buddhi,* and *Manas* or the meaning of the etheric and astral bodies, we are nonetheless alerted to the fact that the human body, *the living human body,* must be understood as the confluence of the activity of high spiritual beings—

---

3. See *The Foundations of Human Experience*, lecture 8, August 29, 1919 and *Toward Imagination*, lecture 3, June 20, 1916.

subtle life-forming and soul-forming forces—with physical matter.[4] The second and third lectures in the section on "Anthroposophy" develop this spiritual understanding of each of the senses. Indeed, these lectures offer what amounts to a short course in the whole of anthroposophy. Fortunately, the editors have provided footnotes throughout, indicating where many of the concepts presented here can be followed up in greater detail in Steiner's other writings and lectures.

Let me now present keys that might be helpful in understanding the importance of Steiner's view of sensing and show how, on this basis, he develops a radically new approach to the human body. It is this new view that I believe to be of the utmost importance for the "psychology of the body."

Steiner describes the human body from an inner perspective. This inner standpoint indicates the capacity to observe and describe the senses and the body from the perspective of consciously developed *imagination, inspiration,* and *intuition.* He states, for example, that a true understanding of the human organism "requires the development of a spiritual-scientific ability to observe and grasp the whole human being from within." We are used to conceiving of the body as viewed from spectator consciousness. This ordinary conception of the body— as currently understood by science and medicine, for example—views the human organism as a closed system. The body that we are, however, is not a closed system as such. The living body is an open field, a locus for the convergence of relationships with the physical world and for more complex relationships with the spiritual worlds.

An example of the human body as an open, dynamic, and interactive field may be seen in Steiner's description of one of the senses—the life sense. In the first lecture, which lists and describes the senses, we learn that the life sense is experienced as a feeling for the body's well-being. In fact, we experience the life sense only when there is some disharmony among the inner organs of the body. We experience hunger,

---

4. *Atma* (spirit body, or spirit human being), *Buddhi* (life spirit), and *Manas* (spirit self) as well as the other aspects of the human being are discussed in detail by Steiner in the first chapter of both *Theosophy* and *An Outline of Esoteric Science.*

thirst, tiredness, or a feeling of energy. The life sense is one of four senses through which we become aware of ourselves as bodily beings. The other physical senses are touch, movement, and balance (though touch is not considered as a separate sense in these lectures). The life sense gives the particular experience of the wholeness of the body.

The second of the four lectures on "Anthroposophy" presents a second description of this life sense from the point of view of clairvoyant perception. This description uses the more specialized language of anthroposophy. There is, for example, a high spiritual being, *Atma*. At some time in the future, human beings will have this spirit being as part of their makeup. But for now it is lent to us. Atma suffuses the etheric body and brings a kind of cramping or a frozen quality to it. This contraction of the etheric body causes the astral body to be "squeezed out." The astral body is the source of experiences such as pleasure, conflict, and tension. This "squeezing out" of the astral body is the process that is lived as our experience of the life sense.

The first description, given from ordinary consciousness, can be comprehended quite easily. The second description, on the other hand, has real meaning only for those who have clairvoyant capacities and—to some extent—for those who accept what Steiner says as true, while others, of course, may take it as equivalent to an abstract theory of the action of the life sense. But there is a third way of working with this description. The description can become the focus of sustained image meditations, from an inner perspective, of a particular functioning of the body. Approached in this way, we can begin to develop an entirely new imagination of the body. We then proceed similarly through all the senses. With regard to the life sense, for example, we can gradually come to a most interesting conclusion. The body itself feels qualities such as pleasure, aversion, pain, joy. But these qualities are not feelings I have; they are the body's ongoing relationship with a spiritual being, the being that provides for us the sense we have of being a body. This is the body as a whole experience, not as a conglomeration of anatomical parts, organs, and physiology. Physiology does not give us an experience of the body at all; it gives us only concepts *about* the body.

We can get to the point of experiencing a strong sense of this quality of bodily life without having developed clairvoyant capacities. As the first step toward developing a "psychology of the body," I would suggest working through each of the senses in image meditations drawn from Steiner's descriptions. Even anthroposophists who work with the senses do not really practice the kind of imaginative procedure that will result in a new imagination of the body—a true spiritual "psychology of the body." Albert Soesman, for example, has written, from other standpoints, a fine book on the twelve senses (*Our Twelve Senses: Wellsprings of the Soul*). But he never mentions the fact that the body is not a product, or something completed, but a dynamic, open relationship with the spiritual worlds.

A set of meditations could be developed in relation to each of the twelve senses. For movement, it would be necessary to develop an imagination of the interplay between *Buddhi*, or life spirit, and the etheric and astral bodies. The specific ways these forces work are described in the text, and it is crucial to develop the meditations based on the specific forms of interaction. For balance, one might meditate on the specific relationship between the spirit being *Manas* and the etheric and astral bodies. These first three senses—the life sense, the sense of movement, and the sense of balance—all give us different qualities of experiencing ourselves as embodied.

The second series of four senses provides experiences of the body's interactions with the surrounding world. These take place through the senses of smell, taste, sight, and warmth. With these four senses, we are more on our own, since they do not involve a higher being, though they do involve the astral body. It may help to think of the astral body as the "soul body," which means here that through these senses we have some bodily experience of the inner qualities of the outer world. As we work meditatively with these four senses, we gradually develop a "psychology of the body." To do so, however, requires that we have a feeling for analogy. Smell, for example, is *like* the body interacting with outer substances through the will. Smell is *like* a struggle, or conflict, between a substance in gaseous form trying to enter the body and a counterforce of will that struggles to penetrate the interior of that substance. Taste is *like* the interaction of the feeling body with the feeling nature of substances. This means that taste is the body's way of experiencing the interaction of feelings. Sight, on the other hand, is analogous to thinking. It is the body's way of thinking that penetrates things of the world. For the sense of temperature, coldness is *like* the uninhibited flow of the soul within the body into the things of the world; warmth is *like* the uninhibited soul within the substance of things, flowing into the body.

With the three higher senses considered in this text—the senses of hearing, speech, and thought—something new enters. Reading, studying, and then meditating what Steiner says concerning these senses and the interactions involved can lead to profound experiences. For here again we are not alone but constantly cared for and helped by very specific spiritual beings. With the sense of hearing we are given the help of angels, who lend their own soul substance so that we can hear. Hearing is thus a truly spiritual sense. In the case of the speech sense, we are given the help of archangels, who lend their own soul substance to help us understand human speech. And with the thought sense, it is the Christ Being, whom Steiner also calls the "Universal Human," who makes possible our access to the thoughts of others in an immediate and sensory way.

In working toward a "psychology of the body" (which is only incipient in this text), it is necessary to understand such terms as *etheric body, astral body, sentient soul, comprehension soul, consciousness soul,* and *sentient body,* none of which are explained in the text. These terms are explained in many of Steiner's other works, and will not be explained here.[5] In keeping with the earlier sections of this introduction, however, it is important to refrain from a static understanding of these concepts.

Most importantly, however, it should have become apparent through these descriptive ways of speaking about the body that the body in its fullness is not something visible. The etheric body is invisible to ordinary perception, as is the astral body. These "bodies" should not be considered separate from the body we are, but as the more-than-physical aspects of

---

5. See the chapters on the makeup of the human being in *Theosophy* and *An Outline of Esoteric Science.*

embodiment. This is also true of the other terms. Furthermore, the body is not just the completed product that we see. In fact, the body-as-completed, finished organism is an illusion. The body, as considered from an inner perspective by Steiner, is at every moment in the process of coming into being and moving out of being. The same forces that form each of the sense processes at the same time form what we might term the "extended" or true body.

We have come to live in our bodies according to the medical-scientific concept of the body. The medical view of the body is based on the anatomy of a corpse and on the physiology of a dismembered human body. Consequently, we must imagine soul and spirit back into our own living being. In this way, we can regain a soul-sense of embodiment. If we approach the lectures on sensing and the body with this need in mind, they can help to awaken the long-forgotten reality of our embodiment. Soul and spirit are not some kind of invisible entities lurking around as ghosts in a machine; the body is ensouled and inspirited through and through. But, to properly understand such a statement, we must keep in mind the body as more invisible than visible.

Our living body is not self-enclosed. The body opens to the surrounding world and is in a constant interchange with it. We take in the world at every moment—not only through the sense processes but also through the life processes. At every moment we return ourselves to the world—not only, for example, through breathing, but also through the activity of sensing. This activity of sensing moves from the exterior nearest the soul (i.e., the immediate body), through an increasing penetration into the world, and finally to a bodily sensing of the soul-spirit being of others. Thus, the living body is more like an open field of forces. However, we must understand such forces in terms of the soul and spirit, and not merely in terms of the physical.

Not only is the body open as a field to the earthly realm, but it is also open to the cosmic world. The body is sensible; it can be sensed in very subtle ways by others. It also senses; it is capable of great knowledge without the use of concepts. The dynamic, full soul-spirit body described by Steiner cannot be conceived of as an object in the world—for example, the way a rock exists as an object in the world. The body, in the mobility of its ongoing soul and spirit processes—its animation, its sensing, its relationship to formative forces and the spiritual worlds—is through and through a *time body*. We do not just exist *in* time; we are a part of the very fabric of time, and a part of the very fabric of pure spirit activity.

The body, in its relationship to the sentient body, sentient soul, consciousness soul, and astral body, is always and in every moment thoroughly an expressive body. It is not true that we have a body that can also have certain kinds of expressions, such as sadness, joy, anger, and so on. Expression *is* body; it is body in its emotional and soul aspect.

Concluding Questions

You might consider *A Psychology of Body, Soul, and Spirit* to be too high, too steep for you. It may not seem to answer your immediate and pressing questions. You may ask, does this book, in fact, present any therapeutic application for understanding the body, soul, and spirit? What does any of this have to do with real people, with people who are suffering? True, this book does not suggest any technical tricks. But therapeutic psychology should not consist of concepts to be used as a bag of tools that a practitioner applies. A perceived need for such "practical" tools is simply a sign of psychological immaturity. Therapy does not, or should not, consist of doing anything. Rather, it is an act of *remembering* the fullness of soul life and the soul's involvement with spirit, and *remembering* the fullness of the soul and spirit fabric of embodiment.

The concepts in this book cannot perhaps be brought directly into the therapeutic situation. But the real therapist in the consulting room must always be able to engage in the art of improvisation—soul in the moment. To improvise, one must really know, understand, and live soul life—one must be able to live it consciously and from within. For this, a true soul education is needed. Unfortunately, however, that kind of education has gone out of psychology. Nevertheless, this book can serve as an extremely valuable starting point for this much needed self-education.

A final question, based on the radically new insights of this book, asks: Shouldn't we abandon the term and field of *psychology* altogether and start something new? We might call it "psychosophy." Indeed, there might be a great temptation to do exactly this in some quarters of anthroposophy. I think this would be a great mistake. Anthroposophy has the opportunity, especially in the field of psychology, to engage a much wider world. It has an opportunity to bring something new and valuable to the field of psychology. I cannot imagine that anyone would wish to confine the considerations of soul life as developed in this book to the small sector of people interested only in anthroposophy. It is more likely, on the other hand, that the understanding of soul life as presented here—if made available to all serious students of psychology—would result in a much wider interest in anthroposophy.

ROBERT SARDELLO, PH.D., is codirector of the School of Spiritual Psychology. A practicing psychotherapist for over twenty years, working in existential, Jungian, and archetypal psychologies, he has developed a spiritual psychology based on the spiritual science of Rudolf Steiner. The School of Spiritual Psychology offers seminars, conferences, correspondence courses, and consultations throughout the country.

Robert Sardello is a faculty member of the Dallas Institute of Humanities and Culture and of the Chalice of Repose Project, Missoula, Montana, and former chairman of the department of psychology, University of Dallas. He is the author of *Facing the World with Soul* (Lindisfarne Books/Harper Collins) and *Love and the Soul* (Harper/Collins). His most recent book, *Freeing the Soul from Fear* (Putman/Riverhead), takes up Rudolf Steiner's understanding of soul life, explores fear in an individual and cultural context, and describes how to cultivate imagination and love as antidotes to fear.

I

"Anthroposophy"

BERLIN 1909

1.

The Human Being and the Senses

D URING RECENT YEARS here in Berlin and wherever the Theosophical Society has been established, we have heard much about the whole range of theosophy—insights drawn, so to speak, from the highest regions of clairvoyant research. This has made it inevitable—even essential—that something be done to provide a basis for our spiritual movement that is both serious and deserving of respect. This General Meeting—which brings our dear members together to celebrate seven years of the German Section's existence—is a suitable occasion to contribute further to a firmer foundation and greater order for this movement. I will try to do this in the four lectures on anthroposophy scheduled for the next few days.[1]

The lectures at Kassel on the Gospel of John, those in Düsseldorf on the hierarchies, the Basel lectures on the Gospel of Luke, and the Munich cycle on the teachings of Eastern theosophy all provided an opportunity to climb to noble heights in spiritual research and bring back spiritual truths that are not easily accessible.[2] It has always been at least a part of our concern in the theosophical movement to ascend to such high peaks of human spiritual knowledge.

---

1. These lectures were given for members on the occasion of the eighth general assembly of the German section of the Theosophical Society. Rudolf Steiner had opened the General Meeting, saying, "On this occasion it may be taken for granted that you have a feeling for what is called a cyclic evolution of events ... the completion of the first seven-year epoch." It also marked a move toward a more Western mode of thinking: "The task of the West is to develop the spirit of synthesis" (Guenther Wachsmuth, *The Life and Work of Rudolf Steiner*, Blauvelt, NY: Garber Communications, 1989, p. 129).

2. See Rudolf Steiner, *The Gospel of St. Luke* (Hudson, NY: Anthroposophic Press, 1964); *The Spiritual Hierarchies and the Physical World* (Hudson, NY: Anthroposophic Press, 1996); and *The East in the Light of the West* (Blauvelt, NY: Garber Communications, 1986).

When we cultivate a feeling for the so-called cycle of cosmic events, we are certainly justified in seeing something of a deeper nature in them. During our first general meeting, when we were establishing the German Section—before an audience, few of whom were theosophists—I delivered lectures that were referred to then as a historic chapter of anthroposophy.[3] Now, seven years later, we seem to have completed a cycle, and it is appropriate to speak more comprehensively about the meaning of the term *anthroposophy.* An analogy may help clarify its meaning. When we wish to examine a region, we go from place to place, looking at the arrangement of villages, woods, meadows, roads, and so on. What we see at any given place or moment at ground level is always just a small, a very small portion of the whole area. But we can also climb a mountain and survey the entire landscape from the peak. Ordinary sight will not then distinguish the details, but the view will provide an overview of the whole.

This analogy illustrates the relationship between theosophy and what we ordinarily think of as *knowledge,* or science. Ordinary cognition moves from detail to detail through the world of fact. Theosophy, on the other hand, ascends a high peak, and the horizon is thereby enlarged. After climbing that peak, however, special methods must be used to make out the details of what lies below. These methods have been described many times—for example, in my book *How to Know Higher Worlds.*[4] There I show how it is possible to reach that ideal peak without sacrificing the capacity to perceive detail.

But there is also a third possibility, which we may infer from our analogy. We may climb only part of the way—stopping, for example, at the halfway point. At ground level, we see only detail with no overview; we look at the heights above us from beneath. When we reach the peak, conversely, there is nothing above us but the heavens, and everything visible lies below. But at the midpoint of ascent there is something

3. The first general meeting took place October 20, 1902. The lectures he refers to were given to the circle of the "Kommenden" and were called *From Zarathustra to Nietzsche: The History of Human Evolution in Relation to the Ancient East and to the Present, or Anthroposophy.*
4. See bibliography in this volume.

beneath us and above us, and we can compare the two perspectives. Every analogy, of course, leaves something to be desired. This one was intended only to illustrate the distinction between theosophy and anthroposophy. Theosophy stands on the peak, anthroposophy at the halfway point, looking both down and up. The only difference is in the place from which the scene is viewed.

This analogy, however, cannot be stretched to cover the following. Taking the theosophical path requires rising above the level of the usual human way of seeing things, rising from the lower to the higher self and attaining the capacity to perceive with the organs of that higher self. The peak from which theosophy is able to perceive is above us, whereas ordinary cognition lies below and we ourselves are halfway between the worlds of nature and spirit. What is above us extends into us, for we are suffused and filled with spirit. We can perceive the spirit there above, but we do not look from the peak of the spirit, but from a place over which the peak towers. We also see beneath us what is merely nature, for it projects into us from below. Theosophy is vulnerable to the danger of overflying the human level when those methods described, for example, in *How to Know Higher Worlds* are not practiced—in which case, it becomes impossible for us to gain sufficient knowledge. The danger with theosophy is that it cannot perceive the reality at its feet. Obviously, this does not mean that such a possibility must be lost, if the appropriate methods are used for developing the organs of perception for the higher self.

In other words, *theosophy is what we investigate when the divine within us speaks.* Essentially, the correct meaning of theosophy is the allowing of the god within us to speak; what it tells you about the world is theosophy. Anthroposophy, for its part, may be characterized as the wisdom spoken by us as human beings when we are between God and nature, and allow the human being in us to speak of what is shining into us from above and of what is projecting into us from below. *Anthroposophy is the wisdom that human beings speak.* This wisdom can serve as an important key to, and support in, the whole realm of theosophy. After we have absorbed theosophy for a while, we can hardly do better than rally to the achievement of such firm support by seeking the wisdom that anthroposophy can provide. Therefore, I will make sure that a brief sketch of the nature of anthroposophy is made available as soon as possible after these lectures.[5]

There is a broad range of historical documentation for what I am saying—there is no need to look very far for it. There is, for example, a science generally known as *anthropology*, about which you can find out through all sorts of popular literature.[6] As ordinarily practiced today, anthropology includes not only the human being but also, when properly understood, everything related to the human being—everything that people can experience in nature and what is necessary for understanding the human being. The starting point of this science of anthropology is an observation of earthly things; it is completely down on earth and moves from detail to detail. It observes what is human through the senses with the help of the microscope. Anthropology, which is widely regarded these days as the only valid science of the human being, takes its standpoint at a level *below* truly human capacities. In its investigations it does not use all the human capacities for research. Now, contrast *anthropology*, which remains stuck at the ground level and cannot work out any of the answers to the burning questions of existence, with what *theosophy* offers. Theosophy climbs to the loftiest heights to find the answers to the most pressing questions of existence.

You will find, however, that those who are too impatient to explore theosophy gradually—those who have not accompanied us step by step in what we have presented over the past few years—have remained stuck at the level of anthropology and consider theosophy a structure of empty air, without any basis whatsoever. They cannot see how the soul ascends stage by stage from incarnation to incarnation, and they cannot rise to an overview of the goal of human and cosmic evolution. Anthropology therefore may be seen as standing on the lowest rung of the ladder and

---

5. *Anthroposophy (A Fragment)*, (Hudson, NY: Anthroposophic Press, 1996).
6. In *Anthropology: A Student's Guide to Theory and Method* (Toronto: University of Toronto Press, 1996), Professor Stanley Barrett describes anthropology as having begun only in the late nineteenth century, just as European colonialism was beginning to lose ground. Modern anthropology as developed by researchers such as Claude Levi-Strauss was still to come when these lectures were delivered.

theosophy on the uppermost level, where the cognitive capacity fades away for many people.

A historical example of what becomes of theosophy when it tries to climb to the peak but cannot apply the methods described in *How to Know Higher Worlds* is that of the German theosophist Solger, who lived from 1780 to 1819.[7] From a theoretical standpoint, his views are thoroughly theosophical. But what are the methods Solger uses to reach the greatest heights? He uses the concepts of philosophy, drained and desiccated products of human thinking. He is like a climber who ascends a peak to look at the view but forgets to take his binoculars along; thus, he cannot see the details of the scene below. The binoculars in this case are of a spiritual nature—that is, *imagination, inspiration,* and *intuition.*[8] Solger tried to climb the peak inadequately equipped in his methods.

Over the centuries, it had been felt for a long time that human capacities were growing more and more inadequate for ascending to the peak. People felt and acknowledged this throughout the Middle Ages. It has been felt recently as well, even though that fact is not readily acknowledged. There had been a feeling for a long time that, at one time, human capacities were enough to reach the peak and that accounts of what was perceived there could be offered, as an older theosophy had actually done. Yes, indeed, at one time there was such a theosophy. The time came, however, when the revelations once attainable on the peak had to end. Such revelations were to be protected from being received through ordinary cognition. Thus, an earlier theosophy became theology, which regarded revelation as finished.

Theology, therefore, stands next to anthropology, which simply goes from detail to detail with ordinary cognition. Theology wants to climb to the peak and learn from what may be seen at such heights. But it too

7. Karl Wilhelm Ferdinand Solger, who published *Philosophical Talks* (1817).
8. Rudolf Steiner uses the terms *imagination, inspiration,* and *intuition* in an extraordinary sense, as will be seen, and they are therefore italicized throughout the text. What we ordinarily call "imagination," for example, could be referred to instead as "mental picturing" or "fantasy." His use of the terms refer to stages of spiritual development as described in the third lecture of "Pneumatosophy" in this volume. See also Rudolf Steiner, *The Stages of Higher Knowledge.*

again relies only on what can be learned through ordinary human means—in this case, historical tradition, what was once revealed—and not what ought to be revealed again and again to the human soul working upward. Anthropology and theology faced each other all through the Middle Ages without one rejecting the other. It is still this way, but with a difference. Contemporary anthropology generally snubs theology by denying it any scientific basis. Yet when, instead of stopping at details, you climb to the midway point I described, you can see that the relationship between anthroposophy and theosophy compares to that of anthropology and theology during the Middle Ages. In modern intellectual life, attempts were also made to substantiate anthroposophy, but again with completely inadequate methodology, namely, with abstract, dried-up philosophical concepts. To comprehend the nature of the problem requires an understanding of what philosophy is, which is possible only for theosophers, not philosophers.

What is philosophy? To answer this question we have to trace the historical development of philosophy. For example, in ancient times there were mystery schools where the higher spiritual life was nurtured. Pupils there could be guided to spiritual vision through the development of their capacities. Ephesus, where the mysteries of Diana were explored, was such a place where pupils looked into the spiritual worlds. Whatever was learned and could be publicly disclosed was communicated accordingly. Those who took in such communications regarded them as perceived in the mysteries and offered as a gift. Among such listeners were those who were aware that they had been told deep secrets learned in the mysteries.

The great sage Heraclitus[9] was such an individual, who came to know secrets of the mystery of Ephesus—especially facts ascertained through clairvoyance. What was communicated to him in this way and

---

9. Heraclitus (ca. 540–ca. 480 B.C.), Greek philosopher who taught that all of reality is in a constant state of dynamic equilibrium, that "opposites" always have an underlying connection, and that all is manifestation of the *Logos*. Plato later interpreted his teachings as a doctrine of constant flow, or flux. Only fragments of Heraclitus's sayings remain. Rudolf Steiner discusses Heraclitus in *Christianity as Mystical Fact* and *Riddles of Philosophy*.

what he owed to his own partial initiation, he proclaimed in a form suited to ordinary understanding. Therefore, anyone who reads the teachings of Heraclitus ("the Obscure") sees a deeper element underlying them, so that the direct experience of higher worlds can still be seen shining through.

Heraclitus's followers could no longer understand that his communications derived from immediate experience of higher worlds, so they became involved in intellectual speculation. They believed, in their merely philosophical mentality, that they were uncovering errors in Heraclitus and busied themselves tinkering around trying to correct them. Concepts continued to be fabricated and passed from generation to generation. The remnants of philosophy that have come down to us are nothing more than an inheritance of ancient teachings with all the life sucked out of them and squeezed dry, to the point where skeletons of concepts are all that have survived. Philosophers themselves are not aware of the concepts' source. Philosophies are mere abstractions, inheritances from an ancient wisdom now reduced to empty concepts. Philosophers are unable to conceive anything for themselves. For that, they would have to make an expedition into higher worlds.

Philosophies of this kind and their dried-up concepts were all that was available to nineteenth-century philosophers when they tackled what may be termed *anthroposophy*. That term was used once when Robert Zimmermann wrote a book by that title.[10] But just as with Solger and his theosophy, Zimmermann was inadequately equipped for the task; thus, his writings were fabricated from the driest, most abstract concepts. This completely dry, abstract conceptual specter, unsuited to its subject, was his view of anthroposophy. It is characteristic of the nineteenth century that whatever transcended individual outer experience or went beyond anthropology and wanted to be anthroposophy became just such a dry conceptual specter.

Through supplying the methods to know the reality within spiritual life, theosophy must restore depth once more to the knowledge of humanity that can be called *anthroposophy*. Anthroposophy is spiritual

10. See *The Anthroposophic Movement*.

insight into the world based unequivocally on the median—the human perspective—not the subhuman, which is the perspective of anthropology. Solger's theosophy occupied a superhuman level, but it lacked content. Concepts conceived at that level fly too high above humankind. Since people up there cannot see anything of the world below, they spin webs of manufactured concepts. We are not interested in doing that; our quest is for reality, and you will see that all reality of human life opens to it. You will still recognize the old friends, the old goals of our seeking, but illumined from a different viewpoint, looking both up and down.

The human being is truly the most important subject for our consideration. When we examine the physical body—if we reflect on what we have learned through theosophy and examine it more closely—we become aware of how complicated it really is. To gain some sense of anthroposophy's true concern, remember that what we call the human physical body is, in a sense, a very ancient creation. We know that it came into existence in its initial seed state on ancient Saturn, changed on the ancient Sun and Moon, and transformed again on the Earth.[11] The ether body was incorporated into it on ancient Sun.[12] The astral

---

11. The use of planetary names to describe stages of cosmic development was a Theosophical convention of the time, used to describe the major stages of cosmic development. These terms do not refer directly to the physical, celestial bodies of the same names or to their specific, physical development. For a thorough discussion of these terms see Rudolf Steiner, *An Outline of Esoteric Science*, chapter 4.

12. Steiner included this note for his book *Theosophy*:
"For a long time after compiling this book, I also spoke of what is here termed 'ether body,' or 'life body,' as 'the body of formative forces.'... I believed one could not do enough to try to prevent the identification of what I meant with the 'life force,' or 'vital force,' of an earlier stage of science.... I agree in some respects with those who would deny the existence of any such force. That term was used in an attempt to explain the unique way of working that inorganic forces took on within a living organism. However, inorganic activity is actually no different inside an organism than it is outside in inorganic nature. Within an organism there is simply something additional present, something that is not inorganic, namely, the formative activity of life whose basis is the ether body, or body of formative forces. Recognizing the existence of the ether body in no way impinges on the legitimate task of science, which is to trace the effects of forces observed in inorganic nature into the world of living organisms. Spiritual science, however, also finds it justified not to imagine these effects as altered by a particular 'vital force' within an organism. A spiritual researcher speaks of an 'ether body' at the point where an organism discloses something that a lifeless object cannot" (p. 36).

body was incorporated into the human body on ancient Moon.[13] These aspects of human nature have gone through continual metamorphosis over the course of evolution. What we recognize today as the complex physical body with the heart and kidneys, the eyes and ears, and so on is the product of a long evolution, during which all its members developed from a primal formative essence that was present on ancient Saturn. Then millions of years passed, bringing further changes before it reached the stage of its present complexity and perfection.

When you study any part of this body today—for example, the heart or lungs—you cannot understand it if you do not have a deeper understanding of how these organs originated and developed. Obviously, nothing of the present form of the heart and lungs existed on ancient Saturn; they developed their present form only very gradually—one earlier, another later—and became incorporated into the physical body. One of these organs may be called the *Sun organ*, because during the Sun evolution it was incorporated and became perceptible. Another may be termed the *Moon organ*, and so on. If we want to understand how this complex structure, the human physical body, really came to be and what it means today, we can get the concepts from the universe— *from a study of the entire cosmos.* This is a theosophical view of the human being. Now, how does the anthropological view differ?

Anthropology views the heart and the stomach in isolation; they are studied separately, as though it didn't matter which was the newer and which the older organ; that aspect is ignored, and each organ is lined up and handled separately. Theosophy ascends to the ultimate heights and

13. In *Theosophy*, Steiner explained his use of the term *astral body*: "The human being can be differentiated into physical body, life body, astral body, and 'I', with the term 'astral body' designating the union of the soul body and the sentient soul. This term is common in older literature and is here freely applied to that aspect of the human being that lies beyond what is sense-perceptible.... What is active in the astral body to begin with are our drives, desires, and passions to the extent that we perceive them, as well as our sense perceptions. Sense perceptions come about through the soul body, a member of our human constitution that comes to us from the outer world. Drives, desires, passions and so on originate in the sentient soul to the extent that it is filled with forces by our inner self before this inner self gives itself over to the spirit self" (p. 59).

explains each individual aspect of the whole out of the spiritual. Anthropology stays at ground level and starts from the individual aspect. By this method, it has arrived at the greatest extreme, viewing individual cells as merely juxtaposed, as though it made no difference that a particular complex of cells originated during ancient Moon evolution and another during ancient Sun. The various cell complexes actually did come to be at very different times. You can list the superficial details, but you will not understand them if you fail to consider them from the spiritual viewpoint. Anthropology walks on the ground, whereas theosophy looks at things from the highest peak.

Matters now become even more complicated. The human heart is one of the most ancient organs, considered in its initial seed form. Its present appearance developed only during a later period. The germinal stage of the heart was dependent on the forces at work on the ancient Sun; evolution continued. During the first period of Moon evolution, old Moon united with the Sun, and the heart passed through another stage of development. Then came the great event of ancient Sun's separation. The Sun worked thereafter from outside the Moon, causing the heart to go through a totally different evolution. From that time on, evolution proceeded with a Sun part *and* a Moon part, and we can understand the heart only if we can differentiate between the Sun and Moon parts. Then the Sun reunited with the Moon, but early in the Earth's development the Sun again separated out and worked with greater intensity on evolution from the outside. Then the Moon separated from the Earth, working on it from without and ushering in a new phase in the heart's long evolution.

We see here, shining into the human physical body, many different forces from the most diverse sources. Belonging as it does to the oldest group of organs, the heart truly has a Sun element, a Moon element, a second Sun element and Moon element, and then, after the separation of the Earth, the addition of an Earth element. If all these elements of an organ (or those of the whole physical body) accord as they do with the harmony of the cosmos, a person is healthy. If one element outweighs another—for example, if the Sun element in the heart overwhelms that of the Moon, the heart becomes ill. You understand the illness when you know what caused the Moon element to fall behind. All illnesses result from various elements becoming unbalanced, or irregular, while restoration of health is found through restoring harmony among them. Speaking of such things is not enough; we must really understand this harmony and immerse ourselves in the wisdom of the world to be able to find the various elements working in a given organ.

The physical body is indeed a tremendously complex structure, as you realize from our considerations so far. You can sense what real occult physiology and anatomy are, since they must consider all these factors and comprehend the human being from the entire cosmos. They speak of Sun and Moon elements in the heart, larynx, brain, and so on. Because all these elements actually work in human beings as they exist before us today, human beings are, so to speak, solidified, crystallized products of all the processes throughout Saturn, Sun, Moon, and Earth phases of evolution. In the human being there stands before us something in which all of those elements are solidified.

Anthroposophy, for its part, begins when we do not look out into the universe but look into human beings themselves as they are today and seek to understand the various human organs—the physical, etheric, and astral bodies, the sentient, intellectual, and consciousness souls. But in anthroposophy we also have to begin at the bottom to ascend to the heights. For human beings the sense-perceptible physical world is the bottom level, made up of everything our senses and sense-oriented intellects perceive. *Theosophy* begins from the whole cosmos and examines the cosmic connections with sense-perceptible physical phenomena, with outer manifestations; that is the theosophical approach. *Anthroposophy* must begin with the human being in studying the physical world; it must study what is of sense-physical nature in the human being. It must begin by studying the human being as a sense being; that is the first step. Then we will have to go on to consider the human etheric body and then the astral body and the I, that which is to be found in the human being itself.

What must be of special interest to us in considering the sense world? The human being! The senses are the first aspect, since they are the means we use to know the physical world. Starting from the physical plane, anthroposophy must begin by speaking about the human senses, since it is through them that we know anything at all about that plane. And we will see how vital it is for a true understanding of the human being to begin by studying the senses. Let us take that as our first chapter, then, and ascend from there to contemplate the various spiritual aspects of human nature.

When anthroposophists study the human senses, they find themselves trespassing on anthropological ground. Anthroposophy must always start with sense reality but must be clear that the spirit works down into it from above. Anthropology limits itself to what can be investigated below and confuses everything. Anthropology views the human senses in a way that misconstrues matters and eliminates what is, because it lacks a guiding thread for discovering the corresponding truths properly. If no thread exists to act as a guide through factual labyrinths, it is impossible to find the way out. Spiritual research must spin the thread that the legendary Theseus used to guide himself out of the labyrinth of the Minotaur. Ordinary anthropology gets caught there and becomes the Minotaur's victim. We shall see that anthroposophy says something different from the usual outer view.

It is interesting to see, however, that contemporary science is forced by the external facts themselves to become more thorough and serious in its observation than it used to be. It is most trivial when speaking of the five senses—touch, smell, taste, sight, and hearing. We shall see that this list of the five senses leads to total confusion. Modern science has, to be sure, recently added three further senses, though it doesn't really know what to do with them. Today, we will lay the very first foundations of an anthroposophic science of the senses. We will list the senses that are really meaningful in light of the guiding thread discussed earlier.

The first human sense for consideration is the one spiritual science might term the *life sense*. It is a real sense that may be spoken of just as we speak of the sense of sight. What is it? It is something we are unaware of when everything is as it should be, and we sense it only when things within us are not in order. We feel faintness, for example, and perceive this state as an inner experience just as we perceive a color. What comes to awareness as thirst or hunger or as a burst of energy is perceived inwardly, just as a sound or color is. We usually notice such states only when things get out of balance. The first human self-perception is transmitted by the life sense, whereby the human being as a whole becomes aware of his or her bodily nature. The life sense is the first true sense, and it must be taken into account just as the senses of sight, smell, and hearing are. We cannot understand the senses if we do not recognize that it is possible to sense ourselves inwardly as a whole, to be inwardly aware of ourselves as a self-enclosed, living bodily totality.

We may become aware of the second sense, which is very different in nature from the life sense, when we move a limb. We would not be human if we could not perceive our own movements. A machine cannot perceive its own motion; this is possible only for a living being equipped with an actual sense to perceive it. The sense we possess for our own movement, from mere blinking to using our legs, is a real second sense, the *self-movement sense.*

We become aware of a third sense when we consider that human beings distinguish between up and down. It is very dangerous to lose this faculty, because then we cannot stand but instead topple over. One of our organs—the ear's three semicircular canals—is involved in this sense. If it is injured, we lose the ability to orient ourselves. Animals also possess this sense. In them, it is based on certain organs of balance known as *otoliths*—tiny pebble-like structures that must be exactly placed; otherwise the animal is likely to stagger. This is the *sense of balance* or the static sense.

We use the senses described thus far to perceive ourselves, to feel something within. We now move outside the human being to where we begin to interact with the outer world. The first interaction we have with the world consists of taking in external substances and perceiving these substances, a process made possible only when those substances become united with the body. Only substances in a gaseous condition actually belong in this category. Organs of the smell sense absorb them. That is our first interaction with the outer world. Things that do not emit gaseous substances cannot be smelled. Roses must emit gaseous matter for us to smell them. The fourth sense, then, is the *sense of smell.*

The fifth sense arises not simply when we perceive the material substance but when we take the first step into it and form a deeper relationship with matter. In this case, the matter must affect us in some way, such as when a watery substance comes into contact with our organs of taste. We do not have a direct perception of the material until the saliva has dissolved it. Here only an interrelationship between the tongue and the substance may be perceived. Things tell us not only what they are as substances but also how they can affect us. The relationship between the human being and nature thus becomes more intimate. That is the *sense of taste*, the fifth sense.

The sixth sense gives us even more intimate information about the nature of the things perceived; we are told more than the taste sense tells us. Here, special conditions have been established so that something can plainly show us what it is. In the case of smell, our bodies take things just as they are. The sense of taste is more complex, allowing substances to reveal more of their inner nature. With the sixth sense, we can discern whether or not an object allows light to shine through. If and how something is colored reveals the particular way it allows light to pass through. An object that allows green light to shine through shows us that its inner nature is such that it can allow this to happen. Whereas the sense of smell reveals only the outermost surface of things, the sense of taste communicates something of the inner nature of a substance. The sense of sight, on the other hand, penetrates all the way to a thing's depths. Such is the sixth sense, the *sense of sight*. The eye is a wonderful organ because it can penetrate more deeply into the nature of things than any of the other sense organs discussed so far. In vision, we have something special; when, for example, our eyes perceive the red color of the rose, the red surface tells us of the rose's inner nature. We see only the surface, but because that surface depends on the rose's inner nature, we learn to know its inner nature to a certain extent.

If we take hold of a piece of ice or hot steel, we penetrate even more deeply into the inner depths of a thing. Color supplies only manifestations of the surface. But ice is cold all the way through, and heat permeates the entire mass of hot metal. Heat and cold thus convey a still deeper knowledge of the inner nature of substances than the sense of sight can, because sight is limited to telling us about surface characteristics. The seventh sense, the *sense of warmth* reaches still further into the foundations of things.

Now let us see what comes of further inquiry and ask whether we can rely on our senses to go even more deeply into these matters. Can we understand their inner nature more precisely than we can through the sense of warmth? Indeed we can, when something expresses its inner nature by beginning to sound forth. Heat is evenly distributed throughout a substance, but that is not true of sound. Sounds make inner nature vibrate, and this gives us evidence as to a certain inner makeup. The more intimate sense of hearing discerns an object's inner mobility. It affords us more intimate knowledge of the outer world than the sense of warmth. This eighth sense is the *sense of hearing*. When an object is struck, it reveals its inner nature in the sound produced. We distinguish between things based on their inner nature, according to how they are able to vibrate when we make them sound. In a certain way, the soul of things speaks to us.

Now are there any senses higher than that of hearing? We must proceed much more cautiously when investigating the higher senses, for we must not confuse the senses with something else. In ordinary life, where one remains at ground level and confounds everything, one speaks of yet other senses, such as the sense of imitation, the sense of secrecy, and so on. The term *sense* is erroneously applied here, however. Sense is that perception through which we obtain knowledge without the help of the mental processes. Where judgment plays a role in acquiring knowledge, the term *sense* is inappropriate; *sense* is a term limited to situations where the power of judgment has not yet become active. We use a sense to perceive a color, but to make a judgment between two colors no sense is necessary.

In this sense (and this is also a misuse of the term!), are there any more senses? Yes, there is a ninth sense. We discover it when we think about the fact that there is indeed a certain capacity of perception in the human being. This is a sense that is especially important in laying the groundwork for anthroposophy. There is a perceptive capacity that, although it is not based on judgment, is present in it. We perceive it when we use speech for the purpose of coming to an understanding with others. In what is conveyed to us through speech there is not simply an expression of judgment; a real speech sense underlies it. This *sense of speech* is the ninth sense, and it is as real as the sense of sight or smell. A child learns to speak before learning to reason. A whole people has one language, but judgment is a function of the individual. What a sense conveys does not depend on the soul activity of the individual human being. Hearing makes us aware of the inner vibration, but the perception of a speech tone's *meaning* is more than just hearing.[14] The meaning conveyed by speech is discerned by a sense other than hearing—the sense of speech, or language. That is why children speak and understand what is spoken to them long before they learn to reason. Reasoning is actually learned through speech. What an educator the speech sense is—just as sight and hearing also are in early childhood! Nothing that the senses perceive can be changed or distorted. That applies to the perception of color exactly as it does to the perception of the inner nature of speech tones. We must recognize the speech sense as a special sense. It is the ninth in the sequence of senses.

And now we come to the tenth sense, the highest among those used in ordinary life. It is our means for understanding concepts expressed through the medium of speech. It, too, is really a sense, just as the others are. We must have concepts to reason. If the soul is to become active, it must be able to perceive concepts, which is possible through the *sense of concept*.

But what about the sense of touch, which seems to have been overlooked entirely? Of course! Touch as a sense is usually lumped together with the sense of warmth. This arises from the confusion created by those who lack the guiding spiritual thread. At first glance, touch indeed has significance only as the sense of warmth. The whole skin can be designated roughly as such a sense. It is also, in a certain way, there for the

---

14. Steiner differentiates between the German words *Ton* and *Laut*. *Ton* is translated as "sound," *Laut* as "tone" or "phonetic tone" (or "speech tone"). The word "tone" is not used here primarily in the musical sense, but in the sense of *feeling-tone* in language, as used by Henry Head in his *Aphasia and Kindred Disorders of Speech* (Cambridge, 1926; cited by Oliver Sacks in his essay on the sense of word, "The President's Speech," in *The Man Who Mistook His Wife for a Hat: and Other Clinical Tales*, (New York: Touchstone Books, 1998). See also Rudolf Steiner, *Anthroposophy (A Fragment)*, chapter 2.

touch sense. But proper observation sees that touching is not only something we do by placing our hands on an object to feel its surface; it also includes seeking something with our eyes. The senses of both smell and taste can be said to touch. We touch a thing when we sniff it with our sense of smell. All the senses, from the fourth through the seventh, or sense of warmth, have the capacity of touch in common and may be properly placed in the touch sense category. Only a crude approach such as that taken by modern physiology can ascribe to a single sense something that belongs to a whole series of them—in this case, the senses of smell, taste, sight, and temperature.[15]

Hearing cannot be considered a sense of touch, and even less so the sense of speech, or language, and less still the sense of concept. These senses may therefore be called *senses of comprehension.* Whereas in the sense of touch we have a sense that stops at the surface of things, unable to penetrate into them, we do penetrate things with the sense of warmth and continue to penetrate more and more deeply with each further sense. These higher senses allow us to understand and comprehend the inner nature of things and may thus be called senses of comprehension. In this way, you can see that three senses have to be listed before arriving at the sense of smell—three senses that inform us concerning our own human inner condition. They obtain their knowledge from our inner condition; the sense of smell then brings us to the boundary between the inner and outer worlds, and the higher senses allow us to penetrate more and more deeply into the outer world.

Are there still lower and higher senses? Yes—those mentioned thus far represent just a partial list. Other senses exist both above and below those we have discussed. We could go on from the sense of comprehension to the first astral sense and from there to consider the senses for gaining access to spiritual realms. If we were to do that, we would come to an eleventh, twelfth, and thirteenth sense. Merely mentioning these unfamiliar senses must be enough for now. More will be said about them tomorrow or the day after, when we will proceed from the physical

---

15. Rudolf Steiner later recognized the sense of touch as separate from the sense of temperature. See Lecture 8, August 29, 1919 in *The Foundations of Human Experience.*

to the spiritual level. They will lead us more deeply into the foundations of spiritual life, into which concepts cannot penetrate. Concepts cannot go beyond a certain point. A realm that requires higher senses for exploration lies beyond concepts. The sense of smell stops short of our inner nature. And just as we have three senses below the sense of smell, three senses are also found above the sense of concept—senses that allow us to penetrate the outer aspect of the spiritual in the same way that the lower three senses delve into external aspects of the physical.

We shall limit ourselves today to the physical plane, and this is the reason we are restricting ourselves to the senses for perceiving the physical. A grounding of this sort cannot be dispensed with. Failure to establish such a grounding has created grave confusion in the sciences, including philosophy and epistemology. A generalized approach is adopted, asking what we can learn through the separate senses. The difference between the senses of sight and hearing cannot be distinguished. Light waves and sound waves are spoken of in a single breath, disregarding the fact that sight penetrates less deeply into the nature of things than does the sense of hearing, which tells us something about the soul nature of the outer world.

Through the higher eleventh, twelfth, and thirteenth senses, we will penetrate into the spirit of things. Every sense has a different nature and different essential characteristics. We need, above all, to take this into account. We can, therefore, regard a large number of presentations today on the nature of vision and its relationship to the world around us, brought to us by physics, as views that never consider the nature of the senses at all. Countless erroneous conclusions are based on this misconception of the nature of the senses. This has to be emphasized, because popular texts in no way do justice to what has been said here. Indeed, popular books often state the exact opposite. In them, you may read statements written by people who haven't the slightest notion of the inner nature of the senses. We must realize that the perspective science takes leaves it no choice but to speak as it does, that it cannot escape making a mistake, since the course of development has been to largely forget what is correct. The true nature and being of the senses thus constitute the first chapter of anthroposophy.

2.

Supersensible Processes in the Human Senses

YESTERDAY, we limited ourselves to a mere listing of the senses—although the way in which it was done was derived from human nature itself. We did not jumble all the senses together, as is typical in sense physiology because of its inability to discern where each sense fits into the picture. We enumerated the senses and then we arranged them in an order that accords with the facts of human makeup. Today, we will proceed to make a closer study of the human sense essence, for this is one of the most important areas from which to approach human nature.

We began with the sense to which we gave the name of "life-feeling," "life sense," or "vital sense." We must now ask, what is the basis, in the true spirit of the word, of this "sense of life." We will have to delve deeply into the unconscious depths of the human organism to make ourselves a picture of this sense's origin—though of course it will be only a sketch.

The first thing encountered will be the remarkable working together of the physical and etheric bodies. This becomes evident when we try to find out what the life sense is based on. The lowest member of the human makeup, the physical body, and the ether body enter into a very specific relationship to each other. That is the result of another factor that appears and sets into the etheric body and suffuses, or, we might say, saturates it; another element flows through and pervades it.

Human beings of our time are not aware of this other element, but spiritual science can tell us what works in the etheric body and, pictorially speaking, saturates it as water does a sponge. Spiritual scientific examination discovers it to be the same as that which, in the distant

future, human beings will develop as Spirit Body, or *Atman*.[1] We do not
yet possess it through our own development; it still has to be lent to us by
the surrounding spiritual world. It is lent to us without any conscious participation on our part. Later, in a still far distant future, we will develop it
through our own effort. It is Spirit Body, or Atman, then, that pervades
and suffuses the etheric body. And what does it do in the ether body?

We are not yet in a position to harbor our own Spirit Body, or
Atman; at the present time it is still a super-human element within us.
This super-human element, this Atman, expresses itself in that it con-
tracts the etheric body, indeed, even cramps it together. If we want to
borrow a picture from the outer sense world, we might say that it could
be compared to the frosty effect of cold. What will one day be the highest human member, for which we are still too immature, cramps us
together. The result of the cramping is that the astral body is as though
squeezed out, and to the degree that the etheric body is compressed,
the physical body, too, experiences tension. Frosty tensions arise in it. It
is as though one were to squeeze out a sponge. The astral body seeks
breathing room and is then pressed out. Processes in the astral body are
feeling experiences, experiences of pleasure and aversion, joy and pain,
and so on. It is this process of being pressed out that makes itself evident in us as the *life sense* in feelings of freedom, energy, or faintness,
for example.

Now, let us take a further step upward. We talked of the "self-movement sense" as the second sense. Again, something is at work in the
etheric body that we do not consciously possess. The etheric body is

---

1. *Atman* refers to the "spirit human being." "When the human I-being gains mastery
over the physical body and when the most powerfully opposing forces of the physical
body are also overcome, the human being bears within itself the *Spirit Human* (Spiritual Body), or Atman. In transforming one's physical body into Atman, or spiritual
body, one thus becomes sevenfold. Outwardly, the physical body appears as a physical
body, but inwardly it is completely controlled and permeated by the I. At this stage, the
physical body is both physical body and Atman" (*The Spiritual Hierarchies and the
Physical World: Reality and Illusion*, p. 68). *Buddhi* is the sixth aspect of the sevenfold
human being, or "Life Spirit," the transformed etheric human body. *Manas* is also
referred to as "Spirit Self," the fifth aspect of the sevenfold human being, "contained" in
the transformed astral human body. See also *Theosophy*, pp. 50–56.

filled, saturated like a sponge filled with water, and the saturating element is the Life Spirit, or *Buddhi*, that we will eventually develop of ourselves. The spiritual world has lent it to us for the time being. Buddhi, or the Life Spirit, works differently from the Spirit Body. Its effect is to establish a state of balance in the astral body reminiscent of still water. Balance in the etheric body, and then in the physical body, brings about balance in the astral body. When this balance is disturbed by some external agency, it seeks to restore itself. If, in making some motion, imbalance is created, balance is restored. Let us say that we stretch a hand out—an astral current flows back in the opposite direction. That is the case in every movement of our organism. Any change of physical position calls forth in the organism an opposing astral streaming. This happens when we blink our eyes or move our legs. The sense of our own motion is experienced in this inwardly felt restoring of balance in the astral body.

Next, comes a third element that can pervade the etheric body. This element—Spirit Self or *Manas*—is also one that we are currently only faintly conscious of, although our developmental task is to become aware of it. It therefore works differently on the etheric body than Life Spirit does. Its effect is to expand the etheric body, bringing about a situation that is the direct opposite of what was characterized as the frost produced by the life sense. The effect of Manas on the etheric body might be likened to an influx of warmth into a space; something resembling a current of warmth is set streaming into the etheric body by Manas, causing an elastic expansion in it. This brings about a thinning process in the astral body, but without pressing it out, so that it is able to remain in the expanding etheric body.

Whereas the sensation experienced with the life sense is based on the pressing out of the astral body, what we have called the "static sense" or sense of balance" originates in the expanding of the etheric body, which gives the astral body inwardly more space. The astral body is then not so compressed; it grows thinner. This thinning of the astral and ether bodies enables physical matter, too, somehow to stretch and expand itself. Whereas Atman's effect is to cramp the physical body and that of Buddhi to maintain it in a state of balance, that of Manas is to relieve pressure on it. And since the etheric body expands, the physical body is able to push out tiny particles of its being at certain places. That is the origin of the three small semicircular ear canals standing in perpendicular relationship to one another, corresponding to the three directions of space. They might be called distentions of the physical substance of the body.

Similar organ formations arise in a great variety of ways as new creations, marvelous structures that owe their existence to a relieving of pressure from outside rather than to being pushed out from within. Owing to the fact that the astral body is able to expand further, it can enter into relationship with the outer world, with which it must establish balance. If that were not to happen, people would stand at an angle or might even fall over. There was no such necessity in the case of the first two senses, but the third sense has the task of establishing balance. When we strive to enter somewhere, we must do it in the way possible for us; for instance, in space we must orient ourselves to the three directions of space. For that reason, the three half-circle canals grow perpendicular to one another in the three directions of space. If these organs in the ear are injured, our static sense no longer functions and we become dizzy or lose consciousness, and so forth. Animals, however, descended prematurely into material existence, so that their physical substance is more hardened. Stony structures called *otoliths* arise within them. They are situated so that they help animals to determine and sense balance.

We have now discussed three senses in a sequence progressing, so to speak, from inside outward. The last sense is just on the borderline between what human beings experience inwardly and what we must experience in order to become a part of the outer world. Modern science, which clings to physical facts, has recently had it pushed under its nose to the point of finally having to recognize these three areas of our sense organization. Here, too, we must make a sharp distinction between the actual findings of research and the opinions held by group-soul cadres of learned men on the basis of inadequate thinking. They have demonstrated in just this area of science how, inevitably, the lack of a thread to guide them through the labyrinth leads to error. That lack is a major stumbling block in this case. It has led to comparing organs in the human ear with certain organs in the plant world, where a kind of balance is brought about in the leaning of a plant through the shifting of the position of such particles in it. Because, as a rule, logic leaves modern thinkers in the lurch just at the moment when a correct view is needed, they sometimes conclude that plants also have a sense of balance.

Logic of this sort is based on a standpoint I have repeatedly cited and characterized. There is a certain plant that rolls up its leaves to trap invading insects. The superficial claim is made that this plant must be credited with possessing a corresponding sense. But I am familiar with another object that is able to perform the same function even more competently and even goes so far as to attract small animals and snap them up, namely, the mousetrap. With the same right then, what is said of the human senses and then extrapolated to the plant world could be equally applied to mousetraps. It would be just as ridiculous to apply the same reasoning to a pair of scales and talk of the scales' sense of balance. Such absurdities are the product of inadequate thinking that is unable to expand and sufficiently penetrate the real nature of a matter.

These are three senses with which science has been concerning itself, but it will learn to understand them only when it finds and makes use of the thread of spiritual science. Only then will it achieve a true understanding of the structure of the human organism, the way it actually is precisely under the effects of the interactions I have described. That requires the development of a spiritual scientific ability to observe and grasp the whole human being from within.

Now we come to the sense of smell. It can be asked why the sense that science calls the sense of touch, the one most dealt with, has been left out here. Since there is to be such a limited number of lectures on the senses, some aspects will have to be covered rather sketchily, and much that is said may then sound somewhat paradoxical. The sense of touch has been left out because the way it is usually described is as a fantasy structure, an invention, of physiology. It cannot be said to exist as such; a whole series of senses can equally well be designated touch senses. There is no such thing as an actual sense of touch.

What goes on when we touch something? Let us say that a person takes hold of an object. We can ascribe the entire process to the sense of balance. Pressure exerted on some part of a body upsets its balance, and what takes place does so only within the sense of balance. Exactly the same thing occurs when we put pressure on a table, stroke a velvet surface, or pull a string: touching calls forth changes in our own state of balance when we press, stroke, pull, and so on. The sense of touch is always to be sought where the sense of balance is active.

Science holds the most disastrous views about the touch sense. People speak of pressing without going into the nature of pressing itself; it is something they do not think about. To spiritual scientific observation, however, it raises the question of what kind of disturbance it causes in the sense of balance and what equalizing adjustment it necessitates in the astral body. We can judge how mistaken it is to view the sense of pressure as an aspect of the sense of touch if we ask why we are not crushed by the huge atmospheric pressure bearing down upon us. If the matter were as ordinarily viewed, there would be tremendous pressure on our bodies. Curious youngsters may ask about this in their physics classes. They are answered with the statement that the pressure from outside and a countering pressure from inside our bodies are equal and thus balance each other, that human bodies are filled with air, as their surroundings are, with the result that the two opposing pressures are the same. This maintains balance, and people cannot be crushed. If the child is awake, he or she might object and say, "I have often dived deep into water and been completely surrounded by water, yet was not crushed, in spite of the fact that my body was not completely filled with water. Otherwise, I would have drowned!"

This is an example of the absurdity to which matters lead when they are explained purely externally and materialistically. The fact in this case is that we are involved in an eminently spiritual process when exposed to pressure. We are led right into our astral bodies whenever disturbances of balance require equalizing. When pressure is exerted on any part of us, our balance shifts, and we push the astral body into that compressed part, thus restoring balance. In fact, we let it extend out slightly beyond the part under pressure. There is, so to speak, always a small astral swelling where the body part is pressed. This purely astral equalizing effect is so powerful that it is able to overcome from within the full pressure of the air outside. The spirit is literally palpable here; it just isn't noticed.

Now, what happens with the sense of smell? The organism is involved here with something of which we are more closely aware than in the case of the other senses—the consciousness soul itself. What spiritual science terms the consciousness soul is brought into operation in the act of smelling. It calls forth at a certain place in the organism a process that is not merely one of thinning or expanding. Here, the astral body extends its influence outward beyond the limits of the organism. Gaseous substance penetrates into the mucous membranes of the nose as we smell, and astral substances simultaneously balance this process by pressing outward in the same measure. When we are engaged in smelling something, these astral substances always desert the organism and plunge into the object; they experience not only in themselves but in the object, too, what we call fragrance, aroma, stench, or whatever.

A "feeler" arises in the astral body through the consciousness soul. The sense of taste functions as it does because the intellectual soul is working on the organism. This soul uses the organ of taste to pour out astral currents and sends them to meet the substances upon the tongue. The process that takes place in smelling is a very special one, for what is streaming out of the astral body in the act of smelling? Nothing other than will-like nature. What we feel inwardly as the will impulse wells up to meet the material flowing in as we smell. Smelling is a process of resisting, a will to repel the influx of matter. Spiritual research can state that such matter is not merely air-like substance—that is only Maya, illusion—but rather will flowing in from outside us. Forces of will engage one another when we smell things. The result, as Schopenhauer guessed, is that wills coming from within and from without fight and obstruct each other mutually. Schopenhauer built his philosophy of the will on this notion.[2] But that is a false metaphysics. His statements about these forces of the will hold true only in the case of smell. Everything else is simply interpreted into it.

---

2. Arthur Schopenhauer (1788–1860), the German philosopher and author of *The Word as Will and Idea* (*Die Welt als Wille und Vorstellung*).

Just as what pours out through the sense of smell is will-like, what streams out toward foods in tasting has the nature of feeling, and what streams in is likewise of a feeling nature. Feeling interacts with feeling in our tasting. Anything else is simply Maya, only an external sign. A feeling reaction functions here as a sense, in that taste is perceived as pleasant or unpleasant, repugnant, and so on. It is not feeling as such that is involved here, just the corresponding interactions of feelings.

The next sense we come to is the sense of sight. What works here on the etheric body and streams into it is the sentient soul. What occurs is of a thought-like nature; a thought-like principle prevails. The sentient soul already harbors in itself, though as a subconscious thought, what is conscious in the consciousness soul. In the sentient soul it is a form of thinking that streams outward through the eyes as genuine thought substance. It has a far greater elasticity than the two other substances that stream out through the senses of smell and taste and for that reason reaches out much further. An astral element really does stream out from the human being to the things. It is not true that ether waves of light enter the eyes and cause them to project an image outward. For that to happen, someone would have to be sitting in the eyes performing the function of projecting images. What a gruesomely superstitious idea this figure doing the projecting is! In a case like this, science—which is so proud of its naturalism—resorts grotesquely to that much despised imagination to help itself.

An astral element streams out as thought substance toward a thing and continues until, at some distant point, it encounters resistance in an opposing astral countercurrent. The conflict that ensues between these two astral elements creates the color that we sense on things; it comes into being at the boundary of the thing, where the astrality streaming out of us meets the astrality streaming forth from the object. Color is produced at the border between the interior and the exterior astral elements.

It is very strange when one considers, for example, that in the sentient soul there is, in fact, a subconscious thinking that appears first in the intellectual soul, and that we first become aware of it in the consciousness soul. If we look at something with both eyes, what seem to be two impressions are in fact caused by a kind of thinking that at first is not conscious. If this is to become conscious, then these two thought moments must cooperate. They must make their way from the sentient soul up into the consciousness soul. To illustrate, here are both hands, each of which can sense things on its own. They must intersect, however, if we are to become conscious of the feeling that the one hand senses the other, just as we become truly aware of external objects only when we touch them. If the impressions developed by thinking activity in the sentient soul are to be lifted into consciousness, they must intersect. In the act of seeing, this is a result of the optic nerves in the brain intersecting. This crossing is based on the sentient soul's subconscious thinking being raised into the consciousness soul through such a crossing, so that one soul perceives the work of the other. Thus, the physical arises out of the spiritual, and the human being can now be understood, down to the finest anatomical details, through anthroposophy.

The next sense is the sense of warmth. Here again is something that, through its effects on human beings, mediates the sense of warmth. This is the sentient body. It activates its astral substance and allows it to stream outward to enable us to experience warmth. This occurs when we are able to send our astral substance outward without being hindered in the act. We don't feel warmed in the bathtub if the water surrounding us is at body temperature; if both are equal, we can't absorb warmth from the water. Only when we stream out warmth or when it can stream into us from outside do we sense either warmth or coldness. When our surroundings lack warmth, our own warmth flows out into them; when we lack warmth, we let warmth stream into us. Here again, it is obvious that an outstreaming and an instreaming are taking place. When inner and outer equilibrium exists, then temperature is not experienced. The experience of temperature is always connected with the activity of the human sentient body. If we touch some object where the temperature is rising, the outstreaming of the sentient body becomes ever stronger.

What wants to come in from outside forces itself more and more upon us, and the sentient body has to meet it with a correspondingly powerful countercurrent. There is a certain limit here, however. When it is no longer possible for the sentient body to let a force flow out to match the heat coming from outside, we cannot endure it and get burned. We would also have to feel a burning sensation on touching something very cold if our sentient body is not able to let its own substance stream out. If we take hold of a cold object that hinders us from letting substance stream out of the sentient body, because the object gives nothing up to us, then the extreme cold manifests as a burning and causes blisters. Both are due to the same effect.

Let us turn now to what is called the sense of hearing. It is the sense with which the etheric body is involved. In its present state, the etheric body, unlike the sentient body, is unable to give up any of its substance without our suffering permanent loss. Since Atlantean times the etheric body has been constituted in such a way that it cannot give up anything further, which would deprive the human being of life forces.[3] Hearing must therefore be based on an entirely different process, for in this area we have nothing more to give up. The highest sense that we can develop out of ourselves is the sense of warmth. If something that we ourselves do not have were not to enter into us here, there could be no such thing as a sense of hearing. Therefore, the human organism is permeated by beings who saturate it like a sponge.

These are the beings we call *Angeloi*, or angels.[4] They went through the human stage in the past. They send their astral substance into us as a foreign astral substance, which we then make our own, allowing it to

---

3. The time of "Atlantis" refers to a period of prehistory and to a specific epoch of cosmic and human evolution on Earth. See Rudolf Steiner, *Cosmic Memory.*

4. The spiritual hierarchies were first outlined by Dionysius the Areopagite, an author who lived about the sixth century A.D. In a lecture during 1921, Steiner said of the hierarchies: "When we ascend into the spiritual, we come to beings arranged above humankind in the same way that human beings have their place above the animal, plant, and mineral realms. As we ascend we therefore have ... the *angeloi* (angelic beings), the *archangeloi* (archangelic beings), and the *archai* (primal beings, or time spirits).... The beings we designate angeloi, or angels, are those who have the strongest relationship to the individual, or single human being.... Those of the second hierarchy above humankind are the archangels ... one of whose functions is to work as "folk spirits," embracing groups of individuals who belong together as a people.... The archai [act as] guiding beings throughout certain epochs of time, beyond the differentiations among various peoples" (*Cosmosophy*, vol 1, pp. 88–89). Steiner also discusses the higher hierarchies at length in *The Spiritual Hierarchies and the Physical World: Reality and Illusion.*

work in us and then to stream out again. It streams out through our ears to meet what sound brings toward us. We move, as it were, on the wings of these beings into that inner realm that we learn to know as the soul of things. Here we are concerned with beings who stand above human beings and fill them but whose substance is of the same nature as our own astral substance.

There is a still higher sense, the sense of speech or words, of *tone*. Here again we are involved with an area in which we human beings have nothing of our own to contribute. For that reason, beings have to intervene whose substance is similar to that of the human etheric body. Of course, they also possess the corresponding astrality, but that is pressed out into the world around us. They have to enter us and give us of their etheric bodies, enabling us to pour this force out again into our surroundings. These beings are the Archangeloi, or archangels. Their role is entirely different from that played by the angels. It is due to their activity in us that we are able not only to hear the tones of speech but also to understand their meaning. We are not limited to the perception of a musical tone—say a G or C-sharp. But on hearing a speech tone we can go further, to an experience of its inner nature; we perceive an "A" ("ah") according to the sense of tone. The beings referred to are the same as those we call "folk spirits"—spirits of the various peoples. In the sense of hearing, angels manifest their work outwardly in air vibrations, which affect the air in our ears, whereas the archangels counter what occurs in the air outside with a different kind of action. They cause patterns of movement in a fluid substance with the result that it circulates in a certain direction. That we perceive the meaning of "A," for example, is also a consequence of the circula-tion of the finer fluids.

This activity comes to outward expression in the shaping of a people's physiognomy, in the particular expression built into the organisms of individuals belonging to a certain race or culture. That is what, in par-ticular, these beings bring about. Therefore, we can say that the fluids in a people flow differently and the whole organism works differently according to how the archangel associated with the people endows them with this or that as a sense of tone. When, for instance, one people says

"Aham" (Sanskrit) for "I," regardless of what theories they may have concerning the human I, these theories play no role. The two consecutive "A" sounds create a basic organization whose result is that individuals within that culture have an experience of the I that corresponds to the two "A" sounds sequence. When a race or culture combines "I" with a "ch" sound (in the German "ich"), it brings about a wholly different effect. Such a people must have an entirely different conception of the I. There is a particular nuance, a special coloring, in the "I," and it is what is implanted by the folk spirit into the organisms of the people concerned in connection with the conception of the I.

It makes a great difference, too, whether something is described by a word containing the sequence "A" and "O" (or an "I") and then an "E." The whole feeling of a people changes accordingly. *Amor* (Latin for "love") conveys a different nuance of feeling than does the German "Liebe." Here we see a typical example of the folk spirit at work. It is not a matter of indifference that "Adam" is used by the Israelites to denote the first human form, whereas in ancient Persia it means "I." Quite different qualities of feeling are evoked thereby in the different peoples. We touch here on the mysteries of language, or rather of its first elements.

We are speaking here of the activity of beings of archangelic rank. They pervade human beings with the speech sense or tone sense and set our fluid substance vibrating. One of the greatest experiences a person who is ascending to higher worlds can have is to begin feeling what a difference there is in the formative force of the various speech tones. The tone force shows its effects best in the fluid element, while that of sound is shown in the air.

We can also sense the significance of someone's feeling prompted to call some person or being "Eva" (sounded: long "a-v-ah"). If the same speaker wants to express something else that reflects the opposite relationship, that of the spirit to the physical, "Eva" can be sounded backwards and thus be turned into "Ave" ("Hail!"), a fitting sequence of syllables with which to greet the Madonna. This evokes an opposite sensation in the human organism from that experienced in "Eva." Another such transposition, adding a "J," is the word "Jahve," as used for God in the Old Testament. A person on the path of higher knowledge can experience every aspect of the relationship between Jahve and Eve ("Eva") by delving into the nature of the speech tones involved.

Language did not spring from arbitrary roots; it is spiritual in origin. And to experience it in its own spiritual nature, we have been given the sense of speech, or tone, which is as true a sense as all the others. It should be added that deeper reasons exist why the senses must follow the sequence in which we have treated them.

We will go on, the next time we meet, to discuss a higher sense, the sense of concept, and still higher ones, in order to be able to explain the microcosm through spiritual scientific means.

3.

The Higher Senses, Inner Forces, and Creative Principles in the Human Organism

OUR STUDY of the senses has progressed to what we call the speech sense. We will now go on to what we might call the "concept sense," using the term "concept" not in its philosophical meaning as pure concept but as it is ordinarily used when we form a mental picture of something someone tells us. We could have equally well called it the "idea sense" or the sense for mental pictures or representations.

First, though, we will have to inquire as to how this "concept" sense arises. To do that, we will have to refer back to the two senses previously discussed—the sense of sound (or hearing) and the sense of speech—and ask ourselves what it means to have a speech (or phonetic) sense and how the perceiving of speech tone, as described here, comes about. I will begin by characterizing the special happenings that occur when a speech tone—an "A," say, or an "I," or some other—is perceived. We need to have a clear idea of the process involved in the perception. Since we cannot spend a whole hour discussing it, I will limit myself to a few remarks that you can verify for yourselves as you think about the matter or that you can research in life.

You know that in music we can distinguish between a single pitch, a melody, and harmony. You are also aware that harmony is based on perceiving simultaneously produced pitches, whereas melody is a series of consecutive sound pitches, in which case, it is the individual tone as such that is considered. We can understand the mechanism involved in the perception of speech tone only when we study the relationship of the resounding element within the speech tone to the speech tone itself.

Let us begin with harmony, in which tones sound together, and melody, in which they sound consecutively. If you imagine that you could make conscious what you unconsciously do in perceiving a speech tone, then the following would occur.

Let us be quite clear that senses have an unconscious—or at least a subconscious—aspect. Senses would not be senses if the unconscious element in sense perception were raised to consciousness; in that case, we would have to speak instead of having reached a judgment, a concept, or the like. Try to imagine the process that would have to take place if we were to carry out consciously what occurs in our unconsciousness when we perceive a speech tone. Imagine that you perceive a melody. When you do that, you hear the tones sounding in sequence. Now picture what it would be if you were able to compress the melodic line in which the tones are heard consecutively to the point of hearing them simultaneously. To do this, you would have to shove the past and the future into each other. You would have to know in the middle of the melody what was coming next, in order to slide the future into the present. This process that we are unable to carry out consciously actually goes on unconsciously in the speech sense. Whenever we hear an "A" or an "I" or some other speech tone, a melody is instantaneously transformed into a harmony by an unconscious activity within us. That is the mystery of tone. This marvelous unconscious activity is carried out on a more spiritual plane, in a manner similar to that taking place within the eye when the various refractions occur according to the strict physical laws that we become conscious of only afterward. We are doing here exactly what the physicist does when he explains how refractions occur in the eye. Melody becomes harmony instantaneously.

That is not enough, however. If that were all that took place, a speech tone would not result. More is necessary. You must realize that no musical tone is just a simple sound. A sound is a musical tone when, no matter how weakly, the overtones always sound with it. They are always perceived, even when they are practically inaudible. That is what accounts for the special quality of musical sound as contrasted with other kinds of sounds and noises. In melody, then, you have not only its single pitches but all the overtones as well. If you instantaneously compress a melody into harmony, you have not only compressed the sequence of its single fundamental tones; you have compressed all the sound's overtones as well.

Unconscious activity has something more to do: it must disregard the fundamental sounds and hear past them, as it were. Our souls actually do that when we hear the "A" or "I" tone. It is not as though the other tones weren't there, but rather that our attention is shifted from them to the overtone harmony they make. Only then do we have the speech tone. Speech tones arise when a melody is instantaneously transformed into a harmony and then the fundamental tones are disregarded in favor of the system of overtones. These overtones then convey the meaning of the tone "A" or "I." Now you have what speech tone perception really is, explained in the same way as the physicist explains the act of seeing.

To take up another equally difficult but vital question—how are ideas or meanings perceived? How is it that we hear words, and even through or beyond words, so that we comprehend the meaning they convey? How does that occur? That something of a very special nature is involved here is at once apparent from a simple weighing of the fact that a great variety of speech tones can designate the same thing in different languages. *Love* is termed "amor" by one language and "Liebe" by another. There is something expressed in each of these different tone pictures that is the same for both of them. This points to the "visualization" or "concept" sense behind them. While one hears a different speech tone with each people and each language, one hears through the tone to the same conception, to that which stands behind it and is the same, in spite of the difference of the tone pictures. That must also be perceived. How does this occur?

As we search for an answer, let us study that process against the background of an assumption that I ask you to keep always in mind, namely, that mental pictures (concepts) are conveyed to us by means of speech tones. In perceiving speech tones, if we have a melody that is transformed into a harmony in which the fundamental tones are disregarded (which provides us with the "tone" or "word" sense), then it is necessary, for the visualization or concept sense to come out, that our attention also be turned away from the whole set of overtones. When this is done on the soul level, we look back to what has been embodied in the overtones, to what is experienced as thought picture or concept. At the same time, however, as we hear the tones and words of the language we speak, there is that which has nuance and is a toned-down experience of a universally human element that pervades all speech tones and all languages: the thought picture or concept.

We have talked of the fact that high spiritual beings, the folk spirits, who have a special mission in connection with earthly life, manifest themselves in the tones of speech.[1] They work not only in mysterious murmurs but also in the equally mysterious forming activity of the fluids of the human being as the system of overtones vibrates into the human organism. And it must be added that the universal human element that underlies the tones of the overtones is the spirit of humankind that we all share and that moves over the face of the entire Earth. We come to know this wielding human spirit only when each of us, in our own particular locality, carefully listens through and beyond the overtones to the inaudible, to the purely imaginative element. In that human beings have received the possibility of looking and hearing beyond nuances and of recognizing something common that flows over the entire Earth, people have first attained the ability, in the course of human development, to grasp what is universally human. For it is only in our life of mental images that we begin to comprehend the Christ Spirit in its true form, that of the universally human. Those spiritual beings whose mission it is to proclaim him in the most varied forms and to each of whom he has assigned a special place—as Goethe so beautifully describes in his poem "The Mysteries"—these spirits, these messengers sent by him are the folk spirits of the various nationalities.

This gives you an idea of the nature of the visualization or concept sense. With that we have traveled a very special path. We have exhausted the list of what is ordinarily said to constitute the human senses. That

---

1. The term *folk soul* refers to the guiding spirit of a particular racial or cultural group. For a further discussion of folk souls in relation to speech, see "History of Language in Its Relation to the Folk Souls" in *The Genius of Language: Observations for Teachers* (Hudson, NY: Anthroposophic Press, 1995).

end was reached when we examined the unconscious capacity of the human soul to disregard the system of overtones. What higher capacity can there still be? What is it that diverts our attention from the overtones? What in us reaches out like tentacles to push the overtones back? It is our astral body that has this capacity. Acquiring the ability to shove back the overtones, which in ordinary terminology simply means disregarding them, signifies a heightening of the astral body's power beyond its previous ability, when it could push back less.

When does the astral body gain such strength? This happens when it has not only the capacity to push the overtones back, which will enable it to form mental images and thus arrive at the boundary of the external world, where tones can be observed as mental pictures, but also when it can thrust its astral substance out with its own inner strength without there being any resistance. Forming mental pictures always requires overcoming the resistance of the system of overtones.

At the moment when we acquire the capacity to extend our astral tentacles without an external cause, spiritual perception begins. The organs of spiritual perception start to develop. When we become able not merely to withdraw attention from the overtones but to thrust out our astral tentacle-like substance from a certain place in the forebrain located between the eyebrows, we develop the two-petal lotus flower there.[2] It is the first spiritual organ, one that might also be called the *imaginative* sense. That is the eleventh sense. And to the extent that we keep on increasing our capacity to put forth our astral substance without any outer compulsion to do so, we develop further higher senses. Work of this kind develops a very complex sense in the region of the larynx, the sixteen-petal lotus flower, the sense of *inspiration*. In the heart region it develops the *intuitive* sense, the twelve-petal lotus flower. And there are other, even higher senses, but since they bring us into purely spiritual realms, they cannot really be spoken of as senses in the ordinary meaning of that term. It will suffice to add to the actual physical

---

2. "Lotus flower" (also called "chakra") refers to the vortex-like centers within the body that form specific spiritual organs. The "petals" roughly describe their appearance to spiritual vision. See "Some Effects of Initiation" in *How to Know Higher Worlds*; also see Florin Lowndes, *Enlivening the Chakra of the Heart* (London: Sophia Books, 1998).

senses the senses of *imagination, inspiration,* and *intuition.* Let us ask now whether these three senses function only in clairvoyant people, or if there is something identifiable as activities of these senses also in ordinary people.

Yes, indeed there is! If you have understood the way these senses function in clairvoyant individuals, you will say that they work by extending themselves outward in a tentacle-like manner. They are present in ordinary people also, but they project themselves inward instead of outward. Just at the place where the two-petal lotus flower develops in clairvoyants, ordinary people have something resembling two such tentacles, directed inward and crossing each other in the area of the forebrain only. The ordinary consciousness turns these tentacles inward instead of outward as in clairvoyant people.

I will have to make use of an analogy to explain the situation here. You would have to do a great deal of meditating to go from the analogy to the actual fact. For it is a fact. You need only consider that we see what is outside us, but not what is inside. We don't, for example, see our own hearts and brains. And this holds true with respect to the spiritual. Not only do we not see our own organs, we are not even aware of them and are therefore unable to make use of them. They are nevertheless active. The fact that something is unconscious does not mean that it is inactive. Consciousness does not determine reality; otherwise everything surrounding us here in Berlin that we are not momentarily looking at would not exist (though that is the reasoning adhered to by people who deny the existence of higher worlds on the ground that they do not perceive them). These higher senses are indeed active, but their activity is directed inward rather than outward. And we perceive its effects. How do we perceive them?

When the imaginative sense directs its activity inward, what we normally call the sense of something—an external sense, the outer perception—arises. The activity of the imaginative sense has to be directed inward for us to see what is outside us. Everything we sense outside ourselves we can perceive only because what appears in the imaginative sense works into us. You must take care to distinguish, however, between what has just been called a sensation and a tone, for example.

There is a difference between hearing a tone or seeing a color and having a sensation in connection with it. To see a color and say it is red is different from having the sensation that it is beautiful or ugly, pleasing or unpleasant in the immediate impression we have of it.

The sense of *inspiration* also pours its activity inward, and that activity accounts for a still more complex form of sensing—that of feeling. The whole feeling life, which has more inwardness than the mere life of sensing, is an activity of the organ of *inspiration* that is directed only inward rather than outward. And the turning inward of the intuitive sense gives rise to what we know as thinking, as the forming of thoughts. That is the result of the inward-turned activity of the intuitive sense. First we have the sensation of a thing, then we have the feeling of it, and finally we form thoughts about it.

You will have seen that we have risen from the life of the senses to that of the soul. From outside, out of the world of senses, we have come to understand the soul in the human being itself in sensing, feeling, and thinking. If we were to now contemplate the still higher senses—they cannot really be called senses at all—that correspond to the other lotus flowers and examine their inward-directed activity, we would find the entire life of the soul. When, for example, the eight-petal lotus flower, located in the lower part of the organism, or the ten-petal lotus flower pours its activity into us, an even more subtle soul force is generated. And at the end of the list we find the very subtlest activity, which can no longer be referred to simply as "thought"; it must be called "pure thought"—purely logical thought. That is what is produced by the inward-directed activity of the various lotus flowers. When this working into us ceases to be limited only to working into us and begins instead to become an outward extending of the tentacles that I have described as ordinarily inward-oriented, and when it undergoes a crossing and outward pouring as lotus flowers, then that higher activity sets in whereby we rise from the soul to the spiritual level. What otherwise appears to us to be just inner life in thinking, feeling, and willing now enters the outside world, carried by spiritual beings.

Thus, you have comprehended the human being, in that you have gone from the senses through the soul and on to that which is no longer in the human being but is rather something spiritual that works into us from outside and belongs to us just as much as to the whole of nature and the universe. What I have been describing to you in today's presentation, as well as in the two previous lectures, is *the true human being, the human being that is an instrument for perceiving the world, for experiencing it through the soul and grasping it spiritually.* That is the true human being. And what the human being is actually forms the physical body. I have not been describing human beings in a finished condition but rather what is active in them. All that activity, everything that works together in the physical, soul, and spiritual planes, is what forms human beings as they stand before us upon this planet.

By what means is that forming accomplished? Here, too, a few indications must suffice, but you will find them confirmed if you study the positive findings of outer observation. What we perceive when we use our outer senses to observe our fellow human beings is an optical illusion; it just isn't there. Fuller study turns up something entirely different. Imagine, just to draw a picture, that you are quite unable to see yourself as a whole physical person, so that as you look at yourself you see only a part of your bodily surface. You can never see your back or the back of your head. You do know that you have them; you know it from information provided by the other senses—the sense of balance, the sense of self-movement, and so on. We are inwardly aware of possessing parts that we cannot perceive with our external senses. There is a good deal of us that we are unable to perceive and can become aware of only by developing the higher organs of perception that I have been describing to you.

Let us now turn our attention to that part of ourselves that we are able to perceive with physical senses, with our eyes, for example, limiting ourselves to that portion of our bodies that we can see. What is the portion of the human being that we can perceive? Take these words in their exact meaning. By what means are we to perceive this visible portion of ourselves?

Everything we discern is perceived essentially through the sentient soul. For if information were not to come to us through the sentient soul, we would not know what to make of it. If only the sentient body received such information, it would be no help at all; the sentient body would only look on without understanding. That the human being can perceive something is brought about by the sentient soul, which grasps what is going on. What is it that confronts the sentient soul there? What is it that faces the sentient soul when the eyes perceive it? It is quite simply the outer appearance, the external illusion of the sentient body.

Of course, you will have to broaden the conception. You perceive yourself not only by casting your eyes over the surface of your body but by reaching out your fingers to touch it as well. Here you perceive it also through the sentient body. The sentient body extends itself over every part of us that is perceptible to touch, to sensing, but what we perceive is not the sentient body itself. If you were really to glimpse the sentient body, you would see at the place where you perceive the semblance of your physical body an astral element pressing forward and being pushed back. And when something is pushed back, it becomes congested. So, first, you have a working together of sentient body and sentient soul. The sentient soul streams from behind, thrusting against the skin on the front of our bodies, and, from the front, the sentient body pushes into it. When two currents become dammed up in this manner, the congestion manifests. It is exactly as if two streams were to collide; something is bound to come to light. There you see the one stream and you see the other. Now imagine that you can see neither of them, observing instead only what emerges at this place through the two streams whirling together. That is the part of your physical makeup that you are able to observe with your eyes or some other outer sense. It is precisely at our skin where the sentient soul and the sentient body meet. We have here an example of what we have been considering from a spiritual point of view, of the way these various members of the human being work formatively on the human being itself. We see how the soul works on the physical body.

Now let's go further. We can see that in human beings, there is an interaction between the front and rear such that the sentient body and the sentient soul collide. There is a similar collision between streams that come from the right and the left. From the left comes the stream belonging to our physical body, while from the right comes the stream belonging to the etheric body. The physical and etheric bodies pour and thrust into each other, and that which arises at the place where they do so, where they work together, that is the sense-perceptible human being.

An illusion, so to speak, appears before us. The stream of the physical body flows from the left, that of the etheric body from the right. They interpenetrate each other and build in the middle that which appears as the sense-perceptible human body. Just as there are streams from the left and the right and from the front and the back, so there is also a stream from above and one from below. The main current of the astral body flows upward from below and that of the I flows downward from above.

The sentient body has been described as reaching a frontal boundary or demarcation. The current of the astral body streams upward from below, but then is taken hold of by a current streaming from behind forward and is thus restricted in a certain way. There is not just a stream coming from below upward and from the rear forward in this astral body, however. There is also a real current moving from front to back, bringing the astral body into being as the result of these various directional streamings, those from below upward and from the front and back. All these currents flow into each other, one from above downward, one from below upward, one from behind forward, one from the front backward, one from right to left, and one from left to right.

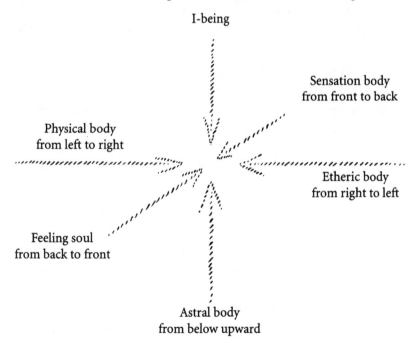

I-being

Sensation body
from front to back

Physical body
from left to right

Etheric body
from right to left

Feeling soul
from back to front

Astral body
from below upward

What comes into being as the result of the flowing against each other of the currents coming from below upward and from above downward? Let me explain it in the following way. One stream flows downward from above. It cannot do so unimpeded because the countercurrent, streaming from below upward, stops it. The same thing applies to the right-left current and so on. Each stream is halted, and that results in creating the illusion of the physical body in the middle.

As we consider the two streams—that from behind forward and that from the front backward—we need to realize that they are intersected by the two currents coming from above and below. This intersecting, in fact, brings about a threefold organization in the human being. So we have to designate the lower portion of the one stream the sentient body in a narrower sense. What the congestion creates corresponds to what can be termed, in the strictest sense, the highest development of the sentient body. That is where the true senses develop, which we can't see because the eyes themselves belong to it and which we can't smell because the organs of smell also belong to it. We cannot see into the inside of our own eyes; we can only look out of them.

Such is the structuring of the complete sentient body of the human being. Why, then, have I been describing two parts if it is all sentient body? The description was correct, because what takes place in the lower part is mainly due to external causation; in the upper part is the physical illusion of what we call the sentient soul. In the countenance we have the expression of the sentient soul; the countenance is built by the sentient soul. The uppermost portion, the part shoved back the least, is the place where the intellectual soul builds its organ. Please note that there are not only these streamings from above and below; there are also currents streaming in from right and left, so that the whole is again intersected. We have one current coursing through the vertical axis of the body, which causes a kind of split to arise there. A piece of the intellectual soul is split off, and this piece, located right at the very top, is the form of the consciousness soul. The consciousness soul forms up above and onward into the depths of the human being, and it shapes there the convolutions of the gray matter of the human brain. That is the work of the consciousness soul on the human being.

Once you know the human being thus as a spiritual being, you can apply that knowledge to understanding every aspect of the human form, for that is how the spirit works on the form of the human body. All the individual organs are, as it were, sculpted out of the spiritual. We can understand the structure of the brain only when we know how the various currents whirl together as in a vortex.

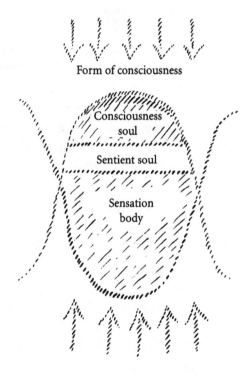

Form of consciousness

Consciousness
soul

Sentient soul

Sensation
body

Now let us consider one detail, so that you see how fruitful these matters can be if they become the common possession of a true science in place of the external science we have today. We have seen that up at the top, the outer organs of the consciousness, intellectual, and sentient souls are brought into being by the various currents. It would require long and complex elaboration to show how these organs continue within, but we do need to concern ourselves with another question. The statement was made that the I works from above downward, while most of the astral body works upward from below so that they touch in a stream. This causes an interaction between the I and the astral body so that they obstruct each other. Where the I is to carry out a conscious action, something has to be generated that arises through the consciousness soul, the intellectual soul, and the sentient soul. Such a thing that the intellectual soul supplies, for example, is human judgment. Where are judgments located?

They are in the head, of course, because it is there that the relevant living forces and members of the human being have found their expression. Let us assume, as a special example, that an organ were to arise in the human being in which the intellectual soul plays no part, in which no judgments are made, and in which only the physical body, the etheric body, the astral body, and the I are allowed to participate as carriers of pleasure and pain, joy and sorrow, and so on. Let us assume that the four members of the human being, the I, the astral body (without the subtler activity of judgments and of consciousness), the physical body, and etheric body were to work together. What would be the nature of an organ in which these four currents were to work together?

Its nature would be such that it would not allow judgments to arise; it would immediately allow a countereffect to emanate from impressions of the astral body. The physical and etheric bodies have to work together, for this organ could otherwise not exist. The astral body and the I also have to work together, for such an organ would otherwise possess no feeling and would lack the ability to respond with sympathy or antipathy to impressions. We will picture the physical and etheric bodies working together and visualize this organ as a physical entity. It must obviously have a corresponding etheric body, because every physical organ must be built by an etheric body. In this case, a current issuing from the right side of the etheric body of this organ would have to work together with a current coming from the left, that of the physical body of the organ. The two currents would become congested in the middle and, since they would not be able to shove past each other, would therefore bring about a thickening. The other two currents, that of the astral body rising from below and that of the I descending from above, would call forth another congestion. Now let us picture schematically the working together of these currents in a single organ. I will make just a schematic representation of it; to fill in details of such an organ would require the inclusion of quite different suppositions.

Let us say, then, that we have an organ that was formed somehow. There is the one current that represents the physical body, and the other represents the etheric body. They bring about a thickening in the middle, where they meet. The other two currents that issue from above and below do likewise, bringing forth their own thickening. This gives us a drawing of the human heart with its right auricle and its right ventricle, its left auricle and left ventricle.

If you bring to mind exactly all that the heart can do, you would have to say that the human heart must be built out of the spirit in exactly this way. This is how the human spirit builds this heart. It cannot be otherwise.

Let us look at another example. A curious statement was made yesterday. It was said that a subconscious thought activity accompanies the act of seeing. Thinking on a conscious level takes place only in the brain. Let us recall how the brain is constructed to enable us to think consciously.

There won't be enough time at our disposal to undertake a study of the chiseling out of the individual forms that compose the brain. It could be shown in the case of every single organ that it has to be the way it is. We want to presuppose, right at the outset, the system of the brain insofar as we need it. Disregarding everything else, we have in the brain an outer skin and then a kind of vascular skin; between the vascular skin and the netlike skin, we find something similar to spinal fluid, which then goes into the spine. The brain's interior is filled with the actual brain substance, with nerve substance. The nerve substance is the external structure for thought activity. This means that when an impression is imparted to the nerve substance by any sense organ, a processing of that external impression by conscious thinking sets in. That is all transmitted to the nerve substance. When an impression is received, it is first worked upon by thinking, and afterward it is processed further by a nervous system into a sensation, and so on.

Now let us suppose that no such conscious thought digestion of an external impression occurs. In that case, a similar process would have to be substituted. There would again have to be a kind of sheath; there would have to be on the back wall that which might be termed a vascular membrane. For certain reasons that could also be explained but would lead us too far afield for now, the spinal fluid would atrophy. To make subconscious thinking possible, we would have to push the brain mass back. This creates space at the front so that subconscious thinking activity arises without being worked through by a nervous system. Something has to be done with what would otherwise be taken up immediately into the nerve substance. The nerve mass would therefore have to be pushed back, for thinking would otherwise take place there. If that is done, however, we can neither think nor have sentient experiences there. If we push all that is the nervous system toward the back wall and, instead of allowing the impression to be processed immediately via nerve substance, allow it to be affected by something that is not permeated by a nervous system, we would have an organ suited to unconscious thought activity.

Now see what we've done: we have made an eye out of the brain! What actually is the eye? It is a small brain, so fashioned by our human spirit that the actual nerve apparatus is pushed back to the rear wall, where it becomes the eye's retina. This is the way in which nature's architects, the modelers of form, work; this is the way they shape. There is basically only one blueprint for all the organs; it is modified only in the particular, as needed. If I could speak for weeks, I would show you how every sense organ is nothing other than a modified little brain and how the brain itself is also a sense organ on a higher level. The whole human organism is built out of the spirit.

Now let us look at another detail. First, allow me to make a preliminary epistemological comment in order to use it anew to clarify anthroposophy's view of the matter. We said that anthropology takes a ground-level standpoint with regard to the details of the life of the senses, theosophy takes its view from the mountain heights, and anthroposophy occupies the middle ground. If you want to cling to the difference between the way people relate, on the one hand, to the outer sense world and, on the other hand, to the spiritual world and to the facts communicated by spiritual investigators, you can say that anybody who possesses senses and uses the intellect, which is bound to the sense world, can convince him- or herself of its existence and its laws. People are therefore more easily convinced about matters that have some resemblance to what their senses perceive than they are about communications from spiritual researchers; they can see it more easily.

It would be easy, however, to show that there is no formal difference between believing facts derived from spiritual research and believing someone who tells you that there was once a Frederick the Great; there is actually no formal difference. The only difference between believing in the existence of spirits of will and that of Frederick the Great is that there is material in archives stating that the deeds of Frederick the Great were thus and such; they happened on the physical plane. And if, on the basis of external facts, someone reviews the course of historical events all the way back to the time of Frederick the Great, you will believe what you are told because there was no one living then who looked other than human. The reason why people believe such reports while refusing to believe in the spiritual world is simply that what they are being told is similar to what they have in their own surroundings. Spiritual researchers are not in a position to speak, on the basis of their investigations, of things and beings that look similar to what we have in our surroundings. Despite the fact that there is no difference between the two kinds of reports, however, and that there are good reasons for this, the comments just made should be kept in mind.

Now we will proceed to another matter. Thus far we have characterized the viewpoints of anthropology and theosophy. There is good reason, as

Dr. Unger has shown, to have well-founded belief and confidence in the presentations of spiritual science.[3] That is a fully justified way of acknowledging its truths. The question arises, however, as to whether there is not a third approach. Are there really only two ways—either acknowledging the truth of something because it is similar to what we are used to experiencing in the sense world or, on the other hand, merely accepting it because it is a communication from higher worlds? Is there not still another approach? In other words, is it reasonable to believe what we perceive through the senses only because we see it or to believe in the spiritually perceptible because spiritual investigators see it? Can there not be a third approach between these two?

Allow me to present an example to show you that a third approach is possible. Imagine a hammer lying here. I take hold of it and stand it upright. Now the hammer has moved. You will say that it moved because a will lifted it. There is nothing miraculous about this, since you see the manipulating will embodied in a person. You won't see anything miraculous about someone lifting a hammer. Let us suppose that this hammer were to rise to a vertical position with no visible being involved. Then what would you say? You would consider it very foolish to believe that a hammer that rose by itself to the vertical was an ordinary hammer, which needs a person to lift it.

What would you have to say next? You would say that it was obviously no ordinary hammer, but one inhabited by an invisible will. As you watch the hammer rise to the vertical, you simply cannot believe it to be ordinary but take it to be something that embodies some other will or some other spirit. If you see a material object doing what you know to be impossible for such material objects according to ordinary sense experience—even though you don't see a spirit in the hammer that lifts itself up—you would not only feel justified in believing that there is a spirit in that hammer, you would even consider yourself a real fool to believe otherwise.

---

3. Carl Unger (1878–1929), one of Rudolf Steiner's closest students, of whom he spoke many times. Dr. Unger wrote *The Language of the Consciousness Soul* (Spring Valley, NY: St. George Books, 1983), an in-depth study guide to Steiner's *Anthroposophical Leading Thoughts*.

If you were not a precise observer and were out walking with a clairvoyant person, you might, let us say, come across a motionless figure lying on the ground. Because you are not capable of exact observation, you would not be able to determine whether the object is a real person or just a papier-mâché figure. The clairvoyant would tell you that it is a real human being and say, "He has an astral body." You would have to believe it. But a third possibility is that the figure lying there might suddenly get up. You would then no longer doubt that the clairvoyant was right—that a soul and spirit inhabited the figure, since it stood up. That is the third possibility.

I want to speak now about a situation where you can have just such an experience, one that may seem remote but is nevertheless within reach. It was said that in the human being the physical body's current flows from left to right, the etheric body's current from right to left, the current originating in the sentient body from front to back, and so on. The astral body's current flows upward from below, and that of the I flows down from above, countering each other. All these currents flow into one another and intermingle.

It was said that the I works from above downward. How, then, must the outer organ be situated for us to be able to use it as an instrument of the I? You know that the outer organ of the I is the circulating blood. The I could not function from above downward without its organ moving vertically through the human body from above downward. Where would it be impossible, then, for the human I to exist? Wherever the main current of the blood flows horizontally instead of vertically. Animals have horizontal bloodstreams; the group I of animals cannot find its own organ because the main circulatory course of animal blood is horizontal. That is the difference—the main circulatory flow of human blood had to be raised to the vertical so that the human I could enter it. On the one hand, we have the animals in which the group I cannot grasp the blood as its organ because the blood flows horizontally; on the other hand, in human beings the I can do so, because the blood's primary course has raised itself to the vertical.

Let us now examine the viewpoint that, for purely external reasons, accepts animals as related to humankind. Indeed, there are animal forms left over from earlier periods, but the time came when the whole circulatory system had to be lifted from the horizontal to the vertical position so that the human being could develop from it. We are looking at a historical case: here we have something that is horizontally aligned. It is obvious from the observable characteristics of animal blood that what is horizontally aligned could no more lift itself into the vertical than could the hammer that is not permeated by a spirit. In the same way that it would be foolish to deny the presence of spirit in something that can lift itself, it would be just as foolish to think that the horizontal bloodstream of animals could, of itself, lift itself up to the vertical stature of the human bloodstream. Only if a spirit were within it, only if a will flowed through it, could the animal group soul transform into the individual human soul. Anyone unwilling to admit that he or she would be a fool to believe that ordinary hammers could lift themselves upright would be just as much a fool to think that that which is in blood could raise itself to the vertical on its own.

This is the third way by which you can verify all spiritual truths, in that we realize that things happen in the context of which it is nonsense to believe that only physically perceptible elements are involved. As we delve more deeply into matters, it becomes more obvious that the middle way of attaining certainty, which is based on spiritual science's fructifying ordinary thinking, can be applied to everything. You have to admit that the human heart could not have been described as it was here without the foregoing spiritual research. Research must be stimulated by spiritual science. When the findings of spiritual science are presented and we then observe the outer phenomena, we see elements that simply could not be explained if we were not to take into account what is said by spiritual science. Thus, there is a method for observing things without bias, for example, when you notice that animal blood follows a horizontal course, whereas human blood flows vertically, and ask yourself what must be present in blood for the whole blood system to lift up to the vertical. And then you receive the answer from spiritual science: *spiritual beings rule the blood.* You may then ask whether or not blood indicates the presence of a spiritual being exactly as a hammer would if it raised itself upright. This is an example of the middle standpoint of anthroposophy that observes physical facts below, observes spiritual facts above and compares them, thus fully explaining what is encountered in the outer world.

I have shown, through individual examples, such as the transforming of the brain into the eye and the schematic internal contraction of the heart, how the form of every organ can be comprehended. We could construe the form of every organ out of the spirit in the same way. Every part of us would be a revelation of how spirit works on us to create the body's forms and organs. Only the principles involved were to be indicated here. But today's indications will give you a feeling that there is much in the world that the experts have never dreamed of, because they have no desire to delve into such matters. If this feeling stays with you, you will see that it is indeed possible to view the world without bias in matters where the communications from investigation of the spiritual world are brought together with earthly things. Not everyone can immediately see such things, but one would be able to say that it is an absurdity not to accept the facts reported by investigators of the spirit concerning certain phenomena. If the described feeling persists, then enough has been accomplished through these lectures on anthroposophy, for progress in spiritual research is slow and gradual.

4.

Supersensible Currents, Group Soul, and the I in Human Beings and Animals

YESTERDAY we discussed the currents of forces that shape the human organism and make its form comprehensible. We saw how, if we get to know the formative forces, the heart and the eye must, in an amazing way, look just as they do. We delineated the supersensible processes that occur in our organism so that its material structure manifests. And we saw how it is built by the currents that flow from left to right and right to left, from above downward and from below upward, and from front to back and vice versa.

Someone might say, "We will catch you in your own trap. You fail to consider a very important phenomenon when you speak of these currents—from right and left, above and below, and front and back. You do not explain the fact that human beings have organs in precise left/right symmetry as well as other organs, such as the heart, stomach, liver, and so on that are asymmetrical." This person would go on to say, "If the human organism were completely asymmetrical, perhaps we could comprehend how it is formed by your currents—if it differed just as much in its left/ right aspect as it does from below upward and from front to back."

Although one could object in this way, it would be shortsighted, because as we already pointed out, the currents flowing left to right and right to left are those that form the physical and etheric bodies. The human being is symmetrical in the direction that the currents of the physical and etheric bodies flow; it is just in this direction where physical and etheric bodies flow that the human being is symmetrically built. Now recall what spiritual scientific research says about the existence of these currents and the anthroposophic explanations of them, and then ask if it is possible to clarify the reason this has to be as it is.

Spiritual scientific research shows that the human physical body is very ancient, having originated on old Saturn. The etheric body was added during the ancient Sun, the astral body during the Moon, and the I first appeared on Earth.[1] We may now ask what the physical body looked like when it was formed on old Saturn. It was, of course, asymmetrical, since it had to work in a direction that corresponds to the left to right orientation of today's physical body. And what about the etheric body in its origin on the Sun? It, too, was asymmetrical, since it had to be laid out in the direction that corresponds to the present right to left orientation in the human body.

Evolution continued, however, and didn't stop with the effect of ancient Sun; the effect of Moon activity now began. The physical body continued to evolve, and its form was shaped further. If the Moon's effect had not been added, human beings would have remained physically asymmetrical. But the physical body's development continued on the Moon, and all the rest evolved further on Earth. Something thus had to enter the picture that changed the earlier formation and transformed it into an entirely different one. The direction had to be reversed in order to avoid one-sidedness, and this had to be done from the opposite side. In other words, the direction from left to right that had been imprinted on the organization of the physical body during Saturn now had to be balanced by a development from right to left. How did this happen?

In previous lectures I spoke about the Sun's separation from the Moon during the ancient Moon evolution, and I said that the Sun's forces no longer worked from the same side, from within the Moon's body, but from outside. This is the same thing that happened to the etheric body as the development progressed. What developed as the physical body until the time of ancient Moon was then taken up from the side under the external influence of the Sun. Now someone might say, "Yes, but we can't

1. Steiner's planetary references do not refer to the physical planets as we understand them today, but to epochs of cosmic evolution. For a more thorough introduction to these planetary phases, see *An Outline of Esoteric Science*; see also *The Spiritual Hierarchies and the Physical World: Reality and Illusion*.

understand why this second side, formed so much later, is not much smaller than the other side. Why are they symmetrical?"

Recall something else I told you; certain more highly evolved beings had to leave both the Moon and the Earth in order to develop a greater impact. These beings had to find a higher functioning position in order to have a stronger influence from right to left on the human structure than those on Saturn. Their task was not so easy as that of the Saturn beings when they formed the one-sided physical body. Those beings had to overcome what existed from previous evolution; the entire formative process was jammed. These beings had to acquire greater powers by shifting their place of action outside Earth to the Sun. That strengthened their powers, and the other side was constructed just like the first. The physical body became a symmetrical structure.

If you enter into this question patiently enough, you will be able to confirm every detail of what was said in the theosophical lectures. The formative forces can be followed even into the most isolated details of the human organs. It would take us too far in these sketchy lectures, of course, to try to explain, for example, the ear lobe, but it could be done.

If you recall what was said yesterday—that currents flow from front to back, that they emanate from the sentient body acting on the human organism, and that the currents of the sentient soul flow from back to front—you will realize that we have two currents that run counter to each other. How should we imagine the currents of the sentient body from front to back and of the sentient soul from back to front forming the human organism? A sketch will help us visualize it.

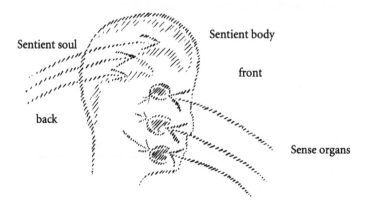

As was said, the physical and etheric bodies and the main portion of the astral body were already present. Now the currents issuing from the sentient body enter the picture to bore their way into the organism from front to back. Their action is such that they build various organs into what was already in the human organism.

Now imagine the sentient soul again working into the organism from back to front. The work is an inner one because it is precisely the sentient soul doing it. The currents congest at the front in such a way that, as they bore into the organism, they form a layer over the structure they are building. The currents of the sentient soul flow forward and penetrate there at the boundary of the physical body. While the currents of the sentient body flow from the outside in (since the sentient body is outside), those of the sentient soul stream from the inside out. This must create various openings where they come together; several holes must be bored there. These currents move forward from behind, and others move from the front back. The former currents issue from the sentient soul, thus from within, and bore into the physical organism.

In viewing this sketch, you see the human face in profile. Coming from the front are currents that bore the sense organs of sight, smell, and taste into the head, and from the rear to the front come the formative forces that build the brain above them. This is how the human head is fashioned, as seen from the side. Thus, we can say that if spiritual science tells us the truth, the human head actually cannot look other than it does. Where can we find proof for that which spiritual science asserts?

Spiritual science demonstrates that if the human head was to arise at all, it would have to appear like this. Let us ask the head if that is how it looks. Yes, it does! The phenomenal world itself presents us with the confirmation, the proof. Or let us consider something else. The action of the sentient body is from the outside in, that of the sentient soul from the inside out, although it is blocked on the way. It does not make it all the way out; it is blocked in the physical brain, so that it can't get out. It can get out only where the openings bored from the front encounter it. The activity of the sentient soul comes out at those places; it strides out. This results in a part of our inner life pouring itself out precisely as sentient soul. The sentient soul can do that.

The comprehension, or intellectual, soul cannot do this. It also lies suspended in us and must also bide its time with respect to its effects. It is completely obstructed. It cannot move outward at all, because no currents come to meet it from outside. This is why our thinking is an inner process; it has no way of getting out. Human beings must contemplate within themselves. Other things cannot think for us, nor do they reveal the thoughts to us from outside; we have to bring the thoughts to meet the things.

This is the great mystery of the relationship of human thought to the outer world. The sense organs do not convey thoughts to us. If a sense organ has an irregularity, the impression it receives is easily distorted. While, however, in normal life the senses do not distort, the intellect can, because it cannot form a relationship with external things. It is the first member of the human being that is able to err, because its activity is dammed up within the brain and cannot get out. And what is the result? It is impossible for human beings to think about the outer world and to have the right thoughts about it unless they have within themselves the capacity to let right thoughts arise. You can see from this that the external world could never give human beings accurate thoughts if the thoughts were not to arise from within. The external world can provide correct sense perceptions, but perceptions cannot think. Thought is subject to error, however, and we human beings must have the power for accuracy of thought in us.

This demonstrates to anyone who cares to contemplate it that if accurate thoughts arise in us about something external that we have not had any contact with in the present incarnation, it points to a previous life. Think for a moment: human beings are supposed to think accurate thoughts about the wisdom of the world but cannot go outside themselves with their thoughts. What permeates the things of the outer world as wisdom must arise within the human beings themselves. There is a boundary between the two, and they can never come together. This can only mean that they must have been together at an earlier time, when the human I did not yet hold back the currents flowing from above downward; the I was still allowing them to pass through. We must conclude, therefore, that human beings must have been organized differently, that today's brain thinking was once, like the sense perceptions of the eye, connected with the external world in such a way that human beings saw their thoughts.

What does it mean to say that people saw thoughts, which we are now limited to merely thinking? It means that they were clairvoyant. Because it is the I that separated them from the ancient clairvoyance, however, the I was thus not yet present. We must, therefore, call it a clairvoyance that was still dim and not yet illuminated by the I. *Dim* is the right term for that ancient clairvoyance; people must have passed through earlier stages in which they possessed a dim clairvoyance.

Again, the present-day organism shows us that the human being of earlier times was organized differently. If what has been stated is true, it has very important implications for practical life, for it implies that sense perception can tell us the truth about all the relationships of the material world, disregarding, of course, the sense illusions. Sense perceptions place us in direct relationship to the outer world; we touch it directly. It also implies that we can know what is within us only through the power of our intellect. When, for example, the I flows inward, it is actually there within us. Therefore, when we direct our thinking to the I, it is very natural that, since the I is inside us, such thinking about it can determine something about it. Dr. Unger's lectures made this clear.

Now you will be able to localize the process. It is the meeting between the intellectual soul and the I that gives rise to pure thinking, thinking directed inward. And it will be clear to you that this thinking, which comprehends itself, cannot be subject to error, like that thinking that rambles all over attempting to draw conclusions out of external things. In pondering the outside world, such thinking gets only as far as the concepts and truth it already finds within itself about the outer things. We have to hold the concepts up to things as a reflection; the things themselves can reveal nothing more than their sense-perceptible aspects. We human beings have to allow the concepts, or thoughts, inherent in the things to arise in us from a real capacity for truth.

What can we judge in the outer world? Indeed, people can assess only what they encounter through the senses in the external world. The senses cannot decide about things that remain hidden to the senses themselves. What is it then about the human being that appears solely in its own truth? Of human beings—and of other natural creatures—the only thing that appears in its reality for the physical plane is that which the senses can actually sense. As soon as something is removed from the senses, no judgment can be made about that thing from the physical plane. At that moment, reasoning, if not accompanied and directed by an inner sense for truth or inner accuracy, must necessarily fall prey to all kinds of errors.

Let me illustrate this with an example that contrasts two different approaches. You are familiar with one of them from spiritual scientific research—the study of the forms human beings have passed through during earlier conditions of existence: the Atlantean and Lemurian periods and all the way back through the Moon, Sun, and Saturn existences. We are shown out of spiritual scientific research what forms the human being has gone through. Today we have studied an example of how what the senses perceive can appear wonderfully comprehensible when we make this approach to human evolution our own and we work through it in relation to the outer world. You will become increasingly convinced of this astounding fact—that everything in the external world confirms what spiritual research discovers out of the facts of the spiritual world.

Now, as a contrast, let us look at the recently formulated theory of evolution offered by ordinary research. We especially notice that an important law that I referred to yesterday has been established. It is the fundamental biogenetic law that states, based on external facts, that the human being, in its germinal state, briefly goes through a series of forms reminiscent of certain animal shapes. At one stage it resembles a small fish and so on, recapitulating the various forms of the animal kingdom. You are all probably aware that when the theory of heredity got out of hand, these facts were interpreted as proof that human beings passed through all the forms observed in embryonic development. One is tempted to comment that it was truly a blessing that the gods' concern for us delayed this observation until, almost simultaneously, after this theory had been publicized in its more extreme interpretation—things almost always overlap—it could be set straight by spiritual science.

The stages passed through before human beings arrived on the physical plane and became perceptible to physical senses were concealed by the gods and could not be observed. If such a discovery had occurred earlier, ideas that are even more absurd might have resulted. The facts themselves are, of course, correct, since they are perceived by the senses. But when conclusions are to be made about it, the forces of the intellectual soul become involved, and that soul has no access to anything the senses have not experienced. If it lacks the inner endowment for discerning truth, it necessarily errs. Here we have a striking example of how the power of reasoning that comes from the intellectual soul can sail into error.

What does it show that at a certain point in embryonic development, human beings resemble fish? It shows that we cannot utilize the fish nature in ourselves and must get rid of it before entering our human phase of existence. The next shape in embryonic development must also be rejected as unsuitable, as must all animal forms because they do not belong to us. We could not have become human beings if we had ever appeared on Earth in such an animal form. We had to separate all such forms from ourselves to enable us to become human beings.

If you pursue these thoughts correctly, you will arrive at correct conclusions. What is demonstrated by the fact that, at a particular point in our embryonic development, we resemble fish? It simply shows that in our line of descent we never looked like fish and rejected the fish shape as unusable, since we were not to resemble it. We may also inquire about the significance of all the other forms of embryonic development that modern science shows us. They show us all that we never were and that had to be expelled in past periods of evolution. Science shows all those pictures that we never resembled. In fact, through embryology we can discover what we never resembled in prehistoric times; we learn which shapes we pushed out rather than went through. If, from the facts, we conclude that we descended from such animal forms, that we passed through them to reach our present evolutionary stage, we place ourselves in the same position as someone who says, "Here is a son, and here the father. As I compare them, I cannot believe that the son descended from the father. Instead, I'll believe that the son descended from himself, or that he was his father's ancestor." Just the opposite sequence of evolution was accepted as the result of a mistake, because the intellect proved unequal to really thinking through the facts of reality. These images of the past are, of course, extremely important, because they make us aware of how we never looked.

Another example brings this fact home to us even better. We can study it in the realms offered by the outer sense world, realms that are not hidden. All these forms are there in the outer world. They lie open to observation by our ordinary disciplined scrutiny. Human beings did not draw false conclusions about human descent as long as they depended only on observation and applied their minds to what was spread before them in the world of the senses rather than to what was not observable. Of course, they didn't judge human evolution out of the intellect, but relied on a natural, exact sense for truth. They looked at apes and felt the same uncanny feeling that any healthy-minded person does when looking at apes— one that can be compared only to a certain sense of shame. That sense was closer to the truth than what was said later by the erring intellect.

In this sense of shame lies the feeling judgment that apes are beings that fell from the human stream, beings that remain behind; they originated in the human evolutionary line and had to be separated out from it. Contained in this was a feeling that human beings could reach today's heights only by first separating from themselves what has now become the ape form. If we had retained it, we could never have developed into human beings. This lies in the natural, healthy feeling. But then the matter was investigated through the intellect, and this gave birth to the erroneous statement that the human form descended from the ape! That is an error. The more you think about it, the more you will find that what was just discussed is deeply justified. That human beings are descended from apes is an error that you can confirm through a very ordinary consideration.

Let us assume that you are observing the members of human nature apparent purely through the senses and that you are studying either yourself or the observable aspect of human nature in other human beings. There are two currents—that of the sentient body flowing from front to back and that of the sentient soul flowing from back to front. And since they converge, we must distinguish, in what appears on the human being, between what is moving from front to back as the current of the sentient body and what is moving from back to front as the current of the sentient soul.

Bearing this in mind, let us look into the countenance of a person. As far as we depend on our senses, the image we perceive is, of course, correct. We cannot be mistaken, since we are dealing with a sense impression. Now the intellect enters the picture, and does so subconsciously. We are confronted immediately with a classic example of erroneous judgment, for how does the mind conceive the human countenance in relation to the forces that formed it? It thinks of it as having been shaped from outside, whereas the face is really the product of the sentient soul working outward from within. We judge incorrectly when we look into a person's countenance and say that it is actually material body. We must say instead that what the senses perceive here is the outer image of the sentient soul, the soul itself, and that soul works outward from within. You have reached the correct conclusion when you view the human face as soul, excluding the possibility that it could be corporeal body.

You are concerned here with a great illusion. You look at a human face—that is, the picture of a soul—and while looking at this picture of the soul (of course, it is only an image), you think of it as corporeal. That view is totally mistaken and demonstrates how wrongly we interpret things as soon as we call on our power of judgment. We form correct views of external images only if we understand them correctly, if we speak of the human countenance as an "image of the soul" and recognize the mistake in trying to explain it only on the basis of the physical and etheric forces. This human countenance must be explained out of the forces of the soul itself; the visible is explained in terms of the invisible in this case.

As you delve into spiritual science, you become increasingly aware of what a lofty training of thinking it is and that the chaotic thinking we encounter everywhere today, especially in scientific circles, must be overcome. Perhaps you occasionally feel that what you hear makes strenuous demands on your thinking. Spiritual science, however, is also a noble training of logical thinking, since it forces us to interpret properly what we encounter in the world. And we must correctly interpret certain manifestations that lead from an anthroposophy that is concerned with the individual to an anthroposophy concerned with all of humankind.

Now let us return to what we have termed the *sense of speech* and the *sense of concept* or *visualization*. Did the sense of speech or tone precede the sense of visualization in earthly human evolution or vice versa? We will have accomplished quite a lot if we succeed in sufficiently penetrating human development on this low plane so as to answer the question whether or not we learn to understand words first or to perceive and understand received mental images first.

This question has little to do with spiritual science, because we can all find the answer by watching the way children learn to speak and perceive thoughts. All of us are aware that children learn to speak first and only then to perceive thoughts. Indeed, speech is necessary for thought perception. Why? Simply because the sense of speech or tone is the prerequisite for the sense of visualization. Children learn to speak because they can hear and listen to what the sense of speech perceives. Their speaking itself then is mere imitation. Thus, you will find that children imitate speech sounds long before they understand anything that might be called a mental representation. Observe carefully, and you will see that the sense of speech or tone develops first and provides the basis for the development of the sense of concept. The speech sense thus enables us to perceive not only sounds but what we call tones of speech as well.

This leads us to ask how, in the course of evolution, human beings became able to perceive speech tones and, as a consequence, developed the ability to speak. How was it that human beings were able to develop speech over the course of their evolution? At this point we have to clarify a certain matter. Learning to speak (not merely hearing) required not only that something come to human beings from outside and be perceived by them but also that something within human beings follow the same route that the currents of the sentient soul take as they press forward from behind. This was essential. Human evolution had to proceed in such a way that the sentient soul became permeated by a current moving in the same direction as the soul's currents, which create through movement toward the front from behind. That was needed for speech. Speaking had to precede the sense of visualization; speaking had to be acquired before human beings were in a position to sense the idea in words themselves, even in the words they spoke themselves. They first had to learn to emit speech tones and live in the sensations such tones generated before relating them to specific mental images. That had to come later. The initial experience was not of concept or mental image, but a feeling for what permeated the tones when they were emitted. Speech proceeded from this experience.

This development had to take place after the blood circulation shifted to an upright position, for animals cannot speak. The I had to work from above downward. Although the I was present by that time, working downward from above, human beings were still unable to imagine it, since the visualizing sense was not yet developed. What was the result? Human beings could not receive speech through their individual I but only through another I, comparable to the group I of animals. In this sense, speech is truly a gift of the gods. It was poured down from above into human beings along the path taken by the I before it could develop speech itself. The human I, flowing down from above, was not capable of developing speech. It did not yet have the organs capable of providing the impulse for speech development, and thus the collective I had to do it. Human beings were already complete, however; they were by that time upright human beings. The collective I had to work from above downward into the physical and etheric organism and so on, in order to bring about speech. Another current flowed from below toward the group I. That group I flowed down from above and met another current that flowed upward from below. They met and created a kind of vortex. If you draw a straight line through the middle of the larynx, it follows the direction of the current used by those spirits who gave speech. Out of these two congesting currents, the peculiar form of the human larynx arose in physical matter. Thus, the human being had to develop speech through the influence of a group soul living in the Earth's environment.

You may recall that I spoke about how group souls actually work on the Earth. I said that the current of the group soul passes through the horizontal spinal cord of the animal. These streams of forces flowing from above downward constantly circulate around the Earth, as they did around ancient Moon. They are currents that do not remain in place, but circulate in a perpendicular manner around the Earth. The vertically oriented group souls sweep around the Earth in circles. What was the result? In order for human beings to develop speech through the influence of group souls, they could not remain at a fixed location, but had to migrate, moving from place to place to encounter the group soul. Human beings could not have learned speech if they had stayed where they were when they could not yet speak.

What was the necessary direction of their movement? This is easily discovered. We know that human etheric currents flow from right to left and the physical currents from left to right. Where, then, are the group souls that endowed human beings with speech? We can answer this through the following consideration. Let us look at the singular form of the Earth. When you consider the fact that human beings learned to speak after they were already complete, you will agree that a strong current was needed, since the larynx, in its soft shape, first had to be transformed into the human larynx. This had to happen under very different conditions on Earth than those we find today. What must they have been?

Let us look at the Earth. Imagine that we are standing on the Earth facing east. The west is behind us, the north to the left, and the south to the right. Now notice the strange fact that emerges. The currents involved in structuring the physical body flow from left to right. They occur in the outer world as well, and they were present when the Earth was formed. Here you have the powerful currents that come from the north and move toward the south. These currents bring physical matter into existence. On the other side are etheric currents, moving from right to left without the goal of condensing physical matter. You can still see this in the Earth's asymmetry. In the direction of the physical currents you have the northern half with its continents. There the condensed physical matter draws itself together, whereas in the other, southern half, you have the expanses of ocean. The current working from the north is identical to the one that acts from left to right in human beings, and the current from the south is identical to the one that acts from right to left.

Now let us consider the other two currents in human beings, the one moving from front to back and the other from back to front. As we have seen, the current from front to back goes from the sentient body into the sentient soul—into the soul in general—whereas the second goes outward.

If you now consider this—and I ask that you consider it very carefully, since it is not so easy—you will realize that in order to learn speech, human beings had to produce a current that flowed from within outward, that made its way into the sentient body. People had to encounter the group-soul current and offer their organization to it, so that what could build the larynx could congest there. Human beings had to meet, within the earthly realm, such a current that could work into the human astral aspect. When human beings were first learning to speak, therefore, they could neither move in a northerly nor a southerly direction but had to move in a direction at a right angle to both. In other words, they had to move east to west or west to east at the time when they were to learn to speak. Spiritual science tells us that human beings at one time lived in ancient Lemuria, there where the sea now extends between Africa and Asia. Then they moved in order to learn to speak. They could not go south or north but had to move west to ancient Atlantis. While moving west to Atlantis, they encountered the group souls who could evoke speech in them. You will find spiritual scientific observation confirmed as you come to understand the organism of human speech. Thus, human beings learned speech in ancient Atlantis.

Human beings then needed to develop the sense of imagery based on speech. They were not to stop at mere speech but were to advance to a sense of mental representation. How could this happen? Of course, they could not continue in the same direction; they had to go in the opposite direction with the same current. Why?

We saw what happens when visualization arises from the sense of tone or speech. We have seen how the speech tone develops from melody when transformed into harmony and when the fundamental tone is disregarded so that only the system of the overtones remains. Then the development of the visualization sense required the suppression in speech, on one side, and on the other, what had to be developed. Human beings had to reverse their direction after learning to speak. They had to return east from Atlantis to develop the sense of pictorial thinking from the speech they had learned. Here we see the significance of migration, as described by spiritual science, during which the ancient Atlanteans who were sufficiently mature began to move from west to east. They were thus able to develop the visualization sense in a fruitful way. Then it would follow that those who moved in the opposite direction—to the west—would not be able to develop a sense of visualization in a fruitful way.

Some people did go in the opposite direction. They are the original inhabitants of America. Why did they not keep with this development? Why was it necessary that that which was learned in the east be brought to them later? It was because they moved in the opposite direction. That was the cosmic destiny of the original inhabitants of America, that they migrated in the opposite direction.

This demonstrates the palpable reality of what is reported by spiritual investigation. One can understand the whole organization of the Earth. The distribution of the continents, firm lands, and oceans and human migrations can all be understood once you comprehend the mystery of the continuous streams affecting human beings, which we have come to understand through anthroposophy. Anthroposophy really guides us into that living realm where human beings and the outer world can be clearly understood.

And now we can go further. We could ask: Did humanity go on to learn more after the sense of visualization was developed? Humanity was not intended to stop short at pictorial imagination, but to progress toward the ability to form concepts. The next step was to ascend out of the mere visualization sense to the soul life. Again, humankind had to move in the reverse direction. First, humanity had to go east to develop the imaginative life. To develop pure concepts, on the other hand, called for a reverse migration, since the ability to conceptualize could be attained only after returning westward. If we had enough time to bring together all the findings of anthroposophic research, we could gain a detailed understanding of the great migrations that occurred during the four post-Atlantean cultural periods. We would obtain a wonderful tapestry of the activity of spiritual forces in every aspect of the formation of Earth and humankind.

Thus far we have considered the currents that flow downward from above, from right to left, from front to back, and so on. But we are somehow stopped there, unable to continue. Spiritual science demonstrates that there are three senses that are higher than the sense of visualization: the senses of *imagination, inspiration,* and *intuition.* In ordinary life they flow into the soul, but they flow outward in clairvoyants. This is reported by spiritual science. In order for these senses to exist in physical human beings, they must all build organs for themselves and must work in a certain way.

Here we must consider something that is found only in human beings—something that animals do not yet possess in the same form. It is the inner soul activity of memory. It is pure scientific invention to say that animals have a faculty for remembering. It is not surprising that animals act in a way that requires the same explanations used to explain human behavior. It is a mistake, however, to call such animal behavior "memory." The primary orientation of animals—which had to be changed to the upright in humankind, so that the I could flow in and memory develop—remains horizontal and, just as in human beings, toward the front. This orientation of animals eliminates obstruction and allows the flow of the currents of the sentient, intellectual, and consciousness souls through it, although without the I. Thus, it is possible for animals to commit acts that are indeed reasonable but definitely are not I-imbued. That is why we cannot speak of animals as having "intelligence." This is where a huge area of error arises in modern science. The facts show only that one can be directed by intelligence without possessing it, and that is how it is for animals. The fact that we encounter phenomena in the animal realm resembling human memory is a natural result of the animal form. But to speak of the form of memory is a gross error and creates complete confusion.

In memory there is something completely different from what may be found in mere reasoned thinking or even in visualization. In memory we have before us a mental image that remains after the impression, or perception itself, is no longer present; memory does not consist of doing something that resembles an earlier action. If that were the case, Professor H. would be correct in saying that when a chick breaks out of an egg and immediately begins to peck, it demonstrates the possession of memory, since it repeats something that its ancestors did. Clearly, what memory is has not been grasped at all when such outrageous things are being done in the field of psychology. We could just as easily say that a clock possesses memory because it repeats the same movements every day.

Such concepts are misleading in the broadest sense. Memory is correctly described as the retention in us of a mental picture; it is not the repetition of an external act. It is the I that retains the mental pictures. The nature of memory is that the I takes hold of a mental picture and retains it. But for this to occur in a human organism, an organ has to be created; the I must produce the necessary currents. Such currents must issue from the I itself and converge with the other currents coming from every direction. The I must flood into the other currents that exist without the I, and the I must conquer them.

If, say, a current flows in from outside, the I must be able to issue a current in the opposite direction. This essential activity—in which the I was unable to engage at the very beginning—becomes apparent when you recall that during the age when the human being was supposed to learn to speak, such a countercurrent had to arise. Because the I was not yet in a position to do so, a group I had to assume the task of driving this current into human souls. When real human soul life began with the participation of the I, however, the I itself sent currents out that penetrated the other, already existing currents.

Does the I notice when it drives a current into an already existing current? Yes, it notices very exactly. Up to the point of visualization, the I is not engaged in penetrating currents. To create higher faculties such as memory, however, the I must issue a countercurrent that penetrates the existent current and must work against it. This becomes obvious as the I continues to develop and another element joins the three currents of space flowing at right angles to one another. As the I begins developing memory, it sends its current to bore somewhat in the opposite direction of space, and this becomes perceptible in the awareness of time. This is why memory is linked with the idea of time. It is an idea that, instead of being spatial, moves in the direction of the past, penetrating the space-related currents. Thus it is with everything the I develops out of itself.

It would lead too far off the subject to develop everything in detail, but we can point to the current that flows as the I develops memory. This is a current flowing from left to right. Currents also flow in the same direction as that in which the I develops characteristics such as habits. These left-to-right currents flow counter to the earlier currents that arose without the I. The I bores into them.

In studying the soul life, we can distinguish between the sentient, intellectual, and consciousness souls. The intellectual soul can still be deceptive. You will recall that I said it is possible to have intellect without possessing intelligence, since intelligence is based on the I-being. To gain inner access to the I, the intellectual soul must develop from within to the level of the I. Then it ascends to the consciousness soul. Now this always involves opposite directions. When it becomes conscious, the consciousness soul always assumes thereby a direction counter to that of the intellectual soul, which still works in the unconscious.

Is there any evidence that the stream of these two souls flow in opposite directions? This can be observed under certain earthly conditions. Think, for example, of learning to read, which in a certain sense is a very intellectual activity, not necessarily based on possessing an intelligent I. What I am about to say applies primarily to Europe, where, as you know, the population waited, as it were, for later cultural conditions to develop. Thus, you arrive at something that was present in Greco-Latin culture, when the intellectual soul first developed what is called writing. People began to learn to read and write as that soul was formed. This was, however, only the very beginning; this feature was retained. Then came the effect of the consciousness soul. Conscious activity must occur in a direction counter to that of the intellectual soul, because the two currents flow in opposite directions. People first learned to calculate once they had developed the consciousness soul, since arithmetic is a conscious activity.

We see these directions reflected in European writing, which is from left to right owing to the involvement of the intellectual soul, whereas their calculation is done from right to left. When they add, for example, they add by columns, right to left. We see here, as in a picture, the two different currents—those of the intellectual soul and the consciousness soul, one superimposed over the other. This is not how it is everywhere. The nature of Europeans can be read from this example. It shows that they were predestined to wait in the development of the intellectual soul until a certain point in time, so that the consciousness soul would not develop prematurely.

By way of contrast, what needed to be developed in the consciousness soul in Western culture, other ethnic groups had developed as capacities of the intellectual soul. These people, therefore, had to be given the possibility of accomplishing something with the intellectual soul that those who waited could accomplish only later through the consciousness soul. It was the Semites who had the mission of preparing for the development of the consciousness soul while developing the intellectual soul, thus becoming pioneers of the consciousness soul. Because of this, they write from right to left.

These findings offer us a means for understanding not only the human being as such but also all cultural phenomena. Such facts explain why, at a certain evolutionary moment, writing and calculation were accomplished in a particular way. We could explore further, right into the forms of the letters of each people, and see whether this or that individual folk formed its letters with strokes from left to right or vice versa. It is a matter that can be understood on the basis of these spiritual facts. You see here the future mission of spiritual science, if it is to bring light into people's heads for an understanding of what would otherwise remain unintelligible.

It is probably not right to end these considerations at this point, so we will continue tomorrow in a certain way to finish them. Even so, it will be only a brief sketch. I will therefore be speaking tomorrow from an anthroposophic perspective about what we might call one of Goethe's "daughters." You are aware that I wrote an essay entitled "Goethe, Father of a New Aesthetic." In it I described Goethe's parental role in connection with the conception and the understanding of the arts. It is my intention tomorrow to describe Goethe's child, a really new conception of the science of art, of aesthetics.[2]

---

2. This refers to the published version of Rudolf Steiner's lecture of October 28, 1909, "The Spiritual Origin of the Arts." It is contained in *Art as Spiritual Activity: Rudolf Steiner's Contribution to the Visual Arts* (Michael Howard, ed., Hudson, NY: Anthroposophic Press, 1997).

II

"Psychosophy"

BERLIN 1910

1.

Aspects of Soul Life

T HE EXAMPLES I will need to use during these evening lectures are best taken from the realm of poetry. Each evening, there will be a short recitation of a poem, which will allow me to demonstrate matters as well as when I use a blackboard. Today's lecture will be introduced by Miss Waller's recitation of a poem from Goethe's youth, an adaptation of the legend of "The Eternal Jew." Please note that this poem from Goethe's youth seems to me to have significance for what I will be speaking of. The recitations used to illustrate these lectures will definitely be of psychosophic interest.[1]

During last year's general meeting, I entitled the lecture series "Anthroposophy." This year another series will be given from a similar viewpoint, entitled "Psychosophy." If the opportunity arises, there will eventually be a third series, or chapter, called "Pneumatosophy." These three series together will serve as a bridge to lead from the world we live in to the higher worlds that are the subject of theosophical study.

Psychosophy is to be a deliberation on the human soul, beginning with the soul's experiences here in the physical world. It then rises to higher realms to demonstrate that whatever we encounter in the physical world as the manifest soul life leads to the perspective where the light of theosophy comes to meet us. We will be occupied with many themes during these evenings.

---

1. A variation on Goethe's early poem "The Eternal Jew" was recited at this point. The original poem is almost unknown in Germany today, and not at all in English-speaking countries. The text has been omitted, since it is unlikely that this variation would have any real meaning for those unfamiliar with the original. The reasons for this "experiment" are explained in the text that follows, and the object of its reading will become clear.

We will begin today with what may seem like very simple matters by looking at certain aspects of soul life, such as attentiveness and memory. We will then progress to passions and emotions and then to matters that might be considered part of the realm of truth, beauty, and goodness. We will study aspects that affect our lives by fostering health or causing illness. We will be concerned with the true soul causes of illness, and as we pursue this theme we will come up against the boundary where soul nature dips into the physical body's life.

Thus, we will need to investigate the interrelationship between the body's state of health and the soul's inner life of activity and work. Then we must rise to a contemplation of high human ideals and consider their effect on the soul. We must look at the phenomena of ordinary life—for example, what makes time pass so quickly? We will see how such phenomena affect soul life and are present in a strange series of events within the soul. We will study the peculiar effects of boredom. Many other things could be mentioned, and we could consider them phenomenologically, or from the perspective of remedying apparent illness in the soul's life—poor reasoning ability, poor memory, and so on. You can also imagine that in speaking of the soul's life, we must touch on other areas as well. Theosophists are, in a certain way, familiar with the ideas needed to relate human soul life to other matters.

You are all familiar with the aspects of human nature that spiritual science recognizes as consisting of body, soul, and spirit. That gives you a basis for saying that we must relate soul life to aspects of bodily nature, on the one side, but also that it extends into spirit, on the other. We have been concerned with the more physical aspects in the lectures called "Anthroposophy." Now we will go into the soul's life in "Psychosophy" and, later, rise to the life of spirit in "Pneumatosophy."

What is soul life when we contemplate it as such, within the limits just spoken of? What we usually refer to as "outer world," or the given world spread before and around us, cannot be considered part of our soul life. The minerals, plants, animals, air, clouds, mountains, rivers, and so on—in other words, everything in our environment—cannot be counted as belonging to the soul life, regardless of what we might bring to them out of our spirit when we visualize them. On the physical level, when we encounter a rose, we do not consider the rose itself to be a part of our soul life. However, if we feel joy or pleasure arising in us as we look at it, we can indeed call that a soul experience. If we meet someone and form a mental picture of that person—hair, face, expression—we do not include that in our soul life. But if we feel an interest in a person through sympathy or antipathy, or if we think of that person with love, all of these feelings must be considered soul experiences. You know that I don't like definitions; I prefer to characterize instead. I don't want to define soul life for you, since definitions accomplish little. I prefer to characterize what belongs to soul life.

Let us look at something else. Suppose we witness someone engaged in an activity, and, according to what we see, we must call it a good deed—one that can be approved of from a certain moral viewpoint. Then we have such a soul experience, which is expressed by our saying: "That deed was good!" This experience is different from that already characterized. We are not describing an action as such or determining the various steps that led to it, and it is not a matter of our liking or disliking the motivation behind it. Other, higher interests are involved. When we call that deed "good," we know that it should not depend on us at all whether we say a deed is good or bad. We must nevertheless make this assessment in the soul if we want to be conscious of the quality of the deed. Nothing in the outer world can tell us whether a deed is good. The judgment that it is good must arise and light up within us out of our own experience. However, if the judgment is to be justified, it must be independent of our own experience. The spirit plays a role in every experience of the soul such as this one; it is an experience in which something must be felt inwardly in order to become aware of it but the significance of which is independent of our consciousness. It makes little difference whether we make a judgment or not.

We have characterized what we might call the relationship of the soul to the outer world with three examples. First, we consider something as the outer world. Second, we consider a purely inner experience, such as an interest in someone else or the pleasure we take in a rose. And third, there is an inner experience of making a judgment, which must be independent of the soul life in order to have validity. The outer world must reveal itself to the soul through the physical body. Soul experience is purely inward, but the spirit also communicates within the soul, as shown in the examples given. It is important to keep firmly in mind that the soul life ebbs and flows in inner facts.

Now we must assume the task of discovering the inner characteristics of soul experience. We have determined the outer boundaries of soul experience—where it borders other realms. Now we want to see how we may characterize this inner life of the soul; in other words, what ideas or pictures must we use to speak of the human soul to make it clear that we are referring only to the soul? We need to find concepts, or images, characteristic of the nature of the soul as such, as exhibited on the physical plane.

What is the essential characteristic of soul experience? There are two ways we can characterize it, two ideas that apply only to the soul experience of the human being, as we will see when we speak strictly in relation to human physical conditions. It will therefore be my task to present an exact description of the characteristics—the basic inner phenomena and manifestations—of the soul's life, studied strictly within its own realm. Two concepts that characterize the inner aspects of that life may be cited. Please do not be put off, because our concern today is with the gathering of ideas. In the following days you will see the value of this precise grasping of concepts in learning to understand manifestations that concern all of us. They will provide us with indications that are of great importance for the health and illness of the ordinary soul life.

One of these two concepts is *judgment*. Judging is one activity of the soul. All other true soul experiences and activities can be summed up by what we can call the inner experiences of *love* [desire] and *hate* [aversion]. Properly understood, these words encompass all of the soul's inner life. We will see how fruitful both conceptions—of judgment and the consideration of the manifestations of love and hate—will be for us. Every aspect of the soul is either a making of judgments or a life in love or hate. Basically, these are the only concepts that pertain to the soul; all others refer to a vehicle for something else coming into the soul, either from without through the body or (due to causes we will learn later) from the spirit within. Thus, on the one hand, we have judgment and, on the other, love and hate. No matter what we call them, forces or activities, they alone belong to the soul life.

If we want to understand the role of these two activities, we must develop a clear idea about judgment for ourselves and then determine the significance of judgment, love, and hate within the soul life. I am not speaking of the logical aspects of judgment; that would be entirely different. I am not talking about the characteristics or laws of judgment. My characterization is not about logic but about the psychosophic nature—strictly from the perspective of inner activity, or soul processes—of judging. Everything you can learn about judgment through logic is ruled out. I am not speaking of "judgment" but of *judging*, the *activity* of judging, using the word as a verb.

When you are motivated—regardless of the motivation itself—to say that "that rose is red," you have judged. You have engaged in the activity of judging. Or you say, "That's a good man," or "The Sistine Madonna is beautiful," or "That church steeple is tall." To the extent you do this as an activity in the inner soul life, that is judging.

Now let us examine the experiences of loving and hating. Those who take the trouble to turn their view inward find that they do not go through the external world in such a way that their souls remain untouched by most things. Let us picture ourselves traveling through a landscape. Not only do we see green hillsides, cloud-covered mountain peaks, and rivers flowing through the valleys; our souls also experience delight in the landscape. This is because we are loving our experience. Even if this love is hidden within our soul experience, it is nevertheless something that accompanies all of us in almost everything we experience during the hours of our waking life.

As you walk along a street, if you see someone doing something wrong that disgusts you, that is really a concealed, a hidden emergence of the inner soul experience of hatred. If you happen to find an evil-smelling plant in a meadow and turn away from it, that, too, is simply another experience of hate that you do not immediately identify as such. Love and hate are continually active in our soul life. The same is true of judging. You are continually judging and continually experiencing love and hate every moment of your waking soul life.

We can understand the events of inner soul life even more exactly when we look at something that plays an important role in judging. Every judgment we make has an affect on our soul life, and this is essential for an understanding of the nature of soul life. When you judge that "the rose is red," or see someone doing a good deed and say, "That is a good person," both judgments have consequences for your soul, which might be characterized as follows. When you judge that "the rose is red," from that time forward, your soul life carries a mental picture of the red rose. That judgment is transformed within the further life of the soul into a mental image of the red rose, and you, as a soul-endowed being, continue to live with it. Every judgment culminates in a mental image in your soul experience. The judgment consists of what we might call two tendencies converging from two directions—one the rose, the other "red." These two then become one: the red rose. They converge into a single image that you carry throughout life. If these two experiences were drawn as two currents, we would have to draw them converging and say that our judging always culminates in the mental image.

mental image: the red rose

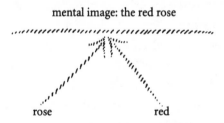

rose   red

Unless we thoroughly understand and impress on our minds the fact that judging always culminates in mental images, we cannot understand human soul life or its relationship to higher worlds, which will be the focus of our study in the days to come.

The phenomena of love and hate require that we ask a different kind of question. We cannot ask, "Where are they going," but rather, "Where do they come from?" With judging, it is a matter of where to, of where it is going; whereas for love and hate, it is a question of where from, of where it comes from. As the soul gives birth to love and hate, we will always discover something there that enters the soul life as though from another side. As soul experiences, loving and hating can always be traced back to what could be called desiring. If we put desiring on the other side of soul life (see drawing), we can say that behind the love and hate that appears in our souls, there always stands desire, which radiates into our soul life.

Thus, desire, as one side of our soul life, flows into it; we will study this in greater depth. And when we look into our soul, what becomes of the desiring? Love or hate! Then we look further into our souls and find the activity of judging. And if we ask what all this leads to on the other side, we see that judging leads to the mental image.

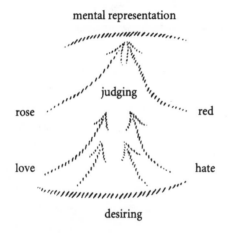

Desiring, as we can easily recognize, must be seen as emerging from the inner life of the soul. Desire cannot be spoken of as something that has an external cause, since it is likely that we are unaware of any such cause. We know one thing for certain; no matter what the source, desires surface in the soul life, and we can observe that as soon as they emerge, love and hate arise as a result. We can be equally certain that our judging that the rose is red must be within the soul. When that judging develops into the mental image of the red rose, however, such an image must have an outer validity and significance to be of any value to us.

Thus, for reasons largely unknown today (though familiar to spiritual investigators), desiring surfaces in the soul and lives as the phenomena of love and hate. And the soul feels impelled to allow the activity of judging to flow from the wellsprings of its own being, sharpening judgments to mental images and aware that if the judging is being done in a certain way, the image can be valid.

It will strike you as odd that I have resorted to so many words instead of just a few in presenting these elementary concepts of soul life; you may be feeling that a shorter statement would have served just as well. What I now say is by way of footnote. It is conceivable that these matters could be covered more briefly, but since they go unnoticed and ignored—even in the broadest reaches of modern scientific life—error upon error is made regarding them. I want, as it were, to insert a footnote to indicate such a significant error, since those who are making this mistake are unclear about these matters with which we have been familiarizing ourselves and are coming to understand more fully. And those making this error are drawing sweeping conclusions with regard to a certain fact that is being completely misunderstood.

In many physiology texts you may read that we are able to move our hands and legs not simply because we have the sense or perception nerves going from the sense organs to the brain and carrying messages to it or to the spinal cord. Everywhere the matter is also presented as if these nerves face others called "motor nerves" (on the physical plane they do, of course). It is said that, whenever we see an object, a message is conveyed along the nerve that goes from the eyes to the brain, which acts as the central organ. The sensation experienced there is then transferred to another nerve connected from the brain to the related muscle, which is stimulated to move. Motor and sensory nerves are distinguished in this way.

To a spiritual scientific perspective, however, the facts are very different. What natural science refers to as "motor nerves" do in fact exist as physical structures, but their purpose is not to stimulate movement but to perceive it, to verify it, to become aware of self-movement. Just as we have nerves for receiving color impressions, so we also have nerves that allow us to check on what we are doing and convey it to our awareness. The prevailing view is a gross error that does widespread damage; it has been ruinous to the whole field of physiology and to psychology as well. (All this should be understood as a footnote.)

We need to clarify the tremendous roles played in the life of the soul by judgment and by the phenomena of love and hate, the two elements we have found active in it. The entire life of soul is composed of various combinations of these two elements. We would arrive at an erroneous view if we failed to include the fact that all along the boundaries of the soul, other elements that do not belong to the soul's life in the strictest sense, enter continuously from outside. Something is certain to occur to us in this context, something encountered everywhere in ordinary life (which we talked about in last year's lectures on anthroposophy). Our soul life is essentially based on what is referred to as sensations experienced by the senses—for example, sounds heard by the organ of hearing, colors perceived by the eyes, taste experienced through the organ of taste, and so on. Experiences of external things conveyed to us by our senses we take into our soul, in a certain way, and they live on in it. When we consider what we take into our souls in this way, we may say that our soul life in fact approaches a boundary presented by the sense organs. Our sense organs are like sentries posted at a frontier, and whatever they report concerning the surrounding world we absorb into our soul life and carry with us.

Now, how does what sense experience gives us behave within the soul life? For soul life, what is the significance of our perceptions and what we then continue to live with—the sounds our ears hear, the colors our eyes see, and so on? What does all this mean for the soul? These experiences are usually studied in a truly one-sided way, without realizing that a combination of two factors, or elements, is encountered at the boundaries of soul life. One is perception, the direct experience we necessarily have of the outer world. We can have an impression of colors or sounds only when the sense organs that convey those impressions are exposed to them. Such impressions last only as long as we are exposed to external objects. An outer impression, or interchange between the outer and the inner, stops as soon as the eyes no longer look at an object or the ears no longer hear it making sounds. What does this prove?

Consider this along with the other fact—that we carry something of these experiences of the outer world with us. You know the sound you heard or the color you saw, although you no longer hear or see them. What happened there? There is something that takes place completely within, something that belongs totally to your soul life and must absolutely occur within. If it belonged to the external world, you couldn't carry it with you. Sense impressions of a color that you have received by looking at the color may be carried within you afterward only if they dwell in your soul, if they become an inner experience of the soul so that they remain in the soul.

Thus, we must distinguish between sense *perception*, which happens between the soul and the outer world, and that which we separate from our interaction with the external world and continue to carry within us. We must sharply distinguish between these two things; this is vital in such matters. Please do not think that I am being pedantic by saying these things; a foundation must be created for what follows.

You can clearly distinguish (for future reference) between the experience you have as long as you have an object before you and that which you carry with you in the soul afterward, if you call the first experience a sense perception and the latter a sensation. In this way you distinguish between the *perception* of a color and the *sensation* of it. Color perception is finished when you look away, but you continue to carry the sensation of color within you. Usually such distinctions are not made in daily life, nor are they necessary. We need them to prepare for coming lectures, however, and they will prove very useful to us.

Our souls carry within them, then, sensations acquired through exposure to external scenes and objects. Should we consider them to be a completely new element of soul life in addition to the elements of judging and love and hate? If that were the situation, you would have to say, "Well, you have forgotten something that is also an element of the soul's life—you failed to mention the sensations derived from the senses, which are found there." That is not the situation, however; such sensations are not a distinct aspect of the soul life. We must distinguish between the subject matter of the sensation and something else. For instance, when sensing the color red, we must separate out the red. If "red" were an inner soul experience, the whole color perception of it as "red" would be meaningless. The subject matter, or color, of the perception is in no way an inner experience of the soul. The object that stood before you is red, but its redness is not produced by your soul. What originates in your soul is something very different—that is, what you did, or your *activity* while the red object stood before you, so that you could carry the impression with you. This activity is the inner soul experience, and it is actually nothing other than the converging of the two fundamental elements of the soul life to which we have been referring. We must look more closely at what occurs when we see a color (red, for example), and then carry the impression of red with us in our soul.

If what I have said is true, that there are two elements in our soul life— that of love and hate, which points back to a desiring, and that of judging, which leads to a mental image—only something connected with these two soul elements may be considered when we have a sense experience before us and want to identify the sensations. Imagine that you have a color impression before you and have a sensation of the color. What emerges as an activity from the soul experience when you expose your- selves to the sense experience of, for example, the color red? Love and hate would emerge from the soul, on the one hand, and judging on the other. Let us make a drawing:

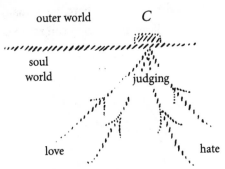

Assume that this is the border between the soul and the outer world. The horizontal line separates the area of the soul (the lower part in the illustration) from the outer world (upper part). If what I have been say- ing is true, then, if something along that boundary makes an impression on a sense organ (let us say that an object at *C* produces a color impres- sion), judgment and the phenomena of love and hate come from within the soul to meet it, for nothing but these elements can flow from the soul. Only judging and the phenomena of love and hate can flow toward this sense experience as we observe the color red.

Please note that there can be important differences between two judg- ments and between two desires. Imagine a dreamy or bored moment— for example, while waiting for a train. A memory surfaces in your soul, evoking the mental image of a previous experience that was unpleasant.

Alongside this fact, there arises in your soul the long, drawn-out, repugnant consequences that resulted from that episode. You can sense how these two mental images now merge into a single intensive visualization of the impression left by the disagreeable event. A judgment is reached entirely within the sphere of soul experience; the outer world has added nothing. Love and hate also play a role, since the image arose from the soul and love and hate immediately joined it from within the soul. Again, nothing gets to the outside. While you sit quietly with this taking place in your soul, someone else can stand near you and not be able to see anything of what is going on in your soul. Nothing in the environment has any significance or in any way affects what your soul is experiencing of love and hate and judging.

While we are engaged in the inner activity I have been describing, where judgment is evoked by love and hate, we remain in a sea of the soul life, so to speak. The following drawing can represent this:

outer world

love and hate

The letter *a* indicates the emergence of the first mental image from within the soul's boundaries, *b* the second. They coalesce to form a new mental image, *x*, or judging. Thereby love and hate come into consideration. None of this extends to the soul's boundary, but remains entirely within the realm of soul experience.

Everything is different when it comes to a sense experience. When a sense experience emerges, we must go as far as the soul's boundary and approach the outer world. It is as though the currents of our soul life flow right up to where the outer world begins and are stopped by the outer world. What is stopped there? *Desire* (we may also say, love and hate) flows as far as the boundary, as does the capacity to judge. They are both halted at the border. As a result, desiring must stop, as must judging. Judging and desiring both arrive at the borderline, but the soul does not perceive them. In that judging and desiring flow to the boundary of the soul life and are halted, a sensation forms. Sensations are nothing more than what flows together out of inner unconscious judging and the unconscious phenomena of love and hate, which strive outward but are hindered and retained. Whatever the soul carries as a sensation arises in this way.

Thus, we can say that what we may call love and hate and what we may call judging surge substantially within the sea of the soul. (We will study all these matters in exact and confirming detail and further clarify them.) When judging leads to a mental image within the soul life, the soul life registers this culmination, the entire activity involved in judging, and finally sees the mental image as the outcome. If the soul allows the same current to flow right up to the boundary, where it comes up against the outer world, it is forced to let the stream of desiring and judging stop; thus, the whole process, the convergence of desiring and judging, results in sensation. Strictly speaking, sensation is the converging of judging and desiring within the life of the soul.

When we consider the usual daily range of our soul life and focus on the source of its rich content, we find it to be sense experience. Self-examination can easily convince you that your inner experiences arise mostly from that which you have taken with you out of sense experience. If you want to visualize something higher—mental images of the nonphysical—you find that it does your soul good when you attempt to perceive sensibly what is not sense-perceptible; in other words, when you picture these things through color or sound sensations, even if quite subtle. Language can show us the soul's frequent deep need to express higher things in terms of sensations. Usually people are unaware of this fact, because in picturing physical things (usually taken from daily life) the picture quality, or symbol quality, is very shadowy and nebulous. People believe they have produced something very different from pictures of combined sensations, but this is not the case.

Just try to imagine an immaterial triangle, one that is colorless and not connected in any way with a sense perception. You will discover the difficulty in this and how totally incapable most people are when they want to imagine something like an intangible triangle. You can do so only when you make it sense-perceptible. If you want to imagine a triangle, you must always imagine it as something physical. You must connect a material idea (one connected with the sense-perceptible) to the concept of the triangle. This is in the nature of our language. You can see how you are always forced to think in sense-perceptible terms through language. I said, for example, that a sense-based image has to be "connected" to the concept of a triangle. Isn't connecting just such a material image? We connect things to one another. The sense-based symbol is present everywhere in the words we use. Thus, we can say that on the broadest scale, human soul life consists of sensations won from the outer world.

There is really only one human mental image that normally accompanies all of us, arising repeatedly from our inner soul experience and not directly attributable to external sense experiences, despite the fact that it must always be linked to them. It is the unique mental image we so often speak of here, that of the I. When we look at the actual soul situation, we find that human beings live, for the most part, in a world of sensations. In that world the mental representation of the I surfaces, occasionally in a very apparent way. There is an underlying awareness of the I.

When you examine your soul life, however, you quickly find that a mental image of the I is not always there. You do not continuously imagine only your I but also other things, such as red, green, or blue, connecting and disconnecting, and so on. You do not, however, continuously imagine the I. Nevertheless, in spite of this, you know that in the I-image, you are picturing something that must be present in every sense experience, for you know that you pit it against sensations in desiring and judging. What we call "soul experience" is, in a certain sense, also "I-experience."

In a certain sense, experiencing sound or color is also an I-experience, but the idea of the I can never be kindled in the external world alone. It always emerges between other images derived from sense experiences, but it cannot (unlike sound and color) enter from the outer world. It comes to the surface from the ocean of soul life and, as a mental image, joins every other mental image, as it were. All these other images also surface from that ocean, but they are caused by external impressions, which are present only when those external impressions exist. The mental picture of the I surfaces without the existence of an external impression. That is the only difference between an image, or perception, of the I and other ideas and perceptions related to sense experiences.

This, therefore, allows us to say that here we encounter the important fact that a unique mental image surfaces in the midst of our soul life, compared with those other, externally induced, mental images. This is a peculiar and significant fact. How can we explain it?

There are a few modern philosophers and psychologists (even beyond the spiritual scientific movement) who stress the importance of the I-image. This is something Dr. Unger has often and penetratingly indicated in his epistemological studies. Nevertheless, the odd thing is that despite their good intentions, such scholars far overshoot the mark. I will mention the example of the French philosopher Bergson.[2] In his works you will encounter numerous references to the I-image with one thing emphasized repeatedly. Such scholars have noted the great significance and unique nature of the I-image. As a result, they conclude that the I represents, or indicates, an enduring presence, because it surfaces from hidden depths rather than external stimuli. Bergson and others defend this view by saying that the I differs from all other soul and sense experiences in that it seems to be centered in itself, in its own experiencing, and thus perceives its own true shape. If the I experiences its own true form in its mental image, it is because something enduring is present, not something ephemeral. You will find that this is the reasoning, based on these significant aspects of the I-image, of several schools of philosophy and psychology, even those outside spiritual scientific circles.

There is a grave error in this reasoning. A certain objection must be raised against Bergson's argument and this proves fatal to his inference. Let us say, for example, that the I-image gives rise to something that

---

2. Henri-Louis Bergson (1859–1941) developed a humanistic philosophy of "process" as an alternative to positivism. He was awarded the Nobel Prize for literature in 1928.

constitutes the true human essence, in other words, that the soul is contained within this self. Let us assume that the I-image does this. Then we must justifiably ask, What happens at night during sleep? The human being is not within the I-image; the mental image has completely disappeared. All concepts of the I-being within its own image are valid only during waking life, since the I-image no longer exists during asleep. It is gone, only to reappear when one awakens. It is in no way something enduring! In order for the I-image to support the theory of a permanent I, it would have to be present as an image during sleep, but it is not. Thus, it is impossible to argue for the permanence or immortality of the I from a mere image of the I. We would be quite justified in concluding that because it is absent during sleep, it is also absent after death. The I-image can be missing. It is in no way immortal, since it vanishes every day. Therefore, we must hold fast to the unique significance of the I-image, which owes its existence to no external factor, a mental image within which the I really feels itself. Nevertheless, that image does not prove the existence of the I, because that picture does not exist at night.

We have reached a conclusion today that we wish to build on from tomorrow onward. We see in the surging sea of our soul life that judging and the phenomena of love and hate are present and basically form our soul life. We see that where the soul and the external world meet, sensations arise as an unconscious flowing together of desiring and judging. We see that sense experiences are taken into our soul life and that within those experiences not caused externally, the image of the I appears. We see that the image of the I has one characteristic in common with all other sense perceptions—at least to the extent they are experienced by the soul. The impressions of sound and color and all other sense impressions sink into the darkness of unconsciousness at night, just as the I-image does.

Now we must ask about the origin of that uniqueness of the I-image and how it relates to judging and the phenomena of love and hate, described as the basic soul elements. I will close today with this question, which involves the relationship between the I-image, or real soul center, and the rest of the soul's life. This is where we will resume tomorrow.

2.

The Activities of Human Soul Forces

W E CONCLUDED yesterday's observations on psychosophy by characterizing the soul's ebb and flow and how it may be attributed to its two essential elements, judging and the inner experience of love and hate. We also pointed out that sensations, given through our senses, emerge and fill the soul life like waves that continually rise and fall on the sea. It was further indicated that there is one aspect that arises in this restless sea that is radically different from everything else we experience while awake to the external world. We experience these sensations when we have contact with the outer world; they then transform themselves in us in such a way that they live on in us.

As we examine the tide of experience arising through the influences of our senses, we become aware of a perception that is very different from any other. All other perceptions in ordinary life are caused by outer stimuli that then go through a process within us. From perceptions they become sensations and live on in what the sensations leave behind in us. Perception of the I is completely different, however. It surfaces among the other, externally caused sensations and is, in a certain sense, always present during our soul life. Perception of the I differs in that it cannot be caused from outside. Thus, there is a contrast in our soul life between the sensation of the I and all other soul experiences. The mysteries hidden behind this contrast will become apparent in the course of these lectures. We must focus on the contrast right from the beginning, to get a feeling for those mysteries.

With all the rest of our experience we depend, as it were, on the external world, and we insert our I-perception into the rest of our experience. Using this completely abstract contrast, we can learn to sense that

that which surges up and down in the soul comes from two directions. It is important that we look with sensitivity at this human soul life, both in an abstract way and concretely, with both a smaller and a larger perspective, since only the study of human soul life will illumine all other soul life.

Essentially, human soul life is anything but unified. It is more like a dramatic battlefield, where opposites struggle continually. Anyone who listens with sensitivity and feeling to this soul life will certainly notice its dramatic character. When confronted by these opposing forces in the human soul, people in fact feel a lack of control, a passivity. The greatest geniuses as well as the least outstanding of individuals are subject to these two opposing natures in the soul's life. Yesterday, I began with a poem by Goethe, to give you a feeling for the contradictions that are active in the human soul, even within the soul of the greatest genius.

If, after hearing that poem, you had looked it up in a Goethe anthology, you would have had a peculiar feeling, which would serve as a good foundation for this whole lecture cycle. I want to describe that feeling in order to avoid considering soul life abstractly and to bring lifeblood into it and to enter into what lives in the soul.

If you had looked up the Goethe poem that was recited yesterday, you might have said, "Well, this is a completely different version! What I see here in Goethe's works is not what I heard." Something was indeed changed for the recitation, which, from an academic perspective, would be tremendously uncaring and barbarous. The poem was specially prepared and not read according to Goethe's text. Certain parts were changed and others omitted, so that a very different impression was created. Of course, this cannot be done in the presence of literature professors, but it is all right when it is done for a very specific purpose. In our case, the purpose was to deepen our perspective of the drama in the human soul. Goethe wrote "The Eternal Jew" in his very early youth. But if Goethe, at a more advanced age, could have looked over the poem as recited here, he might have said, "I can stand behind that." He would have accepted our changes and rejected what we omitted yesterday. He might have admitted to being somewhat ashamed of what he had originally written.

Anyone who shares my own unlimited admiration for Goethe might be allowed to speak as I must today about his "Eternal Jew." It was a product of his early youth, and his youthfulness is expressed there because it was produced when he was still a real good-for-nothing, someone from whom nothing could possibly be learned.

Is it wrong to say that, in certain respects, nothing could be learned from Goethe? We can honestly say that at the time, he could not even spell correctly. Why, then, may we not be allowed to say that certain aspects of "The Eternal Jew" are useless? We certainly cannot condone the rampant poor taste these days that allows, when possible, the light of day to shine on *all* the earliest forms of the works of every great artist. We merely expose our own deficiencies in this way. In this youthful poem, there is something that is not really Goethe himself. Many ideas rumbled around in his youthful soul, influenced by his surroundings, but the nature of his environment is unimportant to us and concerns only him.

Elements were brought together within Goethe's soul that we might refer to as a "marriage" between the temporal and the eternally divine that produced an enduring offspring for all of humanity. It is valuable to us and to everyone who will come after us. These two elements—the one that concerned only Goethe and the one that concerns us and all following generations—were disentangled in yesterday's recitation. These two Goethean souls were cut apart; that which lived in the young Goethe and remained dominant within him until the end of his life was separated from what lived in him only during his youth and later died out.

We see here how forces play into genius and ripen only with time. And we see that there are other, external forces that influenced Goethe. When we view Goethe's youthful soul, it really seems like a battlefield for the struggle between the heroic Goethe—what accompanied him throughout his life as the actual bearer of his genius—and an element in his soul that he fought against. If this battle had not taken place, Goethe would not have become *Goethe*. Here is a clear example of opposites, of contrary forces active in the soul. The soul cannot be a homogenous entity; it would be unable to progress any further. It is vital that we begin by gaining a feeling for this polarity, or contradiction, in the soul life. If we do not have this feeling, we will not be able to value rightly what is said precisely with regard to the soul life. When we have such a typical soul life as Goethe's, we look at it as if at a drama and attempt to approach it with a kind of shy reverence, because in that one incarnation, in the battle that unfolds as soul life, we see the true content, the real destiny, of the individual soul life.

There is still another aspect that we may point out in this soul drama. Let us take another look at the contradictions in Goethe's soul life as they appeared spiritually through yesterday's recitation and through my explanation. What may we conclude? We find that in his later years, Goethe followed only one of the impulses discussed yesterday. Goethe was subjected involuntarily to these two forces in his soul throughout his life. All human beings, as soul beings, are not merely masters of themselves but are also subjected to something within that has power over them and that cannot be grasped knowingly up front. If Goethe, when he wrote "The Eternal Jew," had embraced everything in his soul that could have been embraced, this poem would have been more artistic and a little closer to the version recited yesterday, but certainly not as it appears in Goethe anthologies.

People are given over to their soul lives. There is an aspect there that is essentially just as external to our soul life as anything else around us. When we encounter a red rose, we are powerless to see it any differently; the rose forces us to retain the redness in our image of it. Likewise, there is something that makes it necessary to live out the drama of the soul in a very specific way. In terms of our sense impressions, the outer world dictates to us. We must recognize a similar inner master in our soul life when we examine its polarities and observe how the soul progresses in time from day to day, year to year, and from one stage of life to the next, seeing how it becomes richer as it is driven forward through an inner force.

You can see in these simple, concrete examples—which have been kept entirely at the physical level—that because of the nature of sense perception, we must acknowledge an external force, or master, in external life and an internal master within ourselves. No matter where we are in space, the outer world controls our sense perceptions. It would merely be a fantasy if we refused to recognize this. As we progress inwardly, we must look at the dramatic contradictions of our soul life. We need to recognize that we are subject to a master there, just as we are in the external world—a master who makes sure we have a different soul life at seven years of age, for example, than at twenty, thirty, or later. This example is given at the outset to illustrate much of what we will consider later.

In the final analysis, this soul drama—concretely demonstrated in Goethe—is made up only of the two elements of the soul life, of judging or reasoning and the phenomena of love and hate. As I said yesterday, judging leads to visualization, whereas love and hate come from desire. You might say that my assertion that judging leads to visualization contradicts the simple fact that mental images originate from sense impressions forced on us from the outer world. When we see a rose and have the impression of "red," we visualize red without any reasoning involved. You could further object that judging, thus, does not lead to a mental image, but it is really the other way around; visualization comes first, and reason follows based on the mental image.

Hold on to this apparent contradiction for a moment. It is not easy to resolve or to see through. We must combine several of the insights we can glean from observing soul life to find the key to this apparent contradiction. First, it is important to note that mental images really do have an existence of their own in soul life; they have their own life. Please understand the full significance of that statement. Visualizations are like parasites, like living beings in the soul that lead their own existence there.

On the other hand, desiring also has its own existence in the soul. The soul is really subject to the independent mental images and to longings and desires. You can easily see that mental images live a life of their own in our souls when you consider, for example, that the soul is powerless to easily call a previously formed mental image back into memory. A mental image formed only yesterday may sometimes refuse strongly to allow itself to be recaptured. In ordinary life we then say that we have "forgotten," that it simply will not rise to the surface and resists recall. A battle takes place between something that lives in us as an undeniable soul power wanting to force an image to the surface and something else that is also present in the soul. A battle is waged in our souls with the mental image, though it will eventually return without any external cause. It was present all the time, but refused to reveal itself at the desired moment. You know further that this battle between our own soul forces and the mental image to be called up is different with different human individualities. The mental images indeed live in the soul, but as opponents, so to speak, of our own soul forces. The difference between these two is frighteningly great.

Some people, for example, never seem to suffer the embarrassment of being unable to recall what lives in their souls when needed. Such people can summon in an instant all their memories and knowledge. On the other hand, there are those so incapacitated by forgetfulness that they have absolutely no power over their reservoir of images, and they cannot recall them to consciousness.

A true psychologist finds it very important to know how quickly a person can remember—the speed with which the images of past experiences assert themselves against the forces trying to recall them. Psychologists use this as a measure of a deeper element in the being of the human. They see evidence of inner health or illness in the degree that we are removed from our mental images. Since the nuances of health and illness blend into one another at their extremes, we may say that, from a psychologist's viewpoint, we have subtle indications right into the physical nature of the human constitution in these intimate details. We can even assess just where an individual has a problem by the way a soul must battle with mental images in order to remember them. We look, as it were, right through the soul into something that is other than soul when we understand the soul's experience in battling with the realm of mental images.

Another way of picturing the way mental images lead a life of their own in our souls is through the fact that we cannot completely control the mental images we have at any given moment; we are at their mercy. Certain experiences can convince us of this. It depends on us, on the nature of our soul life, whether or not we understand someone who is speaking with us, for example. You understand me when I am lecturing to you. If, however, you were to bring a person who is unfamiliar with such matters to hear my lectures, such a person would probably get nothing from them, regardless of how well educated that individual might be. Why is this? It is because you have been acquiring the needed mental images over a period of time. You have built up mental images in your souls that now come to meet the new ones in today's talk.

Here you have an example of how we really have very little control over our soul life. There is no point in trying to understand something for which we lack a store of background images. In this case, image comes to meet image. If you observe your soul life, you will be able to notice that your I plays an extremely minimal role in it. You have the best opportunity to forget your I while you are listening to something that fascinates you. The more intently you listen, the more you forget your I. Try, after the lecture, to recall such a moment when you were absorbed in something you understood. You will discover that you must confirm that something was happening in you, with which your I was not very involved, whereby it had indeed forgotten itself. At such times, we say that we were as if given over to it, as if we had lost ourselves. We always lose ourselves when we understand something particularly well. We shut out our I and hold our reservoir of images up to meet those entering the soul. A sort of battle ensues between the old and the new, and we ourselves become the battleground for their confrontation.

In relation to our soul life, something very important depends on whether or not we already have the mental images needed to understand something. Imagine listening to some matter without already having the mental images needed to understand it. We listen "unprepared," as they say. Then something peculiar appears. At the moment we listen unprepared, when the state of the soul life makes it impossible to understand, something demon-like approaches us from behind. What is it? It is the I dwelling in our soul life. It appears to attack as if from behind. As long as we are absorbed, are lost to ourselves, it doesn't show itself, but it arises whenever we lack understanding.

How does it announce itself there? Those who pay close attention to soul life soon notice that what plays into it brings it discomfort—the soul fills itself with some element that brings it discomfort. With this as a background, we may say that this discomfort shows that, in the soul life, the mental images already present affect new mental images trying to enter. Their way of acting is not a matter of indifference. It either brings a sense of comfort and satisfaction into soul life or it brings exactly the opposite. Again, we see the degree to which we are given over to our mental images. Although it is not obvious, this is of vital importance to psychologists. This discomfort is a force created in the soul when confronted with the unfamiliar. It continues to act in the soul's life in such a way that it goes beyond that life and takes hold of an even deeper element of human nature. The results of this misunderstanding and discomfort can have a damaging consequence, even affecting the body's constitution. In diagnosing the finer degrees of sickness or health (those connected with the soul life), it is very important to notice whether or not patients understand the matters they must frequently contend with in life. Such considerations are far more important than is generally believed.

Let us move on now. It was stated that our mental images have an independent life, that they are like beings within us. Further consideration will convince you of this. You will remember moments in your soul life when the external world seemed to have nothing at all to offer you, despite a desire on your part to be stimulated by it, to receive impressions, to experience something. It simply had nothing to offer. It passed you by without leaving any impressions. You then experience something as a result—*boredom.* Boredom causes desire in the soul. It gives birth to a longing for impressions, and the soul life is surrendered to it; yet there is nothing to satisfy that desire. Where does boredom originate?

If you are truly a good observer of nature, you might have observed something not often noticed—that only a human being can become bored. Animals never become bored. Only superficial observers believe that such a thing is possible. You can even become aware of a strange aspect of human boredom. If you investigate the soul life of a simple, primitive people, you will find that they suffer far less boredom than is found among the more cultured people with their more complicated soul life. Those who go about the world and tend to be observant will notice that country people are much less prone to boredom than city dwellers. Of course, you should not think here of studying how bored city people become in the country, but only the degree of boredom country people experience in the country. Your attention should be on the more complex cultural conditioning of soul life. Thus, there is a real difference in the degree to which human beings are prone to boredom.

Then, too, boredom does not emerge from soul life without cause. Why are we bored? It is produced by the independent life of our mental images! The old mental images in us are the source of our desire for new impressions; they want to be re-enlivened and refreshed, to have new impressions. People have little control over boredom, because mental images received in a previous life develop their own life in the soul and seek re-enlivenment. They develop desires. If they remain unsatisfied, their unsatisfied longing—an attribute that we must study in the soul life itself—is expressed as boredom. Therefore, people who have fewer mental images also have fewer desiring images. The fewer desires for new impressions they develop, the less bored they are. We should not conclude, however, that a lasting state of boredom characterizes a highly developed human being. Those who constantly yawn are not among the most highly developed in terms of soul life, though they are more developed than those who can never become bored because they have few mental images. Boredom can be cured, and when the soul has developed sufficiently, boredom is no longer possible.

Why are animals never bored? When the gates of their senses are open to their environment, animals continually receive impressions. Now picture those impressions. The soul life of an animal flows out to the environment and is stimulated. What goes on outside as a continuous external process keeps pace with the inner flow of animal experience. Animals are done with the one impression when a new one is presented, to which they surrender themselves. Outer events and inner experience coincide.

The advantage we have over animals is that we can establish within ourselves a different measure of time. The sequence of mental images that surfaces in our soul life can be based on a time element other than the one in our environment. We may happen to encounter something that has often left an impression with us, but a time comes when we close ourselves to it—we shut out the impression. It is as if our attention is withdrawn from the outer flow of time and events, and we do not accompany them inwardly. Time passes within us as well, but since it is without external impressions, it remains unfilled. As long as people have mental images from a previous life, they work into the time that is empty and in this way continue their activity in the soul.

Consequently, the following might happen. Once again, imagine the soul experience of animals as it runs parallel to the outer flow of time.

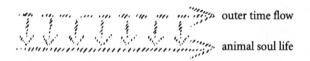

outer time flow

animal soul life

An animal's inner soul life flows in such a way that it is given over to the outer flow of time or the perceptions of its own body. When, for example, an animal digests, the images that arise from within stimulate it inwardly. This is extraordinarily interesting to the animal. For it, the external flow of time has the effect of offering it constant inner stimulation. We could say that it is interested in every moment, which cannot be said of human beings. Outer objects can cease to interest us; nevertheless, the flow of external time continues!

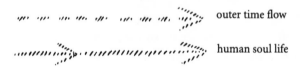

outer time flow

human soul life

Let us picture the inner soul life of the human being and the outer flow of time in relation to it. Human soul life is exposed repeatedly to the same external impressions to the point where they hold no further interest. Soul life then stops, and since time flows on with the soul life, that time remains empty, and we are bored. People are bored because of unfilled time. What works into these unfilled periods? It is the mental images of the past that have a longing but do not receive anything. While animals receive constant stimulation in the course of time, human beings develop, between past and future, longings for impressions as the result of mental images themselves demanding new content and enrichment. Human beings have an advantage over animals owing to the fact that our past mental images continue to live and develop a life of their own. Later, I will point out what can cause illusions in this context.

There is a cure for boredom, which is approximately as follows. Living in our continuing mental images are not only desires, but meaningful content as well—meaning that continues to live in the soul. This is what enables us to carry mental images acquired in the past into the future ourselves. When the mental images themselves bring something to us from the past, that is again the mark of higher soul development. It makes a great difference whether or not we possess mental images that continue to interest and fill our soul life in the future. Thus, there is a stage beyond which one can be bored, but for those who fill themselves with meaningful mental images, such images continue to act in the future. This is the difference between those who can cure their boredom and those who cannot. Such an inability indicates the independent life of one's mental images, a life that cannot be controlled and to which one is subject. If we do no make certain that our mental representations have meaning, we become bored. Only through meaningful mental images can we protect ourselves from boredom.

This is also immensely significant for psychologists, since ordinary human life demands a certain balance between fulfilling the soul's desires and external life in general. A bored soul, empty of meaning—one that nevertheless continues to live with the flow of time (for time waits for no one)—is poisonous also, in a certain connection, for the body. Excessive boredom leads to illness. The phrase *bored to death* reflects an appropriate sense of this fact. Those who suffer from boredom may not be killed instantly by it, but it does in fact work as a psychological toxin far beyond the confines of the soul.

You may have a sense that the things you have heard today are simply pedantic explanations, but they will help us gain even deeper insight into the real life of the soul. Subtle distinctions are vital to familiarizing ourselves with the wonderful drama of the soul, where the I plays the heroic central role. There is "someone" hidden in the soul life of every-one, one who is wiser than we ordinarily are. If this was not true, the outlook for human life would be very grim.

When we examine the way various people view matters, they seem to have the most extraordinary notions about the nature of the soul, the body, and the spirit—subjects over which a great deal of confusion rules. It is especially interesting that during ancient times, when external sci-ence was based more on clairvoyance, people made the appropriate dis-tinctions among the parts played by the body, soul, and spirit in the human being. Then, at a relatively early point in time, a Church council felt impelled to do away with the spirit. The Church established a perma-nent dogma that human beings consist only of body and soul. Yes, the spirit was in fact abolished. If you were to acquaint yourselves with the dogmatism of the Church, you would understand the consequences of that action.

A few individuals, of course, saw that there was something people had to refer to as "spirit," but they were the most vehement heretics. Anyone who could not make do with body and soul, and consequently intro-duced spirit as a third component, was considered a monstrous heretic. This was a consequence of the uncertainty that prevailed about whether or not it was justified to speak of body, soul, and spirit. From the moment when one ceased to speak of body, soul, and spirit, confusion set in—but people tend toward confusion about everything. When peo-ple no longer really know what spirit and soul are, something else can disappear. That is how the clear view of spiritual life disappeared.

Even though human beings are always prone to the error of failing to distinguish properly, we can say that something in the nature of a good spirit keeps watch over humanity and that there is a dim feeling for the truth. We are able to have a dim feeling of the truth because something like the spirit of language is active in our environment. Language is really wiser than human beings. People ruin much of language, but lan-guage does not allow everything related to it to be spoiled. It is more correct and sensible than the average individual. Language, through its stimulation and the impressions it makes on the human soul, can some-times have a very proper effect. People, on the other hand, make errors when they bring their judging to it. I would like to give you an example of how we surrender ourselves to language and yet feel and sense something that is right.

Imagine that you stand before three things: first, a tree; second, a bell; and third, a human being. You begin to judge according to what the outer world presents, based on your immediate sense impressions. You activate your soul life; judging is an activity that takes place in the soul. You make judgments about the tree, then the bell, and then the person. You look at the tree; it is green. You make a judgment that is expressed in accordance with the genius of language with the sentence "The tree is green." Now let us assume that you want to express some fact about the bell as a result of your sense impression—that is, that the bell is ringing and producing a sound. At the moment when the bell is ringing, you express your perception with the speech judgment "The bell rings." You have expressed the tree's greenness with the words "The tree is green" and your experience of the bell with the words "The bell rings." Now let us look at the person. The person speaks. You experience this fact and clothe your outer impression with the words "The person speaks."

Now let us look at all three judgments: "The tree is green," "The bell rings," and "The person speaks." What has arisen in these three? All three have to do with sense impressions. You will have the feeling that each of the three sense impressions, when compared with the spoken judgments, emerges as something quite different. In considering the first judgment, you must ask what it really expresses. It expresses a fact that, through the form of judgment, is related to space. In saying that the tree is green, I am expressing a spatial fact, one that is true now and will remain the same any number of hours from now. It is something enduring. Now take the next judgment: the bell rings. Does that express anything existing in space? It does not. Instead of expressing something spatial, it describes something occurring in time, something in the process of becoming, something in a state of flux. Consequently—and because the genius of language is so wise—you can never speak in the same way about spatial facts as you do about what takes place in time. In terms of judging, language does not allow you to use a verb directly in describing a tree in space. One must resort to an auxiliary verb ("is"), one that helps us live in time with our speech; thus one says, "The tree *is* green." You are allowed to use a verb to express something very similar, but with a different emphasis, saying, "The tree greens." In that instance, however, one is shifting to a description of something taking place in time. Where the genius of language allows a shift from space to time, one must shift to what proceeds in time, to what is becoming, to the arising of greenness. A true genius, a wonderful genius, is at work in language. As human beings, we have damaged it in many ways, but it remains a fact that language simply does not allow us to directly use verbs for spatial matters.[1]

In the case of the second judgment, where a process of becoming is involved, we cannot express such a process with "is," saying, "The bell is rings," which distorts the meaning.[2] To rewrite or paraphrase in such a way ruins language.[3]

As for the third judgment, one's sense perception is expressed by the verb "speaks." Consider for just a moment the difference between the judgments "The bell rings" and "The person speaks." In the first, the sound is the important thing and is expressed with the judgment. If I say, "The person speaks," however, I am making a statement that does not contain that which is of consequence; in this case, the important thing is not in the "speaks" but in what is being said. The stimulus to sense perception expressed in the verb *speaks* is not what holds our interest in this instance, but rather the content, the *what*, expressed with the verb. With the language you stop short of the content there.

Why, in the case of "The bell rings," do you not stop short, and why does the genius of language stop short of content in saying, "The person speaks"? Why do we stop short of what matters to us? It is because we want to confront the living soul directly. In this instance, the genius of language has supplied a word (*speaks*) that stops short of meaning and merely characterizes something external that confronts us. In the case of

---

1. In German, the word for "verb," *Zeitwort*, is literally "time-word."
2. In English, one may say, "The bell is ringing." In German, however, *läutend* ("ringing") becomes an adjective rather than a verb.
3. The genius of the English language *does* allow for a combination of space and time within verb forms.

the bell, the word *rings* conveys the bell's metallic inner quality. When you confront a living human being having inner soul qualities, you guard against bringing that inner quality into the word.

In the genius of language, there is a tangible difference between what refers to place or space, a process or becoming, and the inner aspect of the soul. When we want to describe this from outside, we stop short of the inner aspect, that which matters, in the language as if out of a shy reverence. Through speaking, we recognize the inner soul aspect. In the course of these lectures we will see that it is indeed important to lift ourselves to a certain height of feeling, that we conceive of the soul as a self-contained realm, something that surges from its center, breaking against its confines. When we describe the soul from outside, the genius of language forces us, in a certain way, to stop short of its inner being. It is important that we learn to understand the soul in its true nature as a self-contained inner being and become aware that whatever must approach it from outside confronts an inner resistance coming from it. We should thus imagine the soul as a circle approached from its surroundings by sense experiences and filled internally with surging soul life.

As we saw today, this inner life of the soul is by no means independent; it experiences inwardly its own life of mental images, the reservoir of mental images. Those images, absorbed from without into the soul's inner life, continue to lead an existence in the flow of time.

We will see in the coming days how this self-contained life of mental images, enclosed within the boundaries of the soul, is the source of both our greatest bliss and our deepest suffering, to the extent that they originate in the soul. We will see, too, how the spirit is the greatest healer of the pain and suffering mental images cause in our souls. We may also say that just as hunger must be stilled in external bodily life, and that such stilling is healthy, the same must be done for the inner life of the soul; mental images require, in a certain way, inner nourishment through other mental images. When we overburden ourselves by eating too much, our health is undermined. Thus, the destiny of the soul plays out in such a way that new mental images may promote health or illness. We will see how the spirit functions not only as a health-giver in terms of our hunger for new mental images but also as healer when we suffer from an excess of them.

3.

The Senses, Feeling, and Aesthetic Judging

WE WILL AGAIN begin our lecture by reciting a poem to illustrate certain matters that we will explore today and tomorrow. This time the poem is the work of a non-poet, appearing to be more the incidental by-product of the spiritual activity of the author himself. Thus, we will be dealing with a soul manifestation that does not really arise from his innermost soul impulse, and this will significantly enhance our opportunity to study the theme of our lectures. The poem was written by the German philosopher Hegel about his relationship to certain secrets of human initiation.

ELEUSIS

To Hölderlin

Around me, within me — peace!
The unremitting cares of busy human beings sleep.
And I am given freedom and leisure.
Thank you, Night, my liberator!
The moon shrouds the uncertain boundaries
Of the distant hills with a misty mass.
A bright strip glitters lovingly over the lake.
The memory of the day's tedious clatter recedes,
As if long years lay between it and now.
Your image, dear friend, now rises before me
With the joy of days long gone. Yet, soon these yield
To the sweeter hope of seeing each other again.

I paint our opening scene already—the long anticipated,
Fiery embrace; then the more intimate second act,
When we probe each other with questions, to discover
What new things of feeling, view, and mood
Time has worked within the friend; then, the glad certainty
That the old bond maintains its faith,
Truer, firmer, riper than before;
That bond, not sealed by any oath—
To live for truth alone;
And never, never to make truce
With any convention that would regulate
Our feelings and opinions.
But then the thought, which carried me to you
Winging over streams and high mountains
Must face dull factuality.
Soon a sigh betrays our quarreling — and with the quarrel
Flees the dream of sweet imagining.

My eyes lift to the vault of eternal heavens —
To you, the radiant, starry host of night!
Forgetfulness rains down from your eternity,
Erasing every hope and wish.
My mind loses itself in gazing;
What I call mine disappears;
I surrender to the immeasurable;
I am in it, am All, am nothing else.
Thought, returning, alienated,
Recoils before the infinite, and fails, astounded,
To fathom such depths of vision.
But imagination draws down the mind to the eternal
And marries it to form. Welcome,
Exalted spirits! High shades!
From whose clear brows perfection radiates.
Do not fear! I feel the brilliance and gravity
That surround you are my home too.

Ha! Had the gates of your sanctuary now sprung open,
Ceres, you who are enthroned in Eleusis!
Then enthused, intoxicated, feeling
Your awesome presence near me
I would have comprehended your revelations.
Would have read the symbols' high intent, and overheard
The festive choirs of gods,
The dooms they utter from their council seats!

But today your halls are silenced, O Goddess!
The circle of the gods has flown back to high Olympus,
From their desecrated altars;
The genius of innocence that long ago enchanted
Has fled the grave of profaned humanity.
The wisdom of your priests is silent.
No note of the sacred rite escaped to reach us.
The researchers delve in vain for wisdom, moved more by curiosity
Than by love. Wisdom they possess, you they disdain.
To master her, they dig for words
To find the imprint of your exalted mind.
In vain! They grasp only dust and ash,
And will never conjure back your life!
Yet, in the rotting, unsouled mold they take their pleasure,
Dead themselves, content with the dead!
There remains no sign of your high feasts, no trace of an image.
The children of your mysteries,
The rich essence of that exalted teaching,
The depths of that unspeakable feeling,
Are too holy to be entrusted to a barren symbol.
Even thought itself cannot encompass the soul,
Who, beyond time and space, an aspect of infinity,
Rapt, self-forgotten, awakes once more
To consciousness. Those who would tell others what they know,
Though speaking with angels' tongues,
would feel the poverty of words.

It horrifies them that that holiest thing
Is so pettily thought, made so little by it —
Speaking itself seems a sin —
So shuddering they seal their lips.
This vow, that the initiates laid upon themselves, is a wise law
Laid upon poorer spirits, never to make known
What, on a holy night, they saw, and heard, and felt —
Lest even the nobler ones themselves should find their folly
Troubles the memory of the holy, and their hollow chatter
Stirs it to anger, even with the holiest — lest it should be
Trampled in the mire — become a mere thing of rote,
The plaything of sophists, a wordmonger's ware,
hawked about and bartered, dispensed for pennies,
A cloak for silver-tongued hypocrisy — a birch, perhaps,
To train a mischievous child — and in the end, so void,
So utterly empty, that its only life root
Is in its echo on alien tongues.
Your sons did not vainly flaunt your honor
In the streets and marketplace, Goddess, but bore it
In their bosom's inmost shrine.
Therefore, you do not live in their mouths.
They worshipped you with their lives; in their acts, you live still.

This night, too, Holy Godhead! I have looked upon you—
You, whom your children's lives have often revealed to me,
And felt unseen, as the soul of all their deeds.
You are the higher meaning, the true faith
Of the single Godhead, which
— though all the world should fail —
neither swerves nor shakes.

Let us consider the assertion of the two previous lectures of this series that a survey of soul life demonstrates that it consists of two elements: judging and the experiences of love and hate, which are connected with desiring. It may seem that we are leaving out *feeling*, the most important aspect of soul life, through which the soul keenly experiences its innermost nature. Indeed, someone might be inclined to say that these lectures have described the soul in its least inherent aspects by ignoring the feeling element that surges there, giving it its specific character.

We shall see, however, that the drama of soul life emphasized yesterday may be best understood by approaching feeling from the perspective of the two elements characterized. We must begin with the simple elements of the soul, which have often been mentioned. They are the sense experiences that enter soul life through the portals of our senses and continue their existence there. One fact is that soul life sends its waves surging up to the senses' portals and takes into itself the experiences of sense perception, which continue independently within the soul. Compare that with the fact that whatever is composed of the experience of love and hate, arising from desire, comes from within the soul itself. Mere observation of the soul reveals desires welling up from the very center of the soul, and, even to superficial observation, these desires can be seen to lead to the soul's experiences of love and hate. It would be a mistake to look into the soul for the desires themselves; they are neither to be sought nor found there. You would find in a more thorough study of the soul's life that desires arise through contact with the outer world and that love and hate well up from within the soul itself as the expression of desires. We may say, therefore, that by far the greater content of soul experiences, to the extent that it is concerned with mental images, is generated at the boundaries of the soul through the portals of the senses. On the other hand, what lives within the soul as love and hate wells up out of the very center of the soul.

If we draw this idea we will understand it better. We can characterize the soul life that we want to study in its inner nature by considering it as the inside of a circle that represents the content of our multifarious soul life. Now think of the sense organs as portals; they should be regarded as such. This is something you can also gather from the lectures on anthroposophy.

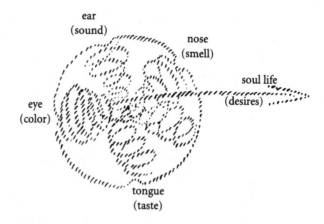

It is enough for now to consider the senses as portals opening to the outer world. Our drawing will best represent the interior life of the soul by showing desires that live on as phenomena of love and hate emerging from the soul's center and welling throughout it. The soul must be represented as completely suffused with desires flooding toward the portals of the senses.

What happens as the result of sense experiences, such as the ear's perception of a sound or the eye's perception of a color? We will disregard the outer world in terms of its content and focus instead on the instant when we have the sense perception—the interaction between the soul and the outer world. Let us really live into that moment when the soul is having an inner experience of color or sound as it enters from the outside world through the portal of the transmitting sense organ. Imagine yourselves turning away from the sense experience; the soul lives on in time and takes with it and retains the memory picture of what was gleaned from the sense experience. The soul carries this with it.

We have said that we must distinguish between what the soul continues to carry as a remembered mental image of a sense perception and the perception itself. If we fail to do this properly, we will not get to the truth but only to Schopenhauer's view of the matter. We must distinguish between the soul experience that continues as a recalled mental image and the experience that arises through the activity of sense perception. What happened when the soul was exposed to the outer world through the portal of sense perception?

As experience demonstrates in a direct way, our souls live inwardly in a surging ocean of desires, of the phenomena of love and hate, in the circumstances that I described yesterday and the day before. To the degree that the soul allows its waves to break against the portals of the senses, desires break against these gateways. Desires actually come into contact with the outer world in the instant of sense experience. It is the desires that are imprinted from the other side.

If you take a signet ring with the name Müller on it and press it into sealing wax, the imprint of Müller's name remains there. What remains is the imprint caused by the signet ring. You cannot say that what was imprinted fails to agree with what the external world brought about! Not only would that not be an unbiased observation, it would be Kantian. In as much as you want to look only at outer matter, it is Kantian. To state the crux of the matter—in this case, the name Müller and not the ring's metallic composition—one would have to say that that which presented itself to the sense experience received an imprint from outside. That imprint is carried further. Just as you do not carry a stamping device with you, you also do not carry the color or sound with you; you do, however, carry what has arisen as imprint in the soul. What we may call desiring, or the phenomena of love and hate, encounters the sense experiences.

Can we really call it that? Can we really detect an element of love or hate in a mere sense experience? Within direct sense experience, is there something like desire that is impelled to reach out? If some of that nature were not reaching out for sense experience, you would have nothing to carry in soul life—no memory image would be formed. There is a fact that speaks for this reaching out of desires toward the perceiving of sound, odors, colors, and so on; it is the existence of *attention*. Naturally, if we merely stare at a sense experience, this also leaves an impression, in keeping with the laws that govern the relationship between sense organs and the outer world. Impressions we only stare at, however, are not carried further within soul life. You must meet them with the power of attention from within. The more intense the attention is, the more easily the soul continues to carry sense experiences in it as memory pictures. The soul's relationship to the external world is such that what lives in it substantially is allowed to surge to the outermost limits of its being, manifesting itself at the extreme boundaries of its being in the fact of attention.

The other attribute of soul life, judging, is completely shut off during direct sense experience. Thus, only desiring, the dedication and openness of the soul to external experiences, remains. A sense impression is characterized by the very fact that attention is concentrated to the point of eliminating judging. When a soul exposes itself to the color red or to a sound, only desire lives in this exposing, and judging, the soul's other function, is suppressed. We must, however, draw a very exact line between them if we do not wish to succumb to fantasy. If, for example, we see a red color and say, "Red is," we have already made a judgment. Only when we go no further than the color impression itself is there still a simple correspondence of the soul with the outer world.

What happens as a consequence of the interaction between the outer world and desiring? We have been concerned with forming exact images, and thus we have distinguished between sense perceptions and sense-derived sensations. Sense perception is the immediate experience that arises from being exposed to external impressions, to what is experienced *while* the impression is made. Sense-derived sensations are what remain with us to be carried afterward. We can say, therefore, that what is carried along in this way represents a modification of desiring. Attention causes us to notice the presence of desires, and what we carry on within us reveals itself as sense-derived sensation. Thus, living on in our souls is sensation in the form of modified desiring. In fact, we also carry the being of our own soul with such sensations or mental images. The force of desiring swirling and surging throughout one's whole soul being gives rise to the sensation.

As we have seen, sensations arise at the gates of the senses, at the border between soul life and the outer world. Now, let us assume for a moment that the force of desiring in us does not go to the boundary of the soul life but remains within the boundary. We would say of a sense experience that the force of desiring goes all the way to the soul's surface. Imagine that a desire appears but does not reach the boundary of the soul's life; it loses its drive in the soul's being, so that it does not reach the portal of the senses. What would happen in this case?

We saw that when a desire presses forward and is forced to retreat, sensation, or the sense-derived sensation, is generated. Such sensations are generated only when a counterforce from outside causes the retreat, as a result of the activity of the senses. Inner sensation is generated when desire is forced back, not through direct contact with the outer world—it is stopped short of the boundary and retained within the soul itself. Inner sensation comes about at that point, and this is what we refer to as "feeling." Thus, in psychological terms, feelings are modified desires that have been turned back upon themselves, but their life has been retained within the soul rather than surging all the way to its boundary with the outer world. We can say, therefore, that in the feelings we have essentially desiring, the substantial aspect of the soul. Feelings as such are not new in the soul life but are substantial and real processes of desire that occur there.

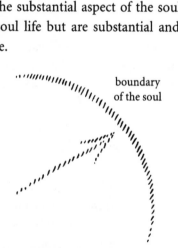

boundary
of the soul

Desiring that does not reach the
boundary of the soul becomes feeling

Let us hold on to the facts we have established and move on to describe, from a certain angle, the characteristics of the two elements of soul life—judging and the experiences of love and hate, which spring from desires. We can say that everything taking place in the soul as judging—and this is the main point—comes to an end at a certain moment. The same also applies to desiring. The soul's judging ceases when a decision is made, when judging has become a valid mental image, one that can be carried on within us. If we ask about the end of desiring, we find thus the satisfaction. Every desire that lives in the soul is trying to attain satisfaction, and judging always strives toward decision. By investigating our soul life, we discover, on the one hand, judging, which presses toward decision until it reaches a conclusion. And, on the other hand, we find in the lively soul life desires pressing toward satisfaction until it is achieved.

We may say then that since our soul life consists of the two elements of judging and desiring, the soul's currents flowing toward satisfaction and decision are its most important aspects, which are present in every soul. If we were to observe soul life in its direction of flow, we would find it fully striving toward both of these goals; this is in fact what happens.

If we study the life of feeling from certain perspectives, we can easily discover the sources of many different feelings, weighing the fact that soul life must display the effect of a continuous flow of striving toward satisfaction and decision. If we consider such manifestations within the soul life that fall, for example, within the concepts of impatience, hope, longing, doubt, and despair, we will have the basis to connect them with something real, something spiritually comprehensible. They all represent ways that the stream flowing in the soul expresses its striving toward the decisions of the forces of judging or toward the satisfaction of the forces of desire.

Live into the feeling of impatience, for example, and you have a vivid experience of striving for satisfaction. You can understand how, living in the feeling of impatience, there is something we may call a desire that continually flows in the stream of the soul. It can reach a conclusion only when it results in satisfaction. The forces of judging are barely developed thereby. Or consider the feeling of hope; the continuous streaming of desire may be easily discerned there, but it is a desiring suffused by the other element of soul life, the one we have described as the movement of our powers of judging toward decision. Anyone who analyzes the feeling of hope will easily see these two elements in it—desire, filled with a striving for judging that can lead to a decision. The feeling of hope is complete in itself, since the two elements in this feeling are perfectly balanced in the soul life, resembling equal weights in a balance scale. There is exactly as much desire for satisfaction as there is a prospect of a favorable decision.

Now picture another feeling arising as the result of a desire pressing for fulfillment but permeated by a soul process of judging that is unable to reach a decision through its own strength and forces. The activity of judging would not be capable of bringing about a decision. The desire nevertheless connects with such an activity of judging that is incapable of bringing about a decision. One then experiences the feeling of doubt. We can discover a remarkable interplay of judgment and desire throughout the feeling realm. When someone fails to find these two elements in a feeling, it is because the person has not searched far enough and should continue to search.

In recognizing the importance of judging for the soul life, we find it necessary to say that the activity of judging concludes in the formation of a mental image but that a mental image is important for life only if it is true. The basis of truth is within itself. The soul as such is incapable of deciding what is true; this is something that we must all feel when comparing our own soul life in its individual uniqueness with the truth we are attempting to uncover. We need only consider that what we are calling "judging" in soul life could just as well be termed "mulling over" or "reflection." This mulling over or reflecting leads finally to the judgment we build out of the mental image. By reflecting, we do not necessarily arrive at the right decision. The result will be correct on quite different grounds that are lifted out of the arbitrariness of the soul. Thus the judgment that the soul strives toward in the decision comes about outside the soul element.

If we inquire now into the origin of the other element, *desiring*— which wells from unplumbed depths at the center of the soul, spreading in every direction throughout the soul's life—we will not initially find it within that soul life itself, but rather outside it. Desires and decisions enter the soul from without. Satisfaction as the product of desire, however, does live within the soul. In considering truth, whose foundation lies outside the soul, a battle for truth or a struggle to arrive at a decision takes place within the soul life. One might be described as a "warrior" in judging, whereas in the inner realm of soul life, one would be called a "hedonist." It is important to note here that only the first part, the start of judging, takes place within the soul, whereas making decisions brings us into a realm beyond it. The opposite is true in terms of desiring. Rather than its beginning, its ending, or satisfaction, occurs within the soul.

Now we should look more closely at what the soul experiences as satisfaction. Let us compare it with the previous statement—that sensation is a surging of desire to the very boundary of the soul's life, whereas feeling stops short halfway, where desiring weakens. What happens at the place in the soul where it experiences satisfaction, the end of desire? It is the place where we discover feeling. Thus, we can say that feeling manifests where, most deeply within the soul, desiring ends in satisfaction.

That is only one kind of feeling found at the halfway point in the soul's depths, where desiring ends. There is another kind of feeling that has a different source, namely, through the fact that relationships exist in the soul's depths between inner life and the external world. That is expressed in that our desires are focused on external objects. Consequently, unlike sense perceptions, they do not always extend all the way to outer objects. When we recognize a color, desiring reaches all the way to the external world. A feeling that has a relationship to an external object, however, can develop within the soul out of the desire. Desire can develop in relation to any object, even when it comes to a halt in the middle of the soul. It is still related in a remote sense to the object, just as the needle of a compass points toward the North Pole without reaching it.

In this way, we can see that desires may shut themselves off within the soul, even while they maintain a relationship to the outer world in such a way that the external world has a connection to the soul life that does not require direct contact with the soul's boundaries. Those feelings can then arise when desire for the object continues to exist, even when the object is not capable of satisfying the desire. Imagine a soul approaching an object; desire for it is generated, but the object is unable to gratify the desire. The desire then remains in the soul and is ungratified.

Let us investigate the situation very precisely and compare it with one where a desire achieves its goal in the soul's life. There is a considerable difference between a situation where a desire attains its goal within the soul and one where it does not. A desire that has attained satisfaction and is then neutralized has an effect on the life of the soul in such a way that it has a healthy influence on it. When desires continue to live in the soul without satisfaction, because the objects cannot provide it, after the object is removed, the soul retains a living connection to a void, so to speak. Consequently, the soul lives on in unsatisfied desiring, as though in an inner fact without any basis in reality. This fact alone is enough so that the soul life has an unfavorable, illness-causing influence upon that connected to it, namely, the spirit and body, owing to the unsatisfied desires. Feelings based on satisfied desires are, therefore, very different for direct observation from those built upon frustrated desiring. In a flagrant case, it is a simple matter to discern this; in subtler cases, people do not always realize what they are confronting.

Let us picture a person looking at some object. Then he goes away. What is referred to here is not a desire extending to an object but one established in the innermost soul. The person can go away and afterward say that the object satisfied him or that it did not. Whether, for example, he says that he was pleased by it or not or expresses it differently, the result is the same. In the one case, there is a desire that has been satisfied, whether or not this is plainly stated, and in the other case there is displeasure, owing to continuing desire.

There is only one category of feelings that shows up in soul life in a somewhat different light, and that is a matter profoundly characteristic of the soul's life. It will be obvious that feelings can be generated not only by external objects but also by inner experiences. This applies to both satisfied and unsatisfied desires. Thus, a feeling that we must characterize as an unsatisfied desire can be generated by a sensation that may recall to memory something that happened long ago. We discover within us causes for our feelings, for satisfied and unsatisfied desires. Let us differentiate for a moment between desires stimulated by external objects and those stimulated from within. There are, for example, striking inner experiences that can show us how our inner life contains desires that stop short of fulfillment.

Imagine yourselves mulling over a matter. Your power of judgment is too weak, and so you cannot reach a decision. Thus, your soul life, your own desires, remains unsatisfied, and you experience pain in this feeling. There is only one kind of feeling in which judgment does not reach a decision nor do our desires actually find satisfaction without causing us pain. Those are feelings in which desires are focused neither directly on external objects nor directly on an inner experience. In ordinary sense experiences, we stand directly before an external object with our desires, but we do not judge in the process. Once judging begins, we have gone beyond the sense experience.

Let us assume that we carry judging and desiring all the way to the boundary of soul life, where the sense impression from the outer world surges directly against us. A desire was thus generated, stimulated by the object—a desire that we then permeate with judgment right up to the boundary, the same place we had the sense impression. This generates a peculiar feeling, an amalgam composed in a very strange way. We can best describe it as follows.

We allow our desiring (horizontal lines) to flow right up to the boundary of our soul life—as far as the eyes, for example.

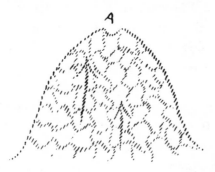

We exert our soul life with respect to our desires and allow it to flow up to point A, the portal of the sense experience. We also exert our powers of judging (vertical lines) and allow them to flow up to the site of the outer impression. We will let this drawing serve as a symbol representative of the very curiously combined feeling that has been referred to.

The difference between these two currents, both of which flow to the site of the external impression, can be appreciated properly when we remember what has already been said. When we develop our powers of judging, the peak of the soul's activity lies beyond the soul rather than within it, for the soul does not determine truth. Truth overwhelms desire, and desiring must surrender to it. When we decide something within our souls, using our power of judgment, in which truth is of imminent importance, we must take an element into the soul that is essentially foreign to it.

We can say, then, that the vertical lines that represent the powers of judging go outside us and circumscribe something of an external nature. Our soul life, as the life of desiring, can go no further than the boundary, where it is either hurled back or halts on its own and remains limited to itself. Desiring feels overwhelmed when the judging in the soul concludes with truth's verdict. Our example, however, specifically assumes that desiring and judging both flow to the point where the impression was received, and they fully coincide. We see that our desiring does not flow out and bring back the alien element, truth; it brings back the judgment that has gone all the way to the boundary of the soul's life. Desiring surges to the soul's boundary, turns around, and returns with the decision. What sort of judgments are we limited to bringing back in this way? They are exclusively aesthetic judgments, relating in some way to art and beauty. Only when we observe works of art does our soul life extend just to the boundary of its activity, turn around on encountering those outer objects, and return with the judgment into itself. You may find this strange initially, but self-observation will convince you that it is true.

Now imagine yourselves viewing the Sistine Madonna or the Venus de Milo or any other true work of art. Could you say that this object arouses your desire? Yes, it stimulates it, but not of itself. If the object itself were to arouse your desiring—which is possible—whether or not a desire is aroused at all would not depend on a certain development of the soul. It is thoroughly conceivable that you could stand before, say, the Venus de Milo and not be the least bit moved inwardly. This could also be true of other objects; there is an ordinary indifference toward them. This indifference also arises in those who experience no soul response to the Venus of Milo.

Those who bring an adequate soul life toward a work of art allow the stream of desiring to flow to the boundary, and then something returns to them; for others, nothing returns. What returns is not a desire. It is also not a desire that yearns to return to the object. It is the desire that expresses itself as a conclusion: that is beautiful. Here, the forces of both desiring and judging interact. We attain satisfaction in the outer world only when it stimulates activity within the soul. How much we experience in relationship to the Venus de Milo depends on how much we already have in our souls, and how much will return to us is in direct proportion to how much we let flow out to the direct impression. The enjoyment of beauty requires the immediate presence of the work of art, because the substance of the soul must strive out to the boundary of the soul's life. Every memory of a work of art results in something other than an aesthetic judgment. An aesthetic judgment originates through the direct influence of a work of art, when the waves of soul life willingly surge to its boundary and return as aesthetic judgments.

Therefore, in truth we have something to which desire capitulates to a certain extent, as if to something outside the soul. And in beauty there is an element wherein desiring directly coincides with judging, where the decision itself is brought about by the voluntary movement of desiring to the boundaries of the soul, returning as a judgment. This is why the soul's inner experience of beauty spreads such an endlessly warm satisfaction throughout the soul. Essentially, the greatest balance exists in the soul's forces when desiring meets the boundary of the soul's life and does not return as desiring, but as a judgment, which the soul then experiences as an element of the outer world. Thus, nothing is so easily found whereby the conditions for a healthy soul life are so strongly developed as when we surrender to beauty. When we strive toward the fruits of thinking of the soul, we work in essence within the soul with a material before which our desiring must continually surrender. This capacity for desire must indeed surrender to the majesty of truth, but this is impossible without impairing the health of the soul and all the other facets of the soul's life. A continual striving in the realm of thought, wherein desire must continually capitulate, is something that must "dry out" the human being in both body and soul. On the other hand, the judgments that return an equal amount of satisfied desires into our souls best balance our desiring and judging.

Do not misunderstand and think that I am saying that it is good for human beings to wallow continuously in the enjoyment of beauty and that truth is unhealthy. If it were stated that I had said that thinking is unhealthy and wallowing in beauty is healthy and thus wallow in beauty, it would make an easy excuse for laziness in pursuing truth. Such should not be the case; instead, the following situation should occur in the soul. Since seeking truth is a duty that furthers the progress of culture in general as well as that of the individual, we are forced to suppress our desiring in favor of truth. Since the decision concerning the truth does not lie with the life of desire, truth forces us to suppress it. We must do this without hesitation in striving for truth. Consequently, it is essentially striving for truth that restrains our self-love to the appropriate degree. When we consider the matter objectively, we can gain a certain satisfaction from our inner experience of how our search for truth continually encounters the boundary of our own capacity for judging.

Seeking truth makes us increasingly humble, but if we were to continue living in a way that reduces us to ever greater humility, we would eventually arrive at a point of dissolution. We would lack an element essential to the fulfillment of the soul life—a sense of our own inner being. We must not sacrifice our own selfhood through exclusive devotion to that before which the inner surging of our desire life must surrender. This is where the activity of aesthetic judgment comes in. The life of aesthetic judging is such that we bring back what we have taken to the soul's border. In this life we are allowed to do what truth requires of us—to arrive at decisions with absolute selflessness, without egoism. There is no other way to seek the truth.

And what is the situation in terms of beauty? This is a very different matter. Here, too, we give ourselves completely to it, allowing the movement of the soul to flow—almost as we do with sense-derived sensations—right to the soul's boundary. And what comes back to us? It is something that cannot possibly be given to us from outside, something that cannot be determined externally; it is ourselves that is returned. We surrender ourselves and then are given back to ourselves. It is the peculiar attribute of aesthetic judgment that it encompasses the moment of selflessness just as it does the truth, while asserting the sense of selfhood that, in the two previous lectures, was referred to as "the inner master." We are given back to ourselves like a free gift in the aesthetic judgment.

As you can see, particularly in these lectures, I must present things in a way that avoids definition. I have often spoken out against defining; for the same reason I will also not say, "This is a feeling" and so on, but I will attempt to characterize by simply laying out the extent of the soul's life—by simply discussing the limits of the soul's life.

In the "Anthroposophy" lectures last year, we saw that the body shares a boundary with the soul. We tried to comprehend the nature of the human being at that common border, to discover how it is related to the outer shape of the body. If you recall that material, you will have a foundation for much that we will discuss in these lectures and in what these lectures on psychosophy are particularly directed toward. It is hoped that they will provide rules to live by and wisdom for living. Thus, it was necessary to lay a broad foundation in those earlier lectures.

Perhaps today's characterizations have indicated the way in which desires surge in the soul's inner life. It was stated yesterday that certain feeling-like experiences, such as judgments, depend on what kind of independent life our mental images lead. The previous lectures ended with the statement that the mental images we have acquired in the past come alive; they are like "bubbles" in the soul as they lead a life of desire of their own there. Much depends, at a given moment in our lives, on what sort of life they lead. What we characterized yesterday as boredom and other soul events that help or adversely affect human beings make all the difference as to whether a person is happy or unhappy at any given moment. Our present soul sensing depends on how the mental images we have previously acquired behave as independent beings.

This raises the question of what our attitude must be when we study the soul life in relation to our lack of control, in a certain way, over specific mental images, images we must take into our present soul life. Other mental images may enter it more easily. You are aware of how much depends on whether we have the capacity to summon a mental image, or recall it from memory, and whether we can do this with a certain ease.

When we recall something in particular, we must ask which images arise more easily and which with more difficulty; this can be extraordinarily important in life.

As we assimilate these mental images, can we impart something to them that makes recalling them easier? Indeed we can. Even to consider such a possibility can have enormous benefit for many people; it can make our inner and outer lives easier if we pay attention to what could ease the recall of mental images, to what we could do to promote it. Those who observe the soul from all sides will see that something must be added to a mental image in order to make it easier to remember. We have found desiring and judging are the two aspects of the soul life. Therefore, we find only within these two elements what must be added to mental images for easier recall. What can we give of our desiring to our mental images? We can give just that: desiring alone.

But how do we do that? We must transfer to the mental image, at the moment we assimilate it, as much of our own desire as possible. It is good for our soul life to give some of our desiring to mental images. We can do this only by taking up the mental image with love, by permeating it with love. The more lovingly we accept a mental image, in other words, the more interest we put into a mental image, the more we can lose ourselves with our egoism when taking up a mental image, the better it can be retained in memory. Those who cannot lose themselves in a mental image cannot easily retain an image in memory. Farther along in these lectures we will discover other indications as to how we can surround mental images with a loving atmosphere.

The other element that we can give to a mental image is our power of judging. Every mental image, in other words, is more easily recalled when taken up through the soul power of judging, rather than merely being imprinted on us. If judgment is exercised when making a mental image part of the soul structure, encircling it with judgment, one adds an element that furthers recall; one surrounds it with something like an atmosphere. The ease or difficulty of recall depends on the way we prepare our mental images. We will see that the way we surround a mental image with love or judgment plays an extraordinarily important role in our soul life.

That subject, however, is for tomorrow. We must also consider the fact that our soul life has a continuous relationship with the I-center. Following this path of inquiry, which has presented us with some difficult challenges today, tomorrow we will find the possibility of bringing together the two directions, that of memory and that of the I-experience.

It might surprise some of you to hear that all human feelings consist essentially of desires. It may especially surprise those of you who are aware that overcoming desiring is a goal of the higher life of the soul, achieved through esoteric development. But the term overcoming desire is not an accurate expression in psychology, since desiring does not originate in the soul itself but instead surges in from unknown depths.

What is it that surges into the soul? Of what is it an expression? We will comprehend this in a more concrete way tomorrow. For now we can think of it more abstractly as something that corresponds to desiring on a higher level, issuing from one's innermost being as *will*. And if we struggle against desiring for the sake of a higher development, we are not battling the will underlying a desire but the several modifications of it, the particular objects of desire. In this way, we purify the will, and it works with purity in us—will divorced from objects. Such an unencumbered will represents, in a certain connection, the highest in us. Do not confuse this with the "will to be," which is not unencumbered. Think rather of a will with a content of desiring but without an object. Will is pure and free only when it is not influenced by a specific desire, but instead leads away from any specific desiring.

We ourselves can witness the life of will surging into the life of feeling. When that is the case, we have a real opportunity to study the fact that will and feeling have something in common. All kinds of fantastic definitions can be formulated for will and feeling. Someone may say, for example, that will must have an object, and its result must be a deed. Such definitions, however, are usually totally unjustified. We will see that they generally have no connection to the reality at all and that those who formulate such ideas would do better to turn to the genius of language, which is wiser than the personal human soul.

Language, for example, has an inspired term for the inner experience of will turning directly into feeling. Imagine the will moving toward a boundary, but it impairs itself inwardly along the way. Picture ourselves inwardly observing such essentially impaired exertion of the will; we allow the will to retreat, as it were, and observe the process.

Will returns back into itself

That is what would happen if someone were to encounter another being and if the will's inner swelling were to reach a certain point and then be restrained. This would certainly leave a deep feeling of dissatisfaction in the will. Language has invented a word for the will that does result in an action but retreats; it is the inspired word, *disgust* (*Widerwille* in German, or "counter-will"). It is perfectly clear to everyone that this is not true will. Such will, it becomes self-evident, is a feeling, or a will that retreats into itself. Language coins the term for the will's viewing of itself and expresses thereby a feeling. We see here how meaningless it is to define the will by stating that it is the starting point of an action. Modified will, or desiring, surges within the will and, depending on how it behaves, shows the various soul forms.

4.

Consciousness and Soul Life

I F WE COMPARE Hegel's poem recited yesterday with Goethe's poem that you have just heard, it will help us understand more deeply the substance of yesterday's lecture as well as what remains to be discussed today.[1] A comparison will be useful, since it can make us aware of the difference between the soul qualities of these two poets. Let us try to become aware of the very great difference between these two poems. Our time here is short, so we can do little more than touch on certain matters. I am certain, however, that we can come to understand them.

Yesterday we listened to the poem of a philosopher, a man who had attained very exalted, pure thought. In his poem "Eleusis," we saw that thought itself became creative in Hegel's soul. If you recall how that poem affected you, you will say that you could sense its powerful thoughts wrestling with humankind's greatest questions as well as the greatest problems of the times, which are linked to the so-called Mysteries. You could feel that someone had penetrated deeply into those great cosmic Mysteries with thinking, but you could feel a certain clumsiness in the poetic handling. You could feel in the poem that it contained something that did not arise from the primary goals in the poet's life. A struggle for poetic form was evident—a difficult struggle to adapt the thought to a suitable poetic form. One realizes that the writer would not have been able to write many poems in his lifetime.

---

1. Goethe's poem "Thoughts about the Descent into Hell of Jesus Christ" was recited at the beginning of this lecture. This poem has been omitted, since it is quite long and adds little to the lecture itself. With a little imagination, it is not difficult to understand the point being made.

Let us compare that poem with the one you've just heard, but keep a certain circumstance in mind. I had a poem of the youthful Goethe read before the first lecture in this series, a poem we changed for our purposes here. It was a vivid demonstration of how two souls lived within Goethe's breast—two soul powers, or forces. We saw the powerful images conjured up by the poem. What we heard was also worthy of what lived as the central core of Goethe's being during his old age. But in this youthful poem, we see that a completely different soul force was active within him than what was active, for instance, in Hegel. Wherever we look in Goethe, we encounter something that may be described as a flow of intensely vivid images. And how full of images is this poem of the young Goethe that we have just heard! The flow of that vivid life of images was an aspect of Goethe's natural talent. When the grandeur of a theme overwhelmed him, we can see that a powerful soul life living itself out in vivid imagery overcame the problems that still disturbed him in his earlier poem.

We can distinguish three elements in the poems recited. In Hegel we see how thinking works, creating imagery only through a tremendous struggle. This is evident in the paleness of his images. In the poem of the younger Goethe, we see how the vivid pictures pour out. We saw in his legend of "The Eternal Jew" how that imaging could be so damaged that he was unable to finish it—the result of the two souls described, which fought for dominance within him. That effort remained only a fragment.

Our attention is drawn here to the myriad possible shapes of soul life. Let us consider for a moment the soul force we might characterize as oriented toward thinking, as it was for Hegel—one that experiences difficulty penetrating into that soul force that was uppermost in Goethe. And let us look at how this soul force in Goethe himself works into just the opposite tendency.

We want to move forward now with our study of psychosophy. We remember that within the soul life, judging and the experiences of love and hate that stem from the capacity for desiring are active. Now we can proceed in a different way than we did yesterday. We can bring together what lives in our souls as the power of judging by reminding ourselves, on the one hand, that this power meets us in the reasoning capacity of the soul, in the capacity to discern the truths of the world, and, on the other hand, that a completely different soul power confronts us when we speak of how the soul is, in this way or that, interested in the external world. A soul is interested in the outer world according to how the experiences of love and hate are working. The phenomena of love and hate themselves, however, have nothing to do with the thinking capacity, with the intelligence. The capacities to judge and to take an interest are two forces in the soul that work very differently from each other, as simple observation demonstrates.

Those who believe that will is a special soul aspect will see, through looking into their own souls, that they meet only the interest in what is wanted. In other words, one discovers nothing in the innermost realm of the soul except the two elements of interest through love and hate and the capacity for judgment expressed in acts of judging. The entire content of one's soul life is summed up in those aspects. However, this leaves *consciousness*, the most important aspect of soul life, entirely out of the matter. Consciousness belongs to the soul life. In other words, when we explore the content of the soul life from all sides, we encounter the capacity of judging and interest. When we examine its inner uniqueness, however—the particulars of soul life—we must conclude that we may consider the experiences of love and hate and the capacity for judgment to be a part of the soul life only to the extent that we associate them with the word *consciousness*. We must ask, therefore: What is consciousness? Again, I will characterize rather than define.

If we approach human consciousness with a background of the matters we have studied thus far, you would say, on the basis of the continuous stream of mental images you have been absorbing, that the conscious state does not coincide with soul life. As we have seen, there is a certain difference between soul life as such and awareness. A mental image formed days or weeks or years ago lives on in us, for it can be remembered. If, however, we cannot recall it at this moment but perhaps only two days later, it has indeed continued to live within us, but unconsciously. That means that it is there in the soul, but not in one's consciousness.

Thus, the soul's stream flows on, but consciousness is something different from this onward-flowing stream of the soul. In short, we must

say that if we represent the soul as a circle and the imaginative pictures
we can remember again at some time as a stream flowing in the direction of the arrow, this stream can contain all mental images that flow in
a person's soul from the past into the future.

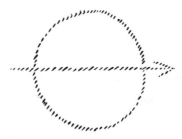

In order for them to become conscious, however, a striving must lift
them from their unconscious life within the soul into consciousness.
Consciousness, therefore, belongs to the soul, but not in the sense that
everything in the soul is within the realm of consciousness. The stream
of mental images flows on, but consciousness illuminates only a certain
part of the soul life at a given moment.

Since we are in contact with others and must be prepared for objections, let me add a parenthesis. Someone might object that what I've
called the "stream of mental images" is simply the disposition of the
soul or brain that, once created, remains. It could also be said that the
only thing required is that the disposition of the brain be illuminated
by consciousness at a certain moment. That would, in fact, be true if it
were unnecessary to separate something from a perception immediately after its reception, so that one could perpetuate it. If the disposition were to be made into a memory by the *perception*, nothing would
have to be released from the whole process, nor would the perception
need to be transformed into a mental image. The perception arises
from the external object, but that is not true of the mental image. The
mental image is a *response* outward from within. We have retained
within us our experience of the world, which continues to flow from
the past into the future with the stream of time—but it does not always
coincide with consciousness. In order to recall it, consciousness must
illuminate it.

How does it happen that this continuous stream of mental images in the soul can be illuminated so that parts of it become visible to memory or in some other way? A fact of ordinary soul life that takes place on the physical plane can explain this. It is a fact that is ignored by outer psychology, since its criterion is bias rather than fact. We prefer to work instead with fact without bias.

Human beings possess a tremendous variety of feelings. I will point to just a few, some of which were mentioned yesterday, and a few others—feelings, for example, that express themselves in longing, impatience, hope, doubt, anxiety, and fear. What do all of these various feelings tell us? If we examine them closely, we find that they all share a peculiar element. They are all related to the future—something that may happen or something that we hope will happen. In our souls, we live in such a way that our feelings are interested not only in the present but also in the future. In fact, they have a very lively interest in the future. Furthermore, the fact that such future-oriented feelings live in us may be compared to something else.

Try to recall an experience of joy or sorrow that you had as a young person or perhaps that you only more recently experienced. Now try to compare for a moment what lives in your feelings from the past of pain that you have gotten over or joy that you have experienced. You can see how extremely pale the summoned memory appears. If it left a mark behind—affected your health or something else, for example—it asserts itself and pushes into your awareness, but that is in the present. What we experience in the past in connection with our feeling life pales the more we distance ourselves from it.

Now let us turn to what is clearly *desiring*. When you desire something that is attainable in the future, try to carefully define the rumblings in your soul. I would like to know how many people are now lamenting a disappointment from ten years ago, unless such longing has continued and is creating a sense of deprivation now. There is a vast difference between our interest in what lies behind and what lies ahead of us. Regardless of how hard we look, there is only one explanation for this. The fact itself is plain, but the only explanation is that desiring flows in the opposite direction of the forward-flowing stream of mental images. You can cast something like a flash of lightning on your soul life by assuming that one fact. All desires, wishes, and interests, the phenomena of love and hate, represent a current in the soul life that flows not from past to future, but toward us from the future. It flows from the future into the past.

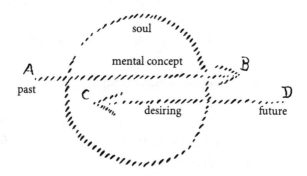

Suddenly, the totality of soul experience is clear. It would take days to go further into this matter, so I will just add the following points.

If you assume that the stream of love and hate, of desires, and so on comes toward a person from the future and encounters the current of mental images previously characterized, what does our soul life consist of now? It consists of the stream flowing from the past into the future meeting another stream flowing from the future into the past. Since that meeting constitutes the soul life of the present moment, you can easily understand that those two streams come together or overlap, so to speak, within the soul; that overlap is consciousness. There is no other explanation for consciousness than this. That is how the soul participates in everything flowing from the past into the future and from the future into the past. You can say, whenever you look into your soul life, that you are involved with an interpenetration of those two streams—what flows from the past into the future and the opposite flow of desires, interests, wishes, and so on. The two streams interpenetrate each other.

We will use two different terms in referring to these two currents, since they are so clearly different. If I were addressing an audience as though there were no spiritual scientific movement, I would choose the strangest names possible to represent those streams. The names are unimportant.

For now, I will choose names that will remind you of things you are already familiar with from another angle. You can then study them from two sides. One is the viewpoint of pure empiricism, which describes soul phenomena according to the way they occur on the physical plane; it can thus choose the names it likes, based on what it finds. And then you examine them on the basis of esoteric investigation. Let us look at this second side. Names are unimportant here, although I prefer to choose such names as someone does who looks at things from a clairvoyant perspective and thus in fact really observes the meeting of those two currents. Such names would be derived from spiritual science; you will rediscover in psychosophy what you have learned from spiritual science. Accordingly, we will call the current that momentarily carries unconscious mental images, those that flow from the past into the future, the *etheric body*. The other stream, which flows from the future into the past and intersects the first stream and becomes congested with it, will be called the *astral body*. And what is consciousness? It is the mutual coming together of the etheric and the astral bodies from their two sides.

Try testing this; apply everything you've learned from investigations of clairvoyant consciousness about the etheric and the astral bodies to what has been said here. You will be able to do that and will recognize there again the truths with which you are familiar. You will only need to ask what causes the intersecting, or damming up. Something congests because the two streams encounter each other in the physical human life. Now imagine removing the physical and etheric bodies. This is the case after death, when the current flowing from the past into the future is no longer present. When that occurs, the current pressing from the future into the past, that of the astral body, becomes free and asserts itself in a direct manner after death. Consequently, life in kamaloca flows in reverse, as I have told you.

You see, then, that we rediscover in psychosophy what we have learned from spiritual science. I hope, though, that you will notice one thing. There can sometimes be a long road to travel from knowledge of spiritual scientific truths gleaned from clairvoyant research to confirming experiences on the physical plane, for that must first be put in order. When that is achieved, you will see that everywhere you look, clairvoyant research is always confirmed by findings made on the physical plane.

Now let us go to another manifestation of our soul life, one usually known as surprise, or wonder. When are we surprised? It is only when something confronts us that we are not immediately able to judge as it makes an impression on the soul life. In that moment when we are able to judge, surprise or wonder vanishes. At times when we are immediately able to judge, we feel no surprise, no wonder.

Thus, we can say that the future forces itself into our soul life when we are confronted by a phenomenon and are consequently surprised, when something makes a conscious impression upon the soul without the immediate occurrence of a judgment. Or we may even feel fear, since that feeling, too, may be characterized as due to an inability to judge something that meets us. Feeling and interest are aroused, but judgment is not yet in a position to function. This can convince us that our interests, feelings, or life of desiring cannot have the direction from the past into the future, because then judging would be able to flow directly from the same direction.

Judging must therefore be distinguished from interest. We have confirmed this by ordinary observation. Judging, however, is not the same as the current within soul life that flows from the past into the future. If it were, judging would have to coincide continually with the current of mental images. One's entire soul life would have to be active at every moment of exercising judgment. In every moment it would have to be finished with mental images. But judging is a conscious activity. Just consider, however, how remote you are at the moment of judging from a conscious possession of all the mental images you could have! Judging occurs in consciousness but cannot assume control of the ongoing flow of soul life. We do not always have all of our mental images at our beck and call. Judging, therefore, cannot coincide with the soul's onward-flowing current, neither can it coincide with the current coursing from the future into the past. Otherwise, that would render it impossible to experience such feelings as fear, surprise, and astonishment. So we must conclude that judging coincides with neither of these directions.

Keep this in mind as we examine the onward-flowing stream of the etheric body as it moves from the past into the future. Its unique feature is that it is able to flow unconsciously through the soul and also become conscious. Let us see what can bring the unconscious mental images flowing through the soul into consciousness. We must bear in mind that these mental images are always present, but what happens at the moment when they become conscious?

Consider a moment when mental images that have escaped us become conscious in a very unusual way. I will suggest such a moment. Assume, for example, that you are touring a picture gallery. You notice a picture and look at it. At that moment the same picture surfaces in your consciousness. Let us assume that you have already seen it. What has evoked that memory? It is the impression of the new picture; the impression of the new picture conjured into visibility within your soul the old mental image of the picture that had continued to live within you. If you had not seen the new picture, the old mental image would not have surfaced.

We can come to a clear understanding of this matter only when we realize something. What happened when you saw that new picture? Your I-being wanted to approach the picture, and it used the senses as a medium. Because your I received a new impression and absorbed a new element, which had a curious effect on something in the ongoing flow of your soul life, your soul life became visible. Let us try to form a picture of this process. Think of all the objects that are behind you when you face a certain direction; you cannot see them, because they are behind you. You can see them only when you hold a mirror; you can then see the objects behind you in the mirror. We can conclude that something very similar must be the case with the mental images living on unconsciously in the soul. When a new impression comes, it affects the soul's life, so that the old impression becomes visible in the soul. If you think of the I as something in the soul's life that stands with the old, unconscious mental images behind it, the moment of remembering may be characterized as mental images being induced to reflect themselves through an inner soul process, in that a cause for their reflection is created. Then you have the process of memory, or the becoming aware of old mental images.

Why does such mirroring occur? You will easily discover this just by thinking about it. You will find the reason such a reflection occurs when you remember a point referred to recently in my public lecture "On Life and Death."[2] We can observe something extraordinarily important in the life of the soul—that the backward-running memory goes back only to a certain point, beyond which it stops, and we cannot recall anything further; memory begins at that point. We might ask what kind of mental images are usually recalled? They are only those in which the I has participated—in which the I was truly involved. I have said before that memory goes back to the moment a child gains the capacity to conceive of the self as "I," when a child develops I-awareness. Ordinarily, we are able to recall only those mental images with which the I was actively engaged, in which the active power of a self-aware I-being was involved.

What happens in an I-being in the process of being "born" during a child's second or third year? Before that, children unconsciously absorb impressions without the I being truly present in them. They then begin really to develop I-consciousness, relating to it all the mental images that they absorb from the outer world. That is the point when the human I situates itself in front of its mental images, placing them behind it. It is an almost physically perceptible event. First, the I was within its life of mental images; it then steps out, free and armed to accept everything coming to meet it from the future, while placing the past mental images behind it.

Using this as a background, what must then happen at the moment the I begins to be conscious, begins to take all the mental images into itself? The I must then form a connection with the onward-flowing current that we have referred to as the etheric body. Now, at the moment children begin developing I-awareness, the current of the soul life imprints an impression of itself on the etheric body. That is the source of the I-image. If you think about it, you will see that the I-image can never be given to you from outside. All other mental images with any

2. Lecture of October 27, 1910; contained in *Antworten der Geisteswissenschaft auf die großen Fragen des Daseins* (GA 60, not translated into English).

relationship to the physical world come from outside; the I-image, on the other hand, or even the perception of the I, can never come to you from outside. That will become clear if you consider a child's incapacity to sense its own etheric body before having an image of the I. As soon as a child begins to develop I-consciousness, it feels its own etheric body and reflects the being of this etheric body back into the I. The child then possesses the required "mirror." Whereas all other mental images related to physical space and life on the physical plane are received through the physical body—that is, through the sense organs—I-consciousness arises because the I fills the etheric body and reflects itself, as it were, on its inner "walls." The essential thing about I-consciousness is that it is the inward reflecting of the etheric body.

What prompts the I to take on such a process of inward mirroring? The only possible cause is that the etheric body comes to a certain inner closure. We saw that the astral body comes toward the etheric body; it is the I that fills out the etheric body and becomes conscious of it, as if through an inner mirroring. This I-image, or I-awareness, has a certain characteristic. It is taken hold of powerfully by all interests and desires, for they anchor themselves firmly in the I. Despite the egoism represented by such interests and desires, there is certainly something unique about this self-perceiving of the I. In a certain sense, it is independent of the desires. There is a certain demand that the human soul places upon itself that we can easily verify in ourselves. Every soul says to itself: I cannot possibly summon my I-being only through desiring. No matter how much I might wish it, wishing does not make it happen. The I no more consists of the current of desires flowing from the future into the past than it does of the ongoing flow of mental images. It is something radically different from both streams, but nevertheless it assimilates them both.

We can represent this in a diagram completely true to the facts by drawing the line of the I-current perpendicular to the time streams. It must be drawn this way to provide a correct picture of the various soul manifestations involved. We remain true to the facts by illustrating the activity of the I as a current that is perpendicular to the two time currents. This corresponds to the I-aspect.

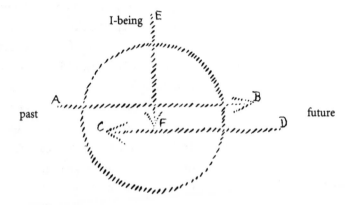

Now there is an element related to the I that self-observation readily discerns as well—the capacity for judging. It enters the soul with the I. You can easily understand this through a feeling such as surprise. If the I works in from the side, an event can approach you that can bring you an abundance of interest. But if the judging activity of the I cannot enter from the side at the same time, then the event cannot meet with the judgment. What happens, then, when the I comes in laterally? We have seen that the I-perception is as an inner mirroring in the soul. Such mirroring would have to occur in such a way that the mental images that flow in unconsciously would be literally behind the I. That would be the case if the I-current in fact flowed in so that its own current entered in the direction of the line *E-F* in the previous drawing, but actually took the direction indicated here by line *G-H*, or toward the future.

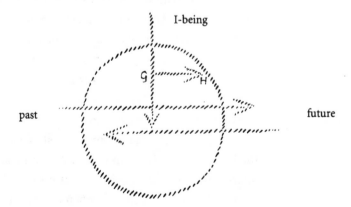

Now picture the I itself becoming a mirror once it enters the etheric body, which fits the facts exactly. If the I has the flow of unconscious mental images behind it, what does it have in front of it as it looks into the future according to its inherent nature? What would it be facing?

Imagine standing before a mirror and gazing into it. If the back of the mirror isn't coated, you see nothing reflected at all. You would be staring into the unending distance. Our perception of the future is like that. This is indeed how we look into the current that approaches us from the future. It flows toward us, but we don't see anything. When do we see something there? We see only what is there from the past. We do not see the future, of course, but we do see the past. You don't see objects in front of you as you look into a mirror; you see only what is behind you.

At the moment a child attains self-awareness as the result of the I entering the etheric body, the I mirrors itself inwardly. From that point on, all soul life is a co-reflecting of experiences and impressions. And this also explains why we are unable to remember anything that happened before the I acquired its mirroring capacity. A child's earliest impressions are not remembered. The important thing is that the human I—to the extent that it has entered the etheric body or to the extent that it receives mental images from the past—becomes, through this, a mirror within the soul. After that, it is open to whatever appears in its mirror.

What has to happen to make it possible for the I really to mirror the past? We could say that if we have an external impression such as I described, such as seeing a picture again that we have seen before, it evokes a reflection in connection with the previous mental picture that we were unconscious of at the time. As the earlier mental image radiates in from the other side, it is restrained so that it falls on the inner mirror of the soul. But when there is no new impression, or a repetition of an earlier one, the I itself must produce what the mirroring should provide. It must work from the other side and create a substitute for what an external impression would have otherwise provided.

What is then this I that is living itself out in our physical life? It is the inner fulfillment of the etheric body. Thus, in order for it to be able to mirror itself on the interior walls of the etheric body, it must make the etheric body into a mirror. This can happen only when the etheric body is complete. For external sense impressions, it is complete when you are in your physical body, since that is when you are surrounded by your eyes, ears, and so on; thus, what lives within the etheric body can be reflected back.

We must have another capacity, however, to allow for a free remembering, since the etheric body must have a "mirror coating" for purposes of reflection. The sense organs—the physical body, in other words—provide such a "coating" for the reflection of new impressions. If, however, the physical body is not involved—as in the case of free remembering, when no new, refreshing impressions are received—the "coating" must be taken from the other side. This is possible only when the primary resource is what counters the I from the side through the involvement of desiring as it flows toward us, which is used for a "coating." Only through a corresponding strengthening of the astral body can we develop the forces for striving, or desiring, which enable us to recall a mental image that resists reflection. Only by strengthening the I as it lives in the physical world can we pull in this stream that flows from the future—a stream we do not otherwise grasp—and make it into a "mirror coating." Thus, only through strengthening the I in this way, by making the I master of the astral body, the stream issuing from the future, can we enable the I to recall mental images that resist reflection. It is a battle we fight with the unconscious mental images. The I lacks the strength to summon them, and so we must borrow something from what is coming toward us.

To make this clearer, let me use an example from real life that will illustrate how we may strengthen the I. Usually, we experience life's events by simply following the onward-flowing stream of experiencing. If a bell rings once, then again, and then a third time, first you hear the first ring, then the second, then the third, but then you are finished. If you attend a play, you hear the individual parts one after another, and then you are done. In other words, you live with your etheric body in the onward-flowing current. Let us suppose, however, that you deliberately try to become familiar with the current flowing in the opposite direction, reversing a sequence of episodes that are otherwise experienced only in the normal order. You decide, for example, to recall in reverse order some events of the day. If you review it backward, you are not following the ordinary flow of the I brought about by the I-being living in the etheric body. Instead, you follow the opposite current, or that of the astral body. If, for example, you pray the Lord's Prayer backward instead of in the usual forward sequence, you are proceeding counter to the usual current, the current resulting from the I filling out the etheric body. In this way, you strengthen your I from the astral current. The result is a tremendous heightening of the capacity to remember.

During my years of teaching, I worked to strengthen the memory of my students for later life by having them learn certain things in reverse order, things usually learned in only one direction, and having them practice this over and over. For example, the scale of hardness in minerals is usually learned as talcum, rock salt, marble, fluorite, apatite, orthoclase, quartz, topaz, corundum, diamond. In addition to having to recite the list in the usual order, the pupils had to be able to recite it in reverse order as well. That is an extraordinarily effective exercise for strengthening the memory, especially when started in a timely fashion in childhood.

There is another exercise, one related to everything we've been talking about today and during the past several days. Imagine a man suffering from a severe loss of memory. He goes to the trouble of resuming with ardor some youthful interest or other. Let us say that this man, who is now forty-seven, was particularly intrigued by a certain book at the age of fifteen. He now decides to read it again. In such a case, if you call the same facts before your soul, a new current flows toward you, an astral current, and you strengthen yourself from it as it flows toward you out of the future. If an elderly person carries out this exercise, deliberately repeating some activity pursued between the ages of seven and fourteen, it will be found to be a very special aid to improving memory.

These things can thus show that if the I really wants to improve memory, it must strengthen itself out of the astral current flowing opposite to the etheric current. These things are all extraordinarily important for practical life. If educators paid more attention to them, it would result in tremendous blessings. If, for example, schools with seven grades were to arrange studies so that the fourth grade existed by itself, after which the fifth grade reviewed on a different level the material taken up in the third grade, the sixth grade reviewed the studies of the second grade, and the seventh grade reviewed the content of the first grade, great benefits could result. There would be a definite strengthening of memory, and people would see how beneficial such practices are, simply because they come from the laws of real life.

This shows us that our I-image, or I-consciousness, is something that must first be created. It arises initially during early childhood from the etheric body's reflecting in an inward direction. It comes as no surprise for those who know spiritual science (since they realize that the human being is outside the physical and etheric bodies in the night) to hear that I-consciousness cannot exist at night, because the I is then unable to reflect itself in the etheric body. Thus, we are not at all surprised that the image of the I submerges into the subconscious during sleep, since the etheric body is the onward-running stream of time. It contains the mental images that must first be illuminated from the other side—by the astral body. Then what swims forward, so to speak, in the etheric body can be illuminated by the soul's life.

The image we have of our own I-being is really only in the etheric body. In fact, it is only the entirety of the etheric body as seen from within. The I-image is active only in the etheric body, but this does not apply to the I itself, for, as stated, the I is the power of judging that enters laterally. You cannot grasp the I by looking to I-consciousness; you must turn to judging.

Although it seems odd, judgment reveals itself as a higher order than I-consciousness. A very exact distinction has been drawn between what is and is not taken hold of by judging. Perceiving the color red does not yet involve any judging by the soul; the capacity to judge is not yet functioning. What decides about the impression rushes in from outside. At the moment of making the simplest judgment, such as "red is"—ascribing existence to the color—the soul life passes judgment. The I arouses itself in that moment when we judge. When the I judges on the basis of the results of external impressions, those impressions participate in the judgment, becoming the object of the judgment, as in "red is."

What must then be possible if the I is an entity distinct from its mental images and also from perceptions of itself? What must be present for the I to be the cause of I-perception? There must be a possibility of judging. Among the various judgments in our soul life, there has to be one that is independent of any external impression, over which the I is master. This is the situation when you state the judgment, "I is," or "I am." There, you have what lives as yet unconsciously in the I, filled with the ability to judge in "I is," or "I am." You have filled out with the power of judgment what was previously an empty bubble that dissolves like foam when the soul's life becomes unconscious.

If that is the case—if the I fills itself out—what happens then? Judging is a soul activity, and soul activities originate in the innermost life of the soul. They lead to mental images. It is in the realm of these images that the I-image surfaces, but we have been unable to learn anything about the I itself from the I-image. One thing now becomes clear, however; no external impression can supply us with the image of the I. In other words, the image does not come from the physical world. Since it is not a product of the physical world but otherwise has exactly the same character as mental images that do originate there, and since judging, which is part of the elementary content of soul life, is applied to the I, the I must enter the life of the soul from some other quarter. In other words, just as the mental image "red" enters the soul from the outer world and is encompassed by the I through judgment, so also something comes into the soul from the other side that is encompassed by judgment.

Let us take the impression "red" and encompass it with a judgment; we end up with "red is." Similarly, let us take the I and say, "I is." Here we have an impression derived from that outer world we call the spiritual world, and we encompass it with a judgment. "Red" as such corresponds to the forms of existence in the physical world, whereas "red is" is a judgment and can originate only within the soul life. "I" is a fact in the same sense that "red" is. It can enter the soul life or, in other words, be encompassed by a judgment only when the judgment approaches the soul from the other side, encompasses the I with the judgment, and says, "I am," or "I is." The genius of language is very wise and expresses things precisely, reversing the "is" from outside the human being and making it the "am" of "I am" from within.

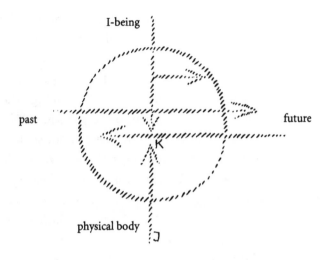

If I now include the fourth direction (the line *J-K*) from below upward, I would have to describe it as the direction of the physical world, running counter to that of the I. It represents the current of the physical body. Presented graphically, the impressions of the physical world move thus from below upward and manifest themselves in the soul as sense impressions. On the one side is the I, placed counter to its sense organs in the physical body. On the other side, the current of the etheric body opposes that of the astral body. When the I collides with the physical body, streaming against the eyes or against the ears, it receives impressions of the physical world. These impressions are brought further into the soul through the consciousness that arises from the counterflowing of the astral and etheric worlds. You will realize from the whole picture that a fairly good representation is afforded of the relationship of the various worlds working together in the human soul when one says that, on the one side, the I and the physical body with its sense organs confront each other in opposite directions. They stand directly across from each other. Then the other two currents, those of the astral and etheric bodies, also oppose each other in that they form right angles, as it were, to both of the other currents.

I can assure you that innumerable riddles of the soul will be solved for you if you refer to this diagram. You will see that this cross, cut by a circle, provides an excellent picture of the life of the soul, showing how it borders on the spiritual world above and on the physical world below, on the etheric to the left and the astral to the right. This requires rising to a concept of time as a current that does not just flow quietly along but that meets with something. The life of the I and the senses, on the other hand, can be understood only when they are seen coming into contact with the stream of time at a right angle. If you keep this in mind, you will understand that very different forces really meet in our souls, which is the scene of an encounter of forces moving in the most varied directions.

Let us assume that we are dealing with an individual (since these forces manifest themselves in a great variety of ways in the great variety of human beings) in whom the judging I prevails. Such a person will find it extremely difficult to fill abstract thoughts with enough lifeblood so that they appeal directly to the feelings. Thus, we can expect that it will not be easy to get something life-filled to engage our feelings out of what a person says whose primary soul activity is judging. On the other hand, the kind of individual whose soul life tends toward a flow rich in interests and astral abundance, which encounters the opposite ongoing stream of physical life, brings a disposition for vivid concepts into life. Such individuals will not turn up on the physical plane as thought people, but they may be characterized by the ease with which they express inner experiences in ways that capture our interest.

Since we incarnate repeatedly and bring with us a tendency to this or that predisposing current, we can picture the soul of Goethe as predisposed to the current coming from the future. If he surrenders to it, then from the beginning he brings life-filled concepts from the future into life. If, however, he allows this element, which is truly his own, to battle a soul content absorbed from his environment—a content that goes floating along in his etheric body as mental images beneath the threshold of his consciousness—the result is a disharmony like the two elements we talked about in his poem "The Eternal Jew," the useless one and the one we emphasized. In the case of someone like Hegel, who brought a judging predisposition with him, such an individual constantly wrestles with everything that streams toward him from the future into the past. The I is placed in such a way that the ongoing stream from the past into the future is always hidden at each present moment; the I hides it, but it is open to the counterflow of the stream of the capacity of desiring. The "I" looks into the never-ending future as though into an uncoated mirror. As soon as the mirror receives a coating, the past experiences become visible.

It has been possible in these lectures to discuss only a few aspects of the infinite wealth of psychosophy, but if you ponder them, you will be able to draw many conclusions from what has been said. Much will become clear if you keep in the background the fact that the stream of soul life flowing from the past into the future—that of the etheric body—contains the unconscious mental images, which are present despite their unconscious state. If you know from spiritual science that the etheric body is the architect of the physical body, you will be able to see that these mental images are indeed present, even if unconsciously, for the etheric body carries them along. And the mental images present there are capable of developing a lively activity toward the other side, especially if they are unconscious. Anyone versed in physiology and psychology is aware how profoundly disturbing mental images can be when they cannot be summoned from the soul's depths into consciousness, but instead continue to swim along with the etheric current in those unconscious depths of the soul life. They then generate all their strength into the physical body.

Here is a relevant fact in life. Let us consider, for example, someone between the ages of ten and twelve who has experienced an event that has been totally forgotten and simply cannot be recalled. This experience nevertheless continues to work in the etheric body and can make the person sick. Below the surface of consciousness, many mental images are active that can cause illness. Those who are aware of this fact also know that there is, in a certain way, help for it. It consists of taking away the power of such images. This means leading them in another direction by trying to provide to the sufferer who is not strong enough to do this alone reference points that allow those images to surface. This is of tremendous help. To assist a person in bringing to consciousness mental images over which the individual is powerless, images that continue to work in the etheric body, can have a truly curative effect.

Some of you are perhaps saying that that is already being tried. There is indeed a school of psychiatry, the Freudians, based on recalling to consciousness past actions and experiences. I cannot equate this school's approach, however, with what I have just suggested, since it applies the method in the very place it does not belong. It is, namely, ineffective precisely with the sum total of the mental images related to sexual life; in every other kind of situation it is valid. The Freudians, however, extend it with predilection to the treatment for mental images of a sexual nature, where it is, in fact, useless. This must be recognized. The point is not that we go tapping around under the influence of materialistic concepts and come across something that the facts have already discovered, but that we know exactly what the facts are.

Perhaps we can thus add something more to the other remarks you will take with you. If we observe conscientiously and with discrimination ordinary life here on the physical plane, we can see that everywhere it confirms the findings of spiritual science. Lectures like these will help give you confidence in information based on the findings of clairvoyant research, though such research certainly does not search the physical plane for the facts it presents. I can assure you that clairvoyants themselves are often surprised, when they test the results of their supersensible research, at the confirmation they find in physical life. Taking the opposite direction would probably not have succeeded; remaining on the physical plane leads to associating things incorrectly and results in misinterpretation of the facts.

Thus, the basic feeling—that of certainty in relation to spiritual scientific research—can also give you confidence in the research of psychosophy. This is why I occasionally try to give you a dry, dispassionate account of supersensible matters in such a way that it meets the criteria of objective scientific investigation of the physical plane. As a result, we are obligated to note that human beings are put on the physical plane for the purpose of understanding it. Our time has two tasks; one is to study, in selfless objective thinking, this physical plane on which the great cosmic laws have placed us for a purpose.

On the other hand, we are at a stage today at which we can no longer master the physical plane by ordinary means if help is not provided through esoteric research. No matter how wisely ordinary science advances, it cannot avoid erring without the guidance and direction provided by esoteric science. After the human race reached the turning point of the fifteenth through the seventeenth centuries and began to emphasize research—when modern physical research began—we progressed and are now again at a point where a different, esoteric kind of research will have to assist and direct physical research. To the extent that esoteric researchers not only know this but also accept it as their duty, they fulfill what must be a dual requirement of modern times. They develop the sense that we must stand firmly upon the physical plane, fearless of the selfless activity of thinking; physical reality, in particular, demands it. The intent of these lectures—and my dry presentation—has been to nurture just such a sense. On the other hand, you have learned much for life if you have absorbed the concept of how the astral stream coming from the future plays its role.

I must admit that I could almost prove these things from the sense-perceptible world. I addressed this matter on another occasion elsewhere. Among all modern psychologists who, without any interest in esotericism, have sensitively approached the phenomena of the soul and have therefore, if in a lopsided way, come to a real sense for the most basic facts, only Franz Brentano's name deserves mention.[3]

In the 1860s and 1870s, Brentano devoted himself to the study of psychological problems. Although his writing on the subject is a scholastic brooding, it contains something that reminds one of a child's first steps, which we would like to pursue further. What he said about desiring and feeling, as well as about judging, misses the mark. The tendency, however, could have led straight to the mark if he had not been so completely ignorant of the esoteric aspects of these matters. This most capable psychologist has stepped onto the physical plane, so to speak. The first volume of his *Psychology* appeared in the spring of 1874, with a second volume promised to follow in the autumn. The

---

3. Franz Clemmens Brentano (1838–1917), German philosopher, Catholic priest, and professor. He wrote on psychology, Aristotle, logic, and ethics. See Steiner's memorial essay on Brentano in *Riddles of the Soul.*

second volume has yet to appear; only the first is available. What is the explanation? You will find the answer in the lectures on psychosophy. He got stuck and could not continue. He had made a nice outline of the chapters yet to come. He even intended to include a view of spiritual life and immortality from the perspective of the I. It was all outlined, but there he got stuck. Esoteric research would have had to be called in from the other side so that soul phenomena would be examined from the perspective of esoteric research. This example proves that Franz Brentano was a child of our time. He began to categorize the facts available on the physical plane, and then he got stuck. He is an old man now, living in Florence.

Everything today will have to become stuck in this way when it has to work with reality. The psychologies of Wundt and Lipps, for example, can, of course, be written, but they are based on preconceived notions rather than on actual processes in soul life.[4] They are based on the preconceived opinions of the authors. It is precisely when they set out into the psychological realm—even in what they have to say on social psychology and linguistics—that they thresh mere empty straw. This is not meant to be unkind, but only to express it clearly. All the branches of science will suffer the same fate if they fail to greet what comes to meet them from the other side.

From this side understand that, through your own interests, you have joined a movement whose goal is to comprehend the mission of our time. Understand also that your confidence, insight, and faith can grow if you comprehend this as manifested karma. Tell yourself that karma has led you to be present and active at the crossroads of a stream of time and that you must become courageous, strong, and confident. This insight should be a source of strength to cooperate energetically in this sphere. And this effort must bear fruit, because the human progress demands it.

---

4. Theodor Lipps (1851–1914), German philosopher and a professor. He developed a theory of aesthetics based on empathy. Wilhelm Wundt (1832–1920), German physiologist and psychologist, considered the founder of experimental psychology. Having studied under Johannes Müller, he went on to become a professor and established the first psychological laboratory. Believing that psychology must be based directly on experience, he developed a methodology of introspection.

One's own participation will provide the opportunity to work selflessly now or in a future for the further evolution of all humanity.

This brings us to the greatest ideal that those who believe in spirit may feel. Think of this not as an abstract ideal but acquire it through persistently returning to our spiritual scientific work. Ample opportunity is given for this in our gatherings. Take away with you a sense that you belong to this work. If I have done anything that can give you such a feeling, it will accompany you on your return home and be a greeting to those scattered in various places. Take it as an emanation of the strength of the unity that should exist among all of the members of our spiritual scientific movement. You should feel this even when we are not together physically. As we depart to various parts of the world, try to draw courage, confidence, and energy from our time together here.

III

"Pneumatosophy"

BERLIN 1911

1.

Franz Brentano and
Aristotle's Doctrine of the Spirit

C ONTRARY TO modern usage, the human being's total makeup will be described here as consisting of three elements—the physical, the soul, and the spiritual. This division, of course, is no different from what we are accustomed to in spiritual science. In these lectures, however, we want to build a bridge from spiritual science to the natural scientific approach in this area. Consequently, we will also consider what is normal for such deliberation of the human being in the modern sciences outside spiritual science.

For a long time now the total makeup of the human being has been viewed as consisting of only two parts—the physical, or bodily, nature and the soul. This has been true even when no open or veiled materialism was involved. Recognized science is not accustomed to speaking of spirit. Indeed, when the Catholic philosopher Anton Günther reverted to a threefold perspective of the human being as body, soul, and spirit, his books, which were interesting from that perspective, were placed on the list of forbidden books by the Church in Rome.[1] The Catholic Church acted contrary to the Bible, where it can be shown, in both the Old and New Testaments, that human nature is threefold and that we can speak of a body, soul, and spirit.

Relatively early, in the very first centuries, the Church prohibited the spirit. That means that, in a certain sense, it led the evolution of dogma

---

1. Anton Günther (1783–1826), a speculative Catholic theologian, placed on the Index in 1857.

in such a way that the human being may consist only of body and soul. Philosophers of the Middle Ages considered it highly heretical to accept a threefold makeup, and this applies today to all those who still base their beliefs on that philosophical outlook. This is still considered to be absolutely heretical in the Catholic Church today. Oddly enough, the Catholic view has made its way into contemporary science. If you try to understand why people working today in the science of psychology—the science of the soul—speak essentially only of body and soul rather than of body, soul, and spirit, there can hardly be any other basis for such a perspective than the fact that, over the course of time, spirit was forgotten. Therefore, people today no longer have within their normal thinking any way of achieving an idea or concept that would enable them to speak of the human spirit as a separate element in addition to the soul.

In this introduction, which may contain concepts that sound foreign to the circle of theosophists, since the corresponding literature is not known here, we must, however, draw attention to the threads that connect us to what otherwise exists as psychology. You can see from what I've just said that we can scarcely find any doctrine of the spirit, aside from Hegel's philosophy. That hardly deserves such a designation, however, since essentially it is also merely a kind of doctrine of the soul. We covered that area a year ago in what was termed "psychosophy."

Our time has become strangely accustomed to thinking without any concept of spirit. We can see the extent of this view by looking, by way of introduction, at the work of a psychologist whom we must also consider from a spiritual scientific perspective as the most outstanding research psychologist among all those who lack a spiritual scientific orientation. I am referring to Franz Brentano. We see in this most significant psychologist (of whom I spoke in last year's lectures on psychosophy) to what degree it is possible, from a standpoint outside spiritual science, to approach what spiritual science has to say about the soul based on pure science rather than clairvoyance. We can see in this very important psychologist, not oriented toward spiritual science, how the modern thought habits work in preventing people from developing any idea or concept of spirit.

Franz Brentano wrote a strange work on psychology (which I referred to last year), or, I should say, he intended to write it. The first volume appeared in the spring of 1874, with the promise of another volume in the autumn. There were to be further volumes in quick succession. The first is the only one that appeared. Nevertheless, a new edition was published very recently. It was not the whole volume, but only a part of the 1874 edition—a special chapter on classifying psychological phenomena. It was published simultaneously in German and Italian. An appendix was added to what was written in 1874.

Considering the promise displayed in the first volume of Brentano's *Psychology,* adherents of spiritual science have reason to bewail the fact that more volumes did not appear. A year ago, however, I reported that the reason for this could be easily understood from a spiritual scientific perspective. As those with a spiritual scientific view will realize, the current scientific orientation made it impossible to continue the series using the assumptions that were the basis for the first volume. Brentano wanted to work on his psychology in the 1870s in keeping with all the thinking habits of modern science. He took particular pride in not going along with a materialistic bias (his own direction was just the opposite) and proceeding, instead, purely methodically. He prided himself on pursuing his research entirely in keeping with the prevailing scientific methodology of the time. He intended to produce a psychology that accorded perfectly with the spirit of modern scientific methodology. When we note that there was to be a discussion of the question of immortality—among other highly interesting topics promised in his first volume—we must, of course, be painfully disappointed that no more appeared.

Do not be surprised that I speak this way about a book of this kind—particularly from the perspective of spiritual science. I had to consider this book and its fate. Indeed, in terms of science, I find the whole scientific fate of its author symptomatic of and extraordinarily important for our time and for what one can call pneumatosophy today, because it promised to discuss the soul's immortality. If, as may be gathered from several of Brentano's remarks, he expresses himself obliquely as intending to prove not the fact of immortality itself but that *hope* of immortality can be justified (please note the difference), then we must agree that this is an extremely interesting fact for the character of current psychological thinking. Brentano, however, did not succeed in producing more than the first volume. It contains only his dispute with other schools of psychology and lays a foundation for a scientific method in the psychological field as well as the previously mentioned classification of the soul's activities or capacities. Nothing further ever appeared, except for the new edition of one section of the book.

The reasons for this are extremely significant and will have to be discussed in this series of lectures. Some of the reasons have to be addressed from a spiritual scientific standpoint, because they relate to the way in which modern science regards the soul, failing to see the spirit as something separate from it. I won't take any of the short time we have here to characterize the human soul, which we covered last year. To connect it to current scientific thinking, however, I will have to use this introduction to discuss Brentano's classification of human soul faculties as it appears in the new edition.

Brentano, a modern psychologist of the greatest significance in this regard for spiritual science, classifies the soul faculties not into the usual categories of thinking, feeling, and willing, but in a very different way as mental picturing, judging, and the phenomena of love and hate, or the emotions. You will be reminded immediately of its similarity to what the psychosophic lectures of a year ago presented from an entirely different source. I need not comment on what mental picturing is in our sense, since these things have been spoken of so often in spiritual science. And we need not go into the concept of a mental picture as such in relation to what we have to say as an introduction to Brentano's psychology. For us, the content of mental picturing is clear when we recall, regardless of how it is otherwise defined, that we think of mental picturing as the recalling of some thought content in the soul. A mental picture is any thought content that is present in the soul and is not in some way connected with an emotion or with anything that is a declaration in connection with something objective.

Judging differs from mental picturing in the previously characterized psychology. Judging is usually said to be a fusing of concepts. A "rose," for example, would be a concept described as a mental image and "red" as another, but to say, "The rose is red," is a judgment. Brentano says that a "fusion of concepts" does not characterize a judgment. If we say,

"The rose is red," however, either we mean nothing special or, if we do, another sentence is hidden within it—in other words, we are saying that the red rose *is*, asserting that there is a red rose among the things of reality. We will have to note Brentano's definition of judging in order to lay a scientific foundation for pneumatosophy. As you can see from superficial observation of your own soul content, there is much that is correct in such a view. Indeed, when we say, "The rose is red," what has been accomplished beyond the creation of a mental picture? There is no essential distinction between imagining "rose" and "red" or fusing the concepts; we are still involved in picturing. I do no more with "the rose is red" than I do when picturing "rose" and "red." To recognize that "the red rose is" is an admission essentially different from a mere fusing of concepts, however, for it points to something *beyond* mental picturing, something not limited to it—that is, to the determination of a reality.

To say, "The rose is red," states only that the mental images "red" and "rose" both exist in someone's soul; it is merely a statement about a thought content. At the moment, however, when something is ascertained and the statement is made that "a red rose is," we then have a judgment in Brentano's sense. According to him, we have no right to speak of transcending the idea of a mental image when merely fusing mental images. We transcend mental picturing only when something is expressed in the life of mental images that is an ascertainment. It is not possible here to go into all of Brentano's brilliant reasoning for his distinctions between mental picturing and judging.

Brentano then distinguishes a third member of the soul, however— the emotions, or phenomena of love and hate. They, too, are different from a simple determination. If I say, "A red rose is," this is not the same as having a *feeling* about the rose. Feelings are manifestations of the soul belonging to a special class that we may categorize as emotions. Feelings represent not only a determination about the object presented by our mental picturing but also something about how the soul experiences the subject. Brentano, however, does not specifically mention will phenomena, because, essentially, he does not find enough difference between the will and the phenomena of love and hate or other emotions. What we love, we *will* with love, and the will that is connected with an object is also included in our feelings of kindness. In terms of hate, "not wanting," or rejection, is also a given. Therefore, it seems unjustified to describe will as separate from love and hate in the same way that separating judgments from mere mental images is justified.

Thus, we have, so to speak, divided the human soul into mental picturing, judging, and the manifestations of the emotions. It is extremely interesting that such a keen thinker divided concepts in this way when he set out to lay the foundation for his psychology. As you will perhaps gather from the commentary today and tomorrow, it is because we have a man here who takes seriously the usual disregard for the spirit. Others have always mixed what are in fact spiritual phenomena into the life of the soul. This inclination led to the creation of a strange hybrid—a kind of spirit-soul or soul-spirit. All kinds of things could be attributed to the spirit-soul—characteristics that, for someone working in an orderly way based on the threefold nature of the human being, would have to be ascribed to the spirit rather than the soul. Brentano, however, was truly serious about answering the question of what could actually be discovered in the soul as such. He was acute enough to discern what had to be excluded from the concept of the soul when spirit is eliminated from consideration. Through taking this tendency seriously, he divided, as it were, the soul cleanly from the spirit. It would have been very interesting to see how, if he had continued his work, Brentano would have found that it had to end somewhere, because, in reality, the soul must receive the spirit and enter into a relationship with it. Otherwise, he would have had to acknowledge the necessity of progressing from the soul to spirit.

Let us look at the two most remote elements of Brentano's classification, mental picturing and the emotions or the phenomena of love and hate, disregarding judgment. In Brentano's conceiving, mental picturing is simply something going on in the soul. Nothing is ascertained through our mental picturing. Making a determination about something real means that judging has to enter into it. This being so, the soul life is not only mental picturing. That would amount to saying that mental picturing is not able to lead of itself to a determination, that it would be impossible to get outside the soul in mental picturing, for only in judging can we get out of the soul, not in mental picturing. On the other hand, it is interesting that Brentano assigns all manifestations of the will to the manifestations of the emotions. There is certainly a good deal to be said for maintaining that the soul's relationship to the world is summed up in the emotions. You can indeed maintain that, basically speaking, the soul contains nothing but emotions. If they are strong enough, they will this or that. No psychologist can find anything in the soul but sympathy or antipathy or the phenomena of love and hate. Even where people's wills are deeply involved, they act, but while they are acting, nothing can be discovered in their souls but the phenomena of love or hate.

That is how it is within the soul. If we now go on to the whole reality, we have to say that the relationship of the soul to the external world does not consist only of the soul's emotional experiences. It is, of course, a step that must be taken, but not wholly within the soul. If we are to go from an emotion to what then becomes will, it must be done out of the soul. The will does not have its totality within the soul but only when the soul goes out of itself. No matter how much we may love an object or a fact, and no matter how great a role our emotions play in us, that hasn't made anything happen. A great deal of emotional agitation may go on in the soul, but that must be disregarded if something is supposed to happen.

Mental picturing, therefore, confronts us in this type of psychology as an activity that does not go beyond itself into reality, and, thus, the emotions stand there, without any ties to true willing, merely as preconditions of the soul to will. This is a matter of extraordinary interest. We will see that in mental picturing, the spirit enters the scene at the exact point where Brentano ended his characterizing. In mental picturing, the bridge leading from the soul to the spirit begins exactly at the place where, if it were not there and the soul were not confronting the spirit, mental picturing would remain self-limited. We will see, on the other hand, that wherever a real transition is made from the emotions to the will, the spirit, in turn, enters in.

We see here, in a significant scientific accomplishment of the last decades, how investigation breaks off at the exact point where spiritual scientific research has to enter the picture if the investigation is to be carried further. And it is interesting to see how the keenest thinkers have to work on the basis of the thought habits of the day. It could not be otherwise.

Going on to other matters, the interesting threads linking today's scientific psychology with spiritual science become apparent in the case of this same man. Those who have concerned themselves with Brentano's writings have always been aware of his intense preoccupation with the Greek philosopher Aristotle throughout almost the whole extent of his professional life. By a strange coincidence, a book by Brentano entitled *Aristotle and His World View*, which contained his research on that philosopher, has just now appeared, giving us an opportunity that was not available three weeks ago. We can now acquaint ourselves with all the research he did on Aristotle during his long lifetime. Brentano does not, of course, view the world in the twentieth century exactly as Aristotle did, but he stands in a certain close relationship to him and presents Aristotle's view of the spirit in a very open-minded, admirable way in this book. This is furthered by the fact that still another book by Brentano, bearing the title *Aristotle's Doctrine of the Origin of the Human Spirit*, has also appeared. It will be useful to say a word or two about this book, because Brentano is, in certain respects, not only the most interesting psychologist of modern times but also the most significant authority on Aristotle's doctrine of the spirit. Let us take a brief look at it.

We find in Aristotle a doctrine of the spirit established centuries before the birth of Christianity and hence uninfluenced by Christian concepts. It was, in a certain sense, however, a compendium of everything represented by the culture of the Occident in the last centuries before the advent of Christianity. That culture had absorbed all that philosophy had achieved with regard to insight into the spirit. It was, therefore, possible for Aristotle to think scientifically in the fourth century B.C. about this matter, about the relationship of the spirit to the soul. Anyone who takes into account Brentano's position on Aristotle, as reflected in the two previously mentioned books—where one can sense so clearly how he thought about Aristotle, to the point of sharing his views on the major questions—will find it extraordinarily interesting to

what extent a doctrine of the spirit that is not spiritual scientific is justified in going beyond Aristotle. It is also extremely interesting to compare the Aristotelian and theosophical doctrines of the spirit, insofar as
the latter is scientific. I would like now to sketch the Aristotelian doctrine without going into a special substantiation of it.

Aristotle speaks unmistakably of the spirit in relation to the human
soul and body. He speaks of the spirit without the slightest trace of
materialistic bias, referring to it as something added to the soul and
body out of the spiritual world. That is a matter with which Brentano is
found in complete agreement, for Brentano, like Aristotle, has to speak
of the spirit as an addition to the soul and body if he has no other explanation for it. When human beings are born into existence on the physical plane, what is involved in Aristotle's sense is not merely the product
of a series of ancestors, though we first encounter inherited attributes of
an ancestral line. Aristotle sees these attributes as constituting the soul,
making the soul in his view ensoul and maintain the body. Both in his
view and in that of Brentano, however, this inherited body-soul complex is not the human essence in its entirety; the spirit also has to be
included. Speaking in Aristotle's sense, we would therefore have to say
that when we are born onto the physical plane, the inherited body-soul
complex is united with the spirit. What, according to Aristotle, is the
spirit's origin?

Aristotle held that our spirits simply did not exist before our birth
into the physical world. He held that they appear with every birth on the
physical plane as a new creation out of the spiritual world, as a divine
creation added to what is inherited from the parents. Brentano states
clearly in his book on Aristotle that we embark on physical existence as
products of the creative cooperation of our parents and God. He means
that the physical body and the soul element are inherited from father
and mother, and, after a certain lapse of time following conception, God
adds the human spirit to the complex.

It is interesting to see how Aristotle, who assumes that God adds the
human spirit to the soul element by a true act of creation, thinks
about immortality. What we would refer to as the incarnated human
spirit is not present before birth. God creates it. For both Aristotle and

Brentano, however, it does not follow that the spirit ceases to exist at the death of the body-soul complex. The spirit thus newly created continues on after death, in spite of having been created for this specific human being, and passes through the gates of death into a "supersensible" world in the same sense that our own use of that term conveys. It is interesting, too, that Aristotle and Brentano, who seems still to be taking the Aristotelian view, trace the human spirit passing into a purely spiritual world. In other words, Aristotle sees this individual spirit, newly created by God, as living on. All investigators of Aristotle seem to agree that there can be no question of any return of this still-living spirit into further bodily incarnations; he doesn't accept reincarnation.

It would lead us too far afield to go into detail on much of Aristotle's purely logical argumentation showing why he did not accept reincarnation. All we really need to do, however, is to consider Aristotle's premise of the human being's origin as a creation of the human spirit by God, a process that he saw continuing throughout all time to come. A return to incarnation by spirits that had lived before could not be looked upon as a new creation. It would not be a new creation if all the old spirits would reincarnate, and it would negate all the theories if a spirit that had already been in a human being were to reincarnate. New creation could no longer be spoken of. Thus, the teaching of reincarnation by Aristotle would stand in contradiction to his *Creation*.

It is a very strange thing, as Brentano's commentary on Aristotle shows, that Aristotle had no other conception of the life of the human spirit after death than that the spirit was actually in a more or less theoretical situation. Any activity that Aristotle can describe presupposes a physical world and a physical body. In his view, the spirit—and this includes the everlasting spirit of God—is engaged in merely theoretical or contemplative activity. This means that there was scarcely room in his conceiving for anything more characteristic of the life of the human spirit after death than contemplation of its life from birth to death, a looking-down of the soul on that life from the spiritual world. Not that Aristotle envisioned this as precluding any further development of the soul. Because, in Aristotle's picturing, this life was significant for the soul, however, the soul had to look down on it continuously, experiencing it as particularly significant and basing its further progress on this one life. That is how he saw the spirit after death—looking back on its life on Earth with all its events, its shortcomings and merits, one perhaps seeing an excellent life and basing further development on it and another contemplating a life of dishonor and crime and having that as a basis for further development. That is approximately Aristotle's picturing of the relationship of the spirit to the soul and body.

Let us ask ourselves how this view of the spirit looks to unprejudiced thinking. It is fully clear that Aristotle does not conceive life on Earth to be a wretched episode in the total range of human existence, a time without significance for further development. There is no question of that with Aristotle. He saw life here as meaningful in a good sense and as exceedingly important. Much is not clear about his view of the soul's further progress after death, but one thing is certain: that this single Earth life is of essential importance for the soul's whole future progress. Even though God created this human spirit, which then appeared only in a single incarnation, he could still take pains to assure its further development despite the lack of more incarnations. We see that Aristotle insisted on a single incarnation as a goal of the godhead and that, in his view, it served a divine purpose as well to lead the human being to an earthly human body. Aristotle thought that it lay in the intention of the godhead not just to create the indwelling human spirit, but to do so in a way that necessitated clothing it in a physical body for its further progress. From the moment of its creation for descent into an earthly body, the human spirit is motivated to enter earthly existence. It is impossible to conceive of the divinely created human spirit as lacking the longing to incarnate in a human body.

Now picture, as Aristotle did, that this human spirit discarded the body, passing through the gates of death into the spiritual world and looking back on its incarnation. And let us suppose that as it looks back on its life on Earth, it finds that life imperfect. Why should it not be a matter of course for most human spirits passing through the gates of death to feel that the Earth existence has been imperfect? For no matter how perfect it may have seemed, there was still room within this earthly life to achieve something still more perfect. In the sense of Aristotle, we must thus recognize in these disincarnated spirits a perfectly natural longing for further bodily incarnations. The spirit needs physical incarnation in order to perfect itself, and if a single incarnation does not accomplish that, it naturally longs to have another one. Otherwise it would fail completely to achieve its goal. It is therefore impossible to conceive of a purposeful single incarnation in the sense of Aristotle, unless such a one-time life were to mean the attainment of a perfect stage of development for the progress of the human spirit. The moment we admit that an Earth life is not perfect, we also have to admit that the divinely created spirit necessarily experiences a longing for another earthly body.

Just consider this strange divine creation envisioned by Aristotle. It produces a human spirit that takes on a physical body and leaves it at death but, if we accept Aristotle's view, necessarily longs for another physical body, without any possibility of entering one again. For the fact is that Aristotle rejects reincarnation, seeing the human spirit as living on after death in a spiritual world with a constant desire for a new incarnation, never to be fulfilled. Aristotle's doctrine requires reincarnation, but rejects it. We will see that from another viewpoint, Aristotle must reject reincarnation.

We confront here a doctrine of the spirit that is by no means materialistic, one that might even be thought of as the West's most intelligent such doctrine still known today, excluding that of spiritual science. You read Brentano and sense how unequivocally he agrees with Aristotle that God, together with a father and a mother, brings forth the spirit for the body-soul element and that this divinely created spirit passes at death into a spiritual world. The God who, according to this assumption, creates the spirit allows it only one incarnation, however, and endows it with an ongoing longing to live that life in a way that permits the spirit really to accomplish its task.

We see here how something that had its origin millennia ago still exercises a powerful influence on present-day science. Justifiably so! We will see that Aristotle's greatness and significance are due to the penetrating intelligence of the conclusions arrived at in his doctrine of the spirit and that it is possible to progress beyond them only if a scientific basis is provided for reincarnation. Such a basis was never provided before our times. We have only just reached the point of transition with regard to the doctrine of the spirit where we can, essentially only through spiritual science, go beyond Aristotle in a true and fundamental way. It is interesting that a man as keen as Brentano has had to stop short at Aristotle's point of view but was forced, on the other hand, by that very acuity to end up with nothing more than a psychology, because he took the exclusion of the spirit seriously. We will see from the mistakes made by the fact that the exclusion of the spirit led to a self-contradictory doctrine of the spirit—or rather of the soul—that from the standpoint of modern science, it is impossible to arrive at a noncontradictory view of the world if spiritual science is ignored.

2.

Truth and Error in Light of
the Spiritual World

I N DISCUSSING important themes in these lectures at our annual
gathering, my comments on contemporary scholarship and on the
statements of modern authorities may seem excessive to some in our
group. It may also seem extravagant for me to speak of the statements of
earlier authorities who are recognized by those of today. It is not as
though we are attempting an extensive bridge building between those
authorities and this group. That may be unnecessary, if only because
most of those who enter our group do so because of deep longing and a
connection to spiritual life. They are not here for scientific proof of the
spiritual world's existence, but to understand the reality of what their
hearts and souls long for. Consequently, many of us may consider the
inclusion of today's scholarship to be excessive. A reason that could be
proposed for considering modern scholarship is that while it is perhaps
not completely valid, it has some usefulness. We could say that theosophists meet people in the ordinary world and are challenged to show reason for their views. It is therefore necessary that they have some
knowledge of how non-theosophists think, to have the possibility to
refute objections and to support this spiritual scientific view of the world.

We have often discussed the fact that it is possible only to a small extent
to convince contemporary opponents of spiritual science with proofs of
any kind. The worldviews of people, in as much as they are opponents of
this spiritual science, are based on their thinking habits rather than on
proof. Those people whose thought habits preclude their seeing the world
in a spiritually scientific way will certainly not be open to proof.

The reasoning I have just characterized is barely valid in terms of presenting matters such as those discussed yesterday. Within our circle, such matters should serve primarily to alleviate any confusion that might arise in us, since we must continually listen to statements about how our perspective of the world is unjustifiable—at least, scientifically. We are, therefore, not concerned with refuting our opponents or with supporting the spiritual scientific outlook, but rather with helping theosophists develop the feeling that our worldview is solidly grounded, even compared with what recognized science has to say. Our concern is, therefore, that theosophists do not become confused. Much more time would be needed if I were to present a fuller commentary on officially recognized science. During these lectures (which can also be important to broadening our overall view), if there is an opportunity to consider modern science, the basic purpose would be merely to arouse a feeling that there are ways to discuss conventional science while also standing on firm ground when depicting spiritual science. Thus, we intend to suggest a *way* of discussion when you have the time and opportunity to do so, rather than providing any comprehensive content for such discussions.

When we speak of the physical body in scientific terms today, there may be many inner contradictions—doubts may arise. But this kind of science has one advantage; the physical body is undeniably a reality. When we speak of psychology—or psychosophy, as we did last year—we enter a domain in which some people, in fact, deny the existence of the soul, the object of psychology. In our time, we must deal not only with materialism but also with a certain kind of psychology that wants to be a "soul-science without a soul." Yesterday, in our discussion of Aristotle and one of the modern authorities on Aristotle, we saw an example of how it would not occur to their science to deny the soul. They scientifically consider the soul in a very intelligent manner. As will be clear from the few indications given yesterday, there can be no question in Aristotle's case of his denying the existence of the spirit. But we saw in the example of Brentano's psychology how a keen modern observer has to stop short in describing the various soul capacities of what we term the spirit. In studying pneumatosophy, or the science of the spirit, we thus enter a field where it is possible to find people not only disputing certain laws of that science—denying aspects of the inner being—but also denying the objective existence of the very object of their study. As can be taken from what I said yesterday, the existence of the spirit has become a very arguable question for a good many people. We must seriously take up the question of why such a controversy about the reality of the spirit exists for many human beings.

The logical answer is obviously that we perceive the body, what is corporeal in us, with our external senses. Physical facts act upon people with such strength, act upon them automatically, that people are not in a position to deny what those facts say. A somewhat similar situation exists for people with respect to the soul, for we experience feelings, mental images, impulses of will, and everything else that of necessity arises from the experiences of the soul, all the sufferings and pleasures, the joys and the pain, and so on. Those who do not begin by denying all such experiences and do not describe them merely as "foam" on the surface of physical phenomena must recognizing that the soul—in some sense—has reality. Although present, spirit is supersensible and not directly perceptible. From there, it is only a short step to complete denial of spirit.

Now all seeking for the spirit could seem astounding if it were true that the spirit actually belongs to the supersensible world only and never becomes involved with the world in which we ordinarily live. In spiritual science we concern ourselves with research about the spiritual world, and it is often emphasized that the facts presented are derived from a view of the human being based upon self-development by means of meditation and concentration exercises. This is to say that spiritual facts are not simply given us to start with; they must be obtained by ascending to insight of a higher kind than what is at our disposal in ordinary life. Thus, it could seem as though the spiritual world, unlike the physical world, is wholly hidden and could become known to us only by leaping over our ordinary capacity for knowledge and climbing to a higher level of insight. If that is true, we have to ask how it is that human beings long for a world that never really reveals itself to their everyday selves.

This is an objection that only believers, not scientists, are prepared to answer. A believer will be able to counter it with another argument—

that through evolution the spiritual world has revealed itself to humanity, and that our knowledge of it arises from the revelations to us from the supersensible realm. Those who are inclined to reject supersensible revelation, however, find what has just been said to be all there really is. Consequently, even the most broadminded scientists might say that there may be a spiritual world but that, since no evidence of it exists in the material world, we are not encouraged to consider it.

Philosophers who are idealistic or spiritually minded may object to that viewpoint. Such objections have surfaced repeatedly with the passing of time. Indeed, recognition of the spiritual by certain philosophers has been based on objecting to that argument being considered seriously. It is said that there exists a possibility of transcending the given world of external perception. We can build a world of truth within ourselves and—simply because we are human beings—find the material world of our perception unsatisfactory. In this way, we build a world of truth within us. And when we truly examine that world, we see something there that transcends all physicality. We then cite the great comprehensive views and ideas about the universe that could never have come into the human being as a result of merely external perception. They must enter us from a side different from that of the senses. The existence of the world of truth thus suffices to convince us that we are sharers of a spiritual world, for we live in it with our truth.

This would have been sufficient reason for a philosopher such as Hegel to reject the argument just described and to justify accepting the existence of that spiritual world to which sense-free thinking also belongs. Those philosophers whose whole orientation enables them to recognize the total independence of the world of truth as opposed to the rest of reality always find sufficient justification in the spirit's self-movement for accepting spirit. Thus, we could say that there are enough people in the world for whom the existence of truth, the concrete existence of truth, of the real world of ideas proves the reality of spirit. We can, in fact, say of Aristotle that his view was similar, that he, too, held the belief that human beings inhabit a spiritual world with their concepts and ideas, with what he called the *nous*, or reason. And since this spiritual world is present in human beings, it thus exists and is sufficiently proved to exist. On the basis of what we can know of that world as we move in it, we can draw conclusions about other facts and beings of the spiritual world. That is how Aristotle came to his conclusions about the godhead and the soul's immortality and to other such results that were discussed yesterday. The modern philosopher Hegel speaks of a "self-movement" of the spirit, meaning the self-movement, self-energized activity of concepts that, in their lawfulness, have nothing to do with the external world around us. He is referring to the independent activity of the spirit, and he sees in this activity that the spirit appears, reveals itself, and proves its existence. Later attempts, such as that of Rudolf Eucken (who, from a spiritual scientific perspective, is not regarded as very impressive), speak of a self-comprehending and, thus, of a proving of its own self by spiritual life.[1]

A closer examination of this reasoning, however, does not show it to be proof of the spirit. It is extremely important for theosophists to be aware of this in order to realize how hard it is to get a clear picture of all that the external world, including its philosophy, has to offer when it comes to proving the existence of the spirit as such. We are much too casual about this. The fact that truth exists is not a proof of spirit. For let us assume that nothing exists beyond the corporeal, physical world. (I am going to use little more than an analogy to speak of something that, in fact, would need a whole lecture series to discuss thoroughly.) This external world with its forces or, as it is now fashionable to say, with its energies expresses itself in what we call the mineral kingdom and then develops, without enriching itself with new energy, into the greater complexity of the plant and animal kingdoms. Let us imagine that it finally works in such a way as to build the human being out of the pure combination and pure working together of all the energies in the physical world, so that, in the complicated instrument of the brain, the world of thought can spring up and form itself in the bodily nature as physical processes do. Let us suppose that this seemingly crude assertion by many materialists that the

---

1. Rudolf Christoph Euken (1846–1926), German philosopher and professor. He wrote works on historical philosophy, especially Aristotle, on religion, and on his own philosophy of "ethical activism." He was awarded the Nobel Prize for literature in 1908.

brain secretes thought as the liver does gall were to be taken seriously. Let us do so briefly, picturing the human brain being built in such a complicated way out of purely inorganic physical energies that it produces, through its activity, what appears to us to be our spiritual life. For a moment let us assume that the materialists are right in asserting that there is no such thing as spirit. Would it not still be possible, in the sense of these materialists, to speak of a world of truth such as is found in Hegel's philosophy as the "self-movement of concepts"?

You see that it isn't meaningless to raise this question. For if it is answered with any sort of affirmation, it shows that even a philosophy like Hegel's could be materialistically explained, and this means nothing less than that all philosophy that calls itself idealistic or spiritualistic could be dismissed. We need only imagine that what is produced as thoughts by this complicated brain, in the sense that it is thoughts that compose this world of truth, is really only reflections of the external world, though it would take a great deal more than this brief statement to indicate why that is so. Put an object in front of a mirror, and you get an image of it. The image is like the object. It isn't the object; just an image of it is produced in the mirror as the result of purely material processes. Nothing more need be admitted than that you are dealing with a mere reflection. You do not have to prove the reflection's reality.

All you have to do is take the materialist's position and say that nothing is involved but the physical energies that develop the complexity of the human brain and call forth a kind of reflection of the external world, that all thought reflections are merely representations of the external world. Then it becomes unnecessary to prove the existence of the spirit. For thoughts, which are all there is, are mere pictures of the outer world, and it is as unnecessary to prove the reality of thoughts as it is to prove the reality of mirror images. Not much can be done when people say that there are concepts not derived from external perceptions, since we never find a circle as we know it in geometry, nor a triangle—in general, we find none of the mathematical truths. Then, however, we could say we see them as pictures that arise in the brain. They may not exist outside us, but there are many close approximations to them, and thus is formed what appears as an abstract concept. People create within

themselves the supersensible truth and it is supersensible—that is truth
and cannot be denied. Materialists, however, can certainly do away with
that objection. Truth does not, as such, constitute a viable refutation of
the materialistic view.

Now we are in a fine predicament. Truth, whose existence suffices to
convince numberless individuals of the existence of a spiritual world or,
at the very least, serves as an indication of it, since it is indubitably
supersensible, does not actually prove it. Yes, it is supersensible, but that
does not mean it has to be real. It may be just a collection of images, in
which case nobody needs to accept it as real. We must keep in mind that
our possession of truth does not prove the existence of a spiritual world.
Although we comprehend the truth and live in it and according to it, we
can never fully arrive at spirit in this way, since we are always confronted
by the fact that truth can be a mere reflection of the physical world.

It could be said that it is almost impossible to conceive that there is
anything in the world through which ordinary people may be led to
acknowledge spirit. People such as the nineteenth-century philosopher
Feuerbach come along and ask what the gods were and what a god
means to humanity.[2] Their answer is that people simply experience
their soul content, their thoughts, and project them out into the universe. That is what they make into their god. Then it is easy to prove the
unreality of the divine, because it is just the projection of an unreal
world of thoughts. Feuerbach thought Aristotle to be in error for building proof of the existence of God out of the presence and objectivity of
the human thought world, of the world of reason. He said that the
human being has reason in the soul, which can be applied to things.
That presupposes that the all-powerful "nous" is present everywhere. As
he describes it, however, it is only the projected human reason. And if
that is only a reflection, it is nothing to build on.

Exponents of spiritual science must achieve such clarity as this on
these matters. They must be able to see clearly that the paths usually

---

2. Ludwig Andreas Feuerbach (1804–1872), a student of Hegel in Berlin; he abandoned
Hegelian idealism for a naturalistic materialism and subsequently attacked orthodox
religion and the concept of immortality. He believed that God is a projection of inner
human nature.

traveled to get from external reality to acceptance of the spiritual world appear rather unreliable. On closer examination, they prove to be completely so.

Should we now therefore admit that before penetrating into the world of clairvoyance, there is no possibility of becoming convinced of the existence of the spirit? It could almost seem so. It could appear as though there were no justification for anyone other than clairvoyants who perceive it and those who believe them to speak of the spirit. That is how it could seem, but it is not the case. We come at this point to a question. The external world with its material content does not in itself give us any inkling of a spiritual world if we do not already know of its existence. Nor does the inner world of truth point to any such world, since that may be just a mirror image of the external world. Have we anything else at all besides the sketchy indications given? Yes, we do! It is error. Not a single item should be overlooked when it is a matter of establishing complete understanding of the world.

Besides the truth, there is error. Now you will say that error cannot, of course, lead to truth, and it would be strange indeed to use error as a starting point. I also absolutely did not say, however, that because it is fruitless to take a stand on truth we should therefore base our stand on error. For it would not lessen the number of our opponents if we were to suggest basing insight into the reality of the spiritual world on error. Error should also not be suggested as a starting point in the quest for truth. That would be worse than foolish; it would be absurd. With regard to error, however, something that cannot be denied is that it exists, has presence, and is real. Most important, it can crop up in human nature and become an entity there. If the external world has created an apparatus for mirroring itself in the brain and if the content of truth is the sum of all the mirror images, there is still the possibility of error surfacing instead of truth, in that someone could be like a defective mirror or a mirror that creates caricatures of the external scene. A mirror that distorts instead of reflecting properly is false. Error could be comparatively easily explained by the statement that it is made possible by the false mirroring on the part of an organ of perception that has been formed by the external world. Truth can be seen as a reflection, or mirror image, and error likewise. One thing is impossible, however, and that is to explain the correction, the transforming of the error into the truth as a reflection. Try as you may to persuade a reflection that is presenting a caricature of some external object to turn itself into a correct representation, it will not change; it remains as it is. It shows an incorrect picture and remains in error.

Human beings do not have to live with error, however; they have the possibility of overcoming it and transforming it into truth. That is what is important! We can demonstrate in this way that there is indeed a reflection of external reality in the fact of truth. By transforming error into truth, we also demonstrate that error is not, as such, a reflection of external reality; to put it in other words, when error crops up, its existence in the real world around us is not justified. The existence of truth in the world around us is justified, and to accept the truth we need to accept nothing other than the existence of the external physical world. Nothing is reflected from the external world that could serve as a basis for accepting the existence of an error. There would have to be a factor not belonging to or in any way directly related to the external world. If the sense perceptible reflects itself as a supersensible picture in truth, then if the sense perceptible is reflected as an error, there must be a reason other than that lying in the sense perceptible itself for the resulting error. What are we looking at, then, when we perceive that the error is there? We are looking at a world that consists of more than a material world of the senses, more than the world of external physical facts. Error can originate in a supersensible world only.

Let us leave that topic for the moment. Now let's see what supersensible research has to say, not for the sake of proving anything, but just for clarity's sake, about this curious place of error in the external world. Let us imagine that we are given to such self-contempt as to be driven by some impulse to think a thought that we know to be erroneous. Let us thus assume that we are purposely thinking an error. This would appear at first glance to be an undesirable act, but it can serve a useful purpose in a higher sense. Anyone who does this with all the necessary energy and attention and keeps repeating it will notice that the error becomes something very real in the soul, that it is doing something. Such an error, deliberately entertained and recognized to be an error, proves nothing and explains nothing, but it affects us. Its effect is extremely significant, because we are not distracted by any awareness of a truth when we deliberately think an error. We are absorbed in our own activity as we think it. If this process is carried on long enough, we find that it brings about the situation described in *How to Know Higher Worlds* as an evoking of hidden soul forces, of forces not previously there. Giving oneself up continuously to external truth does not lead a person very far in the direction of what is meant here, but the deliberate strengthening of error in one's soul can indeed result in evoking certain hidden soul forces.

Put as I've just put it, this is not meant to be a recommendation. You will therefore find that I have quite properly left out of my book *How to Know Higher Worlds* the advice to think deliberately, repeatedly, and energetically as much error as possible in order to develop hidden soul forces. This exercise actually somewhat resembles what is described there, however, demonstrating that we are indeed not to proceed on the basis of some clumsy error, but need rather to meet two requirements. We must form a mental image that does not correspond with outer reality. Take, for example, the often-recommended meditation on the rose cross. Viewed one-sidedly from the standpoint of external reality, that is an erroneous image, an error. Roses do not grow on dead, black wood. However, we are dealing here with a symbolic image, an allegorical picturing. It does not give a direct representation of a truth; it symbolizes one. From the standpoint of physical fact, it is, therefore, erroneous— yet, in a sense, not entirely so, since it then again symbolizes significant spiritual reality. When we meditate on the rose cross, we give ourselves to a mental image that, though it is indeed erroneous looked at with material reality in mind, meets the requirement that we take an error into our souls. It isn't error in the ordinary sense. We are fulfilling quite special requirements by giving ourselves not to ordinary error, but to a significant symbolization. We now come to the second condition, which is that we must fulfill certain other requirements if we thus devote ourselves to meditation, to concentration, and so forth. If you penetrate into the whole spirit of what is set forth in *How to Know Higher Worlds* or the second half of *An Outline of Esoteric Science*, you will see that a

particular state of soul is needed for proper meditation and concentration. The soul must possess certain moral qualities in order for that
which is to happen to come about in the right way. Why is this a
requirement? Why are certain moral qualities demanded as a prerequisite to devoting oneself to such a symbolic—and externally erroneous—
mental image?

That is again a matter that must be thoroughly taken into account.
Nothing good is normally achieved by giving oneself up to meditation
and concentration and the like without attempting to achieve that state
of the soul that has been so often characterized. Experience shows that
unless we have built a foundation in the characterized condition, the
world that opens to us by waking hidden soul forces has a destructive,
disintegrative effect on human life rather than a health-giving, con-
structive one. The outcome will be healthy, helping to develop further
what is already present in us, only if meditation and concentration grow
in the soil of the indicated soul condition. That is proved by experience.
Experience also demonstrates clearly to what pathological phenomena
fall victim those who fail to base themselves on the characterized state of
soul and are driven instead by mere curiosity or passion or the like to
seek to ascend to higher worlds by means of meditation and so on. They
have taken in a reality, for error is a reality, and it affects their souls. It is
a reality that does not belong to the external sense world. Such individuals actually take into their souls a supersensible force, a supersensible
entity. The error, with its forces and its being, is an effect-causing element that cannot have a foundation in the physical world. But it may
not be allowed to work in this way. Its supersensible energies must not
be permitted to act without special grounding in the proper soul condition. The reason for this is that though we have a supersensible force in
error, if this force makes its appearance and shows itself as error, it is
quite certainly not a good force. It can become a good force only if it is
grounded in the soil of a right soul condition.

Translate that into the terms in which spiritual science often discusses
these matters. It would be said that we can come to know a supersensible
world, for we learn to know error. We do not need artificial means of
ascending to that world, since it extends into us by way of sending us

error. And it has an effect. The world that we come to know in this way, however, is not a good one. We must bring, from the other side, a good world in a soul condition out of which alone the error can work in the right way in the soul. If I were to express this paradoxically, I would have to say that we learn to know the supersensible world in the sense-perceptible world because we have error there. We thus first come to know the devil without recourse to the supersensible world; we become acquainted with something not good, something that even announces its presence and reveals itself as such. There was good reason for the statement "People do not notice the devil, even when he has them by the collar." For he, like error, is indeed present. If we use our accustomed terms to state this, we would say that we come to know the luciferic forces, to know the supersensible world at first in the form of the luciferic forces. Our only escape is to play ostrich, sticking our heads into the sand and refusing to recognize this world. We can do that, but it does not solve the problem. That is the fact. The fact that the existence of error in the outer world is an inner proof of the existence of the supersensible—of the luciferic aspect of the supersensible that is the opponent of human nature—would require a great many lectures to provide more than a mere sketch. We fall prey to Lucifer if we penetrate into the supersensible world by deliberately taking error into our thinking without providing a safeguard through the necessary moral state of soul.

Is there a particular reason for discussing these matters? Yesterday we quoted the statement of Aristotle that in addition to what we inherit from our ancestral line through our parents, God gives us our supersensible nature. Thus, God, in connection with the parents, creates the supersensible part for every human being that enters the physical world. If you recall what was said at the close of yesterday's lecture, we could not just accept that assertion. We found all kinds of things that were not compatible with this Aristotelian assertion. Now our dear friend Dr. Unger has shown and proved clearly, very rightly so, that the existence of the contradiction is justified. Again, I would have to give a whole series of explanations to prove to you that a contradiction is not justifiable when someone makes an assertion that leads to consequences at odds with that assertion. That holds in Aristotle's' case. For if God were to create the supersensible element in human beings at their entrance into the physical world, a state of unfulfillment would be the lot of everyone living after death in that supersensible world, a situation observable in Aristotle's own development. It would have to be assumed that God created human beings to be dissatisfied. That cannot be right in Aristotle's opinion, either. We cannot possibly agree with any wise person that what comes into existence through the ancestral line is linked with a direct God-given supersensible element. In the first place, this is founded on a proof out of the truth. Aristotle seeks to give only a proof out of the truth, but that is impossible, as we have seen, for the existence of truth is no proof of anything supersensible. Therefore, proof of a supersensible world on the basis of truth is of no use. In the second place, if we assume that our supersensible element is created by God as we enter the physical world, it would be beyond explaining that we could go on after death into an imperfect state of being.

What was described yesterday as "Aristotle's supposition" is consequently illogical. He fails to consider the luciferic principle, which is the nearest supersensible element that has been given to human beings, revealing itself as very powerful and experienced by us as such. Nor does he consider the fact that we do not properly come to terms with the luciferic principle until we allow it to gain access to us, permit its participation in us, at the moment of our origin as supersensible beings, in as far as we look upward from human beings as they are in the physical world to the supersensible world. Thus, the human being cannot be born of God alone, but only of his joint activity with Lucifer. We stand here on ground that you would do well to note—and I urge you to do so—because it is owing to the aforementioned fact, which has taken hold of the unconscious feeling of Occidental peoples with regard to the accepting of a spiritual world, that right up to our time the leading lights in academia have been unable to achieve an open mind about what we call reincarnation.

What I have explained today when I stated that people can more easily believe in the devil than in anything else of a supersensible nature, and that he is a real concern of theirs, would not have applied to people of earlier times. They felt the same things, however, that I have now expressed in ideas. They sensed Lucifer's presence alongside God's. And they felt something further, the justification of which will become clear only later in these lectures. They felt that a spiritual God-created element was given to us in and with the corporeal. They simply could not see how to reconcile the recognition of the physical human being on the physical plane with the acceptance of the human being having a divine, supersensible origin or a supersensible basis at all. They simply couldn't grasp this. People of Western traditions experienced a very different problem than did Buddhists, for example, whose entire thinking and feeling made it easy for them to accept the idea of reincarnation. Buddhists are as though born with the feeling that our physical bodies represent a kind of denial of the divine, that our corporeality is a waste product of divinity, and that our striving to attain freedom from it and ascend to higher worlds, where it possesses no significance, is justified.

Aristotle saw it differently from the viewpoint of the disciples of Buddha. Aristotle says that we take our supersensible element through the gates of death but must then look down on what we were during our embodiment and that our development in the supersensible world depends on that life in an earthly body. There was nothing useless in it. God put us into bodies because he saw it as necessary for our total development. He could not have provided us with that development if we had not been given a body. In other words, Aristotle valued the experience to be had in physical existence. Here the concern is not with concepts and abstractions but with the content of sensations. Buddhists do not have such a content of sensations, as I have often shown. They have a real feeling that human beings passed through a state of not knowing that brought them into touch with the sense world and that they must free themselves from that through which they have come into contact with the sense-perceptible world. There is a feeling in Buddhism that human beings are rightly human only after they have cast off all aspects of the physical, sense-perceptible existence. As an exponent of the spiritual life of the Occident, Aristotle could not share that feeling, nor can any who stand in the spiritual life of the Occident. They may persuade themselves that they do; they can honor the Buddhist point of view and

even take extraordinary pleasure in it, but that is always the result of dis-
avowing the feelings of their own souls.

It is characteristic of Western people to recognize divinity within the
sensible world, to see that world as imbued with spirit and permeated
with God. Even for those in the West who have been influenced by Buddhism and temporarily disavow the spirit inherent in the sense-perceptible world, a feeling for it continues to live within them and will always
be present. Precisely this valuing of the physical lived in Aristotle, not
for its own sake but as a necessary point through which evolution must
pass, as an essential prerequisite in the total evolution of humanity. It
was something that lived on in Western cultures until the nineteenth
century. It is one of the reasons why outstanding Western minds could
not befriend the idea of reincarnation. The feeling that the luciferic
principle is justified and the acceptance that the divine exists also in
external things worked together. This evoked feelings of a kind that I
want to comment on with reference to a man who truly belongs in the
category of the most profound personalities of the Western world.

I want to point out the presence of this feeling in the significant philosopher Frohschammer.[3] You will find it described in his book on the
philosophy of Thomas Aquinas. He set down in it a very extensive comparison of his own philosophy with that of Thomism, and there is a section where he expresses his feeling about the possibility of
reincarnation. He is certainly to be regarded as a representative of the
Western worldview—in other words, as a person in whom we can see
how difficult it was for the preceding centuries to acknowledge the
teaching of reincarnation, which must be a basic nerve of our pneumatosophy. Frohschammer says,

> Deriving as it does from God, the human soul can only be
> regarded as the product or work of divine imagination, for the

---

3. Jakob Frohschammer (1821–1893), liberal Roman Catholic priest and scholar of
Thomas Aquinas's philosophy. He wrote books on "generationism" (or traducianism),
which states that the soul is inherited materially, along with the physical body, from the
parents. His books were placed on the Index of works officially banned by the Church.
He was excommunicated in 1871.

human soul and the world itself indeed must originate out of divine force and activity (since nothing can derive from mere nothingness). Yet this force and activity of God must act as a preparation for creation and as formative forces for its realization and perpetuation—that is, as a creative force, not merely formal, but actual. It must be an imagination immanent in the world, continually working and creating, a sustaining force or potency; a world imagination, as was explained earlier.[4]

I would like to mention that Frohschammer also wrote a book entitled *Fantasy as a Basic Principle of the World Process*.[5] There he shows that fantasy itself is the universal creative principle. He presents fantasy as this principle, where Hegel indicates the idea and Schopenhauer the will. In this book he says:

As concerns the doctrine of the pre-existence of the soul (souls are regarded either as eternal or as transitory, but in any case created in the beginning and all together), a doctrine that has been resurrected in recent times and is considered capable of solving all sorts of psychological problems, it is connected with the doctrine of the transmigration of souls and their confinement in earthly bodies.

This was written in 1889. I indicated in the Karlsruhe cycle that there were always those in the nineteenth century who were exponents of the doctrine of reincarnation.[6] Frohschammer knew that too, of course, and therefore he continued:

According to this doctrine, neither the direct, divine creation of souls nor the creative production of new human beings, with regard to the body and soul, would take place at procreation,

4. Jokob Frohschammer, *Die Philosophie des Thomas von Aquino*, Leipzig, 1889, pp. 418–419.
5. Here the word *fantasy* (*phantasie* in German) indicates "imagination" in the more usual sense of the term—that is, a creative thought process.
6. Lecture of October 6, 1911, *From Jesus to Christ* (Sussex, UK: Rudolf Steiner Press, 1973).

but only a new union of the soul with the body. It is a kind of becoming flesh or a sinking of the soul into the body, at least partially, so that one part would be encompassed and bound by the body and the other would extend beyond and above it, asserting a certain independence as spirit. The soul, however, cannot break away from the body until death severs the union and brings liberation and deliverance, at least from this union. In that case, the spirit of the human being would resemble, in its relation to the body, the poor souls in Purgatory as they are usually represented on votive tablets by daubers, that is, as bodies half engulfed in roaring flames, but with their upper parts, the souls, protruding and gesticulating. Consider the position and significance this conception would imply for the contrast of the sexes, the concept of human species, wedlock, and the relation of parents to their children! The contrast of sexes would be but a system of bondage; wedlock, an institution for fulfilling the task this involves; parents, minions of the law for holding and imprisoning the souls of their children, while children themselves owe this miserable, weary imprisonment to their parents, with whom they have nothing further in common. Everything connected with this relationship would be based on wretched illusion, as would all that humanity associates with the contrast of the sexes.

What a formidable role the sex relationship plays! How greatly all the human being's aspirations are determined by it! What yearning it excites, what bliss it yields, what a source of bodily and spiritual transport! What an inexhaustible subject of artistic and particularly poetic creation! Now we are to believe that this contrast is but an arrangement for embodying and imprisoning poor souls that are thereby committed to earthly misery; consigned to the toils, passions, temptations and dangers of this earthly existence; rising at best with only a portion of their being into a Beyond, or as one says, the transcendental—or actually, transcendent. The significance of such a sex relationship, then, is not to be found in a continuous renewal, a rejuvenation corresponding to the spring of existence—quite the contrary. And the underlying longing and

rapture it engenders would not be based upon the satisfaction
of a lofty creative urge, as one would assume should be the case,
but would emanate from a pitiful ambition to imprison new
souls in bodily forms that obscure and estrange the greater part
of their real selves.

This, you see, is an individual who speaks sincerely and honestly out
of the spiritual life of his period. There is plenty of reason for us to
acquaint ourselves with the difficulties that Western thinkers of the past
centuries experienced with the problem of acknowledging what must be
the basic nerve of our own worldview. It is just in dealing with problems
as vital as those in these lectures that it becomes essential to be clearly
aware that people who come honestly to spiritual science encounter
great difficulties. One of our tasks as theosophists is not to take things
lightly, but to acquaint ourselves with the problems experienced by individuals who come from Western culture and want to lift themselves into
the life of the spirit as this is presented to us in general by spiritual science and in particular by what we can call pneumatosophy.

3.

Imagination—Imagination
Inspiration—Self-Fulfillment
Intuition—Conscience

W E SAW YESTERDAY that in a sense there is proof of the existence of the spirit for ordinary consciousness, if that consciousness has the appropriate self-understanding. We found that for this ordinary consciousness, to begin with, error and the possibility of overcoming error are evidence of the presence of spirit. In order to understand this, we drew on an attribute of the spirit that appears self-evident. We call it "supersensibility," for our case was built on the fact of error having to have its roots in the supersensible. I said that it obviously is not possible to cite all the details to thoroughly prove such a statement, though that could be done. It could actually be a very interesting matter to show how the possibility of error turns up first in the realm to which we ascend in freeing ourselves from the compulsion of the external world, in freeing ourselves from all that which we can know through sense perception. Only a single fact is needed to indicate the method that shows that only human beings can be exposed to the temptation of error as a result of their relationship to the physical world—that is, "exposed" through their own inner nature and being. It has been shown on other occasions how, in a basic sense, modern science, too, has provided proof for the findings of spiritual science. The only trouble is that the adherents of modern science do not interpret its proofs in a sufficiently unprejudiced manner.

Take, for example, a fact such as that established by the natural scientist Huber (1777–1840). He examined a caterpillar that was just spinning its cocoon. There are caterpillars that spin their cocoons in a series of stages, so that one can speak of their being in the first or second or third stage and so on. Huber took a caterpillar that had reached the third stage of its spinning and placed it in another caterpillar's cocoon that had already completed the sixth stage. A strange thing happened. The caterpillar that had reached the third stage only and had then been transferred to another cocoon, that of a caterpillar that had completed all six stages, continued calmly on its normal course, despite some problems, spinning not a seventh and eighth stage, but the fourth and fifth stages. It thus followed its instinctive course from the stage that it had completed on its own. In other words, it followed an unerring directive within its own being, an inner life that can follow only itself. When such a caterpillar that had arrived at the third stage was taken out of its own cocoon and put it into another cocoon where the third stage was complete, it calmly continued to finish this cocoon in a regular manner. There also it was following not an external impression but its own inner drive to spin the fourth stage after the third. However, it also did this despite receiving an external impression of already having completed the sixth stage.

This is an extraordinarily interesting fact, for it shows that in creatures of the animal kingdom, external impressions cannot bring about the effect that in human beings can be described as right or wrong, as belonging in the sphere of the possibility of error. We human beings are susceptible to error from external causes because we are so organized that we do not simply follow inborn drives and impulses; in our acts, we are obliged to follow impulses entering us from without. In that sense, we see that only human beings confront an external world. That is basically the source of all the delusions that people can harbor in reference to the spirit. There is a close connection here.

Today, to find from the scientific outlook the right link to our spiritual scientific view concerning the spirit, we want to look once again at how that intelligent, modern psychologist Brentano characterized the soul and its capacities. I will make a diagram to help us find the right transition to the realm of the spirit. Brentano divided the soul capacities, as I reported in the first lecture, into mental picturing, judging, and what we could call the movements of the soul—the phenomena of love and hate.

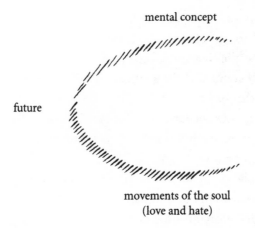

mental concept

future

movements of the soul
(love and hate)

If we think of the whole area of soul life as distributed in this way, we would have to say that on closer scrutiny, mental picturing and the movements of the soul are differently related to the soul than are judging and deliberating. That is just what that psychologist claims—he separates judging from mental picturing in such a way that judging is something different from a mere combination of mental images. I reported in the first lecture that judging is usually described as the product of combining mental images. "Tree" is a mental image, as is "green." "The tree is green" is a combination of mental images that would add up to a judgment. Our psychologist does not in the least regard that as judging, where a conclusion is involved, for he says—and all his reasoning is well-founded—that when it comes to combining mental images, it can also be a question of establishing the impossibility of combining them. An example might be an attempt to combine the mental images "tree" and "golden." If we are trying to combine these images instead of "tree" and "green" in a true statement, we would have to say that no tree is golden or something of the sort. What, in a case like this, is the prerequisite for making a judgment? It is that we have to make an existential statement in every such judgment and that this statement be valid. Out of the combination of the mental images involved in "The tree is green," we can form the existential statement "A green tree is." Then we have made a judgment. And only in trying to make the existential statement do we notice that the combining of mental images can establish a fact. "A golden tree is," however, does not work. The question, then, is whether a judgment can issue from a combining of mental images, whether an existential statement can be made.

Now I ask you whether, after examining the whole content of your soul life, you find it possible to shape an existential statement without the involvement of anything else but a combining of mental images. What impels you to shape the existential statement "A green tree is" out of the combination of mental images in "A tree is green"? Only something that is not, at first, present in your soul, for you can find nothing to support it in your whole soul content. And if you want to find the transition from a combination of mental images to an existential statement, to a sentence that decides something, you have to go beyond your own soul life to what you feel to be a relating of your soul to some element other than itself. This means that there is no other possibility of finding the transition from a combining of mental images to a judgment than by way of perception.

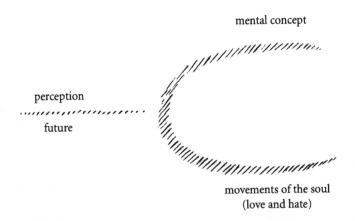

mental concept

perception

future

movements of the soul
(love and hate)

If what we can call perception is added to the combination of mental images, then and then only is it possible to say that we can form a judgment in the sense of this presentation. Then we have shown, however, that we cannot state anything else concerning our mental picturing than that it simply lives in our soul and that we need something more than what is in our soul if we want to progress from mental picturing to judging. When we consider the movements of the soul, or emotions, everyone will surely find it easier than it was in the case of mental images to reach a conviction that they live in the soul only, for they could not otherwise have such an individual character in such a variety of human beings. We do not need to waste many words about the fact that our emotions live in the soul.

Now let's ask whether it is at all possible to attribute existence to mental images and emotions in the soul, despite our awareness that they cannot afford us a judgment in the first place, since they are inner soul processes. If contact with the outer world does not take place through perception, if we cannot properly speak of percepts, the question has to be whether there is any justification to speak of our mental images and emotions as though they lived only in the soul. It might be pointed out where the life of mental images is concerned that individuals living in mental images do not have a sense of being complete masters of these images; they do not have a sense that there is nothing compulsory about them. If we keep in mind what was learned in the lecture of two days ago—that error is something spiritual, that it is supersensible, and that it can enter the realm of our mental images, and our mental images can, in turn, overcome error (for if they couldn't, there would be no possibility of surmounting error), then we would have to acknowledge that our souls are the scene of a battle between error and another element.

Error, however, is a spiritual element; consequently, we must have something to oppose to it that can hold its own; otherwise, we would never be able to surmount it. There is such a possibility. Everyone knows that. Since error is of the spirit, we cannot conquer it through purely external perceptions. In the lectures on anthroposophy, I pointed out that the senses cannot really err. Goethe once stressed this especially strongly. The senses cannot deceive; what goes on in the soul is the only source of error. It doesn't take much thought to see that error can be overcome only within the soul, and this by resorting to mental picturing. Mental picturing enables us to surmount error. We saw yesterday, however, that error is a distorted species of something else, of what was referred to as the element that lifts us into higher regions of our soul life. Error's basic characteristic is its lack of agreement with the world of perception. We realized that on the path that we have to take to enter the spiritual world, we also have to devote ourselves in meditation and concentration to mental images that are not in keeping with external perceptions. The rose cross was cited as an example of a mental image that does not harmonize with external perception and is, therefore, like error in that it is not consistent with external perception. We saw, however, that if error were to be used on the path of spiritual life, it would affect us destructively and that experience shows this to be so.

Now how do we arrive at mental images that have something in common with error in that they are not in keeping with the external world of perception but nevertheless awaken healthy higher soul forces in us in an entirely sound and proper way? How, in other words, do we come from a merely false mental image to a symbolic image such as has often been described and of which the rose cross is one of the most outstanding examples? We do so when we do not allow ourselves to be guided by the external sense world, the world of perception, or by the forces responsible for causing us to err. We must turn away from both kinds of influence, that of the external world of sense perception and that of the world that induces us to err. We must appeal to forces in our souls that have first to be awakened. They were characterized two days ago as stirrings prompted in us only by the moral and the beautiful. We have to break with our drives and passions in the way they are impressed into us by a world that can be described only as external. We must work upon ourselves to call forth on a trial basis soul forces that we do not as yet actually possess.

When we awaken in our souls forces not as yet actually in our possession, we attain the possibility of forming symbolic mental images that, in a certain sense, have objective validity, though it is a validity that does not apply to the world of percepts. We form something often described as the mental image of a human being standing before us as a being who, in a certain sense, cannot affirm itself, but must rather declare that its nature, as it is at present, must be overcome. Then we set beside this image another, one impossible to perceive because it belongs neither to the present nor to the past but to the future. It is an image that expresses the fact that human beings sense that they must strive to develop a higher nature, one that enables us to become master of everything not yet recognized as belonging to us in our present form. Then, out of such inner stirrings, we put together mental images that the world of percepts would never prompt us to connect. We put together the black cross, the symbol of everything that must be eradicated, and the red roses, the symbol of life that must sprout from it. In meditation, we picture the rose cross as a mental image that can only be described as unreal, but that we have not been able to put together in the way a simple error originates, but rather as born of the loftiest striving of our soul.

We have thus given birth out of our loftiest soul stirrings to a mental image that does not correspond to any external perception. If we make use of this mental image, devoting ourselves to it in deepest meditation and allowing it to take effect on our soul, we become aware that our soul is being developed in a wholesome manner and that it can rise to greater heights than it has reached before. We experience the fact that our soul is capable of evolving. Here we have a picture that in its relationship to the external world of perception really coincides with an error, at least to the extent that it does not picture anything from that external world. We have thus done something that leads to what is right, that leads to something that reveals that it, in itself, is right.

Now we ask ourselves if we can give everything entering us from external perception control over such a mental picture that has absolutely nothing in common with external perceptions? Can we lend it the power to exercise any force that will make of the mental image something different in our soul from what it makes of error? We have to answer that the element in us that makes of this symbol something so entirely different from what error could give rise to is the polar opposite of the force at work in error. And if, two days ago, we could say that we perceive luciferic forces in error, we can now say that in the transforming of the symbolic mental image that takes place in our own soul, in the wholesome guiding of the symbolic image to a higher level of perception, it becomes apparent that we have in the lofty stirrings we sense in ourselves the divine spiritual element that is the exact opposite of the luciferic.

As you ponder this connection more deeply, you will see more clearly that through the inner experience of transforming a symbolic picture you directly perceive and sense the inner activity of the supersensible. When it becomes apparent that the supersensible acts in us, that it causes a certain completion and strengthening, then something very different grows from what was previously a mere image in the soul, from what lived within the soul. This must now be referred to as a conclusion, something not produced by the soul as it exists initially. Perception can produce a conclusion in the act of judging. Similarly, a mental image can inwardly accomplish the result just described by means of the process I have delineated. Just as a mental image coming, as a result of perception, into contact with the ordinary external world leads to judgment, so does the inner life of the mental image, which is not directionless but allows itself to be guided in the manner described, lead beyond itself as a mere mental image and become something that, though it is not a judgment, makes it a meaningful image, pointing beyond the soul. This is what we may call *imagination* in the term's true meaning.

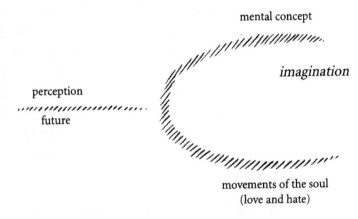

mental concept

imagination

perception

future

movements of the soul
(love and hate)

So we may say that the mental image, in coming into connection with the external world, points on the one side to judgment, and in undergoing the described process, points on the other to true *imagination*. Just as a percept is not simply a mental image, so an *imagination* is not merely a mental image. Through perception, the life of mental pictures touches an external world that is still undefined at first. Through the process described, mental imaging moves into what we could call the imaginative world. Just as there is, in fact, a transition from simply putting mental pictures together in "A tree is green," to the judgment "A green tree is," so, too, there exists a transition from simply the life of mental images to what lies in the filled image in the *imagination*. This image is not filled from some external spatial world. Thus, we have the process before us that fills the pictures in imaginative life.

Now there is something occupying a position between *imagination* and mental picturing. The nature of *imagination* is such that it makes its reality keenly felt at the moment it appears. When our soul really achieves *imaginations*, it senses in its life of mental picturing something entirely similar to its life in perception. In the latter, it feels itself in immediate touch with an external physical world. In imagining, it feels itself immediately in touch with an external world, but an external world of the spirit. When it enters mental images that are really pressing toward *imagination*, that spirit is as compelling as the material world is. We find it difficult to imagine a tree as golden while we are connected with external reality. Such contact compels us to imagine in a specific way, and it is only our contact with the outer world that compels us. Similarly, we experience a sense of necessity exerted by spirit when mental representation rises to the level of *imagination*. When the mental images rise to imagination, however, we know at once that the life of mental images goes on independent of all the routes whereby mental images otherwise make up their content. In ordinary life, mental images fill themselves with a content derived from percepts conveyed by our eyes and ears and so on, all of which provide the nourishment for their life. In imagining, we allow the spirit to do the filling of the mental pictures. Nothing springing from the bodily organs that might affect our soul content is allowed to participate; nothing that enters through our eyes and ears may or does take part. There we have a direct awareness of the fact that we are free of everything that might have its source in our bodily makeup. We are as free of all that as we are when, looking at the matter in an unprejudiced way, we can say that we are free in sleep of all the processes of our physical body. For a person engaged in imagining, everything is as it is in sleep, the only difference being that imaginative consciousness takes the place of sleep's unconsciousness. That which is otherwise empty, that which has separated itself from the body, is filled with the mental images of *imagination*. There is no other difference between a person sleeping and another imagining than that ordinary sleepers are outside their physical bodies with a consciousness empty of mental images, in a certain sense, whereas those imagining are filled with mental images.

An intermediate state can also come about, in that a sleeper might be teeming with imaginative mental images but lack the power to bring them to consciousness. That could happen; it is a possible condition. You can see from ordinary life that it is possible. I will just call your attention to the fact that in your ordinary life you perceive a great deal that you do not bring to consciousness. You may, for example, walk along a street perceiving all sorts of things, but much of it unconsciously. Often you can convince yourselves that you've perceived things unconsciously when, for example, you have a dream about strange things. There are dreams that are very strange in this respect. Imagine, for example, dreaming of a man standing with a woman and saying something to her. You remember the dream. You have to admit, as you think it over, that such a situation did indeed take place, but you would not have known of it if you had not dreamed about it. This same man and this woman actually stood before you somewhere, but you paid no attention to them. Only when you were free of all other impressions and began to dream did this otherwise unnoticed picture enter your consciousness. Such things often occur; thus perceptions that really did arise can leave the consciousness completely untouched.

Imaginations, too, can live in the soul without registering in our consciousness; they cannot appear immediately as *imaginations*. Then they enter into our awareness in a way similar to the perceptions just described. Such perceptions that we have had without registering them appear occasionally in the semiconsciousness of dreaming. In the same way, *imaginations* that we have not had the power to register in consciousness can shine into our waking life and become active there, transformed as dreams are, fluctuating and flowing into such perceptions that would ordinarily stand clearly before us. Thus it happens that such *imaginations* actually intrude into what is otherwise everyday awareness, undergoing thereby a transformation when what is termed *fantasy* is active in our consciousness, genuine fantasy based on cosmic truth, the true source of all artistic and other creation that springs from human productivity.

It was because of that fact that Goethe, who was well acquainted with the artistic process, so often stressed that fantasy is by no means an element that assembles phenomena in an arbitrary manner but that it is subject to the laws of truth. The laws of truth work entirely out of the world of *imagination*. Only because they take effect in everyday life do they undergo change and interweave with the everyday content of consciousness, shaping the world of ordinary percepts in a free way. Thus we really have in genuine fantasy something midway between mere mental picturing and *imagination*. When fantasy is not conceived of as something of which it can be said (as often happens), "Fantasy is not true," but rather when it is realistically grasped, it bears witness to a further development of mental images in the direction in which they can pour themselves into the realm of the supersensible, the world of *imagination*. Here we have one of the points where we can witness the streaming of the spiritual world directly into our ordinary world.

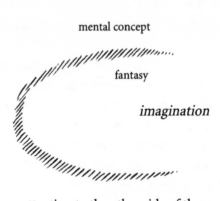

mental concept

fantasy

imagination

Now let's turn our attention to the other side of the matter, the side of the emotions. It has already been stated that the soul investigator whom we are discussing remains within the realm of the soul and therefore follows the impulses of the will only to the point of examining the emotions. When a person carries out an action, underlying that action, of course, is a desire, a passion, a feeling, or an urge that, looked at from within the soul, is considered an emotion. Nothing happens through an emotion alone, however. So long as we remain in the soul, nothing needs to happen. We can experience an emotion very intensely but still nothing is achieved that should be achieved through the will, namely, that something takes place that is independent of the soul. What remains within the soul is not a true expression of the will.

If the soul were never able to go beyond itself, if it experienced only in desiring this or that emotion, ranging from reverence to deepest disgust, nothing would happen independent of the soul. We must, therefore, say that in having to recognize the will in its true form as a fact, the whole realm of emotion directs us beyond the soul. The realm of the emotions, however, points beyond the soul in a most unusual way. To where, then, does it direct us? In the case of simplest acts of will—moving a hand, taking a step, striking a table with an object, doing anything in which the will is involved—we can see that, in reality, something occurs that we can call a transition of our emotions, the inner impulse to action, to something that is no longer within our soul and yet, in a certain way, is still within us. What happens as the result of a genuine will impulse that brings our body into motion and causes such activity to continue into an external act is not by any means summed up in the soul's content. For no one can follow all the actions that run their course from the decision to lift a hand to actually lifting it. On the one hand, we are led by our emotions into an external element, but it is an external element of an entirely different nature—our own exterior, or bodily nature. We descend from the soul into our own corporeality, but we do not understand how we do that in external life.

Think what an effort we would have to make if instead of moving a hand, we had to construct some apparatus to do the same thing by means of springs and so on, producing the same effect as if we were to say, "I want to pick up the chalk" and move a hand to do so. Picture what would have to be set up in order to have a tool accomplish what goes on between the idea of wanting to pick up the chalk and actually lifting it. Just think of everything that you would have to do! We cannot conceive of it for the simple reason that we are not capable of it, and there is also no such device. One does exist in our human organism, however. Something occurs in the world that is very clearly not in our consciousness. If it were in our everyday consciousness, we could easily fashion such a device. If we knew everything that goes on between the idea "I want to pick up the chalk" and actually lifting it, we could construct the corresponding apparatus to do the job. There is something taking place that must be counted as belonging to our bodily nature, yet it remains wholly unknown to us.

We must ask, "What would have to take place to make us aware of the activity behind the movement of one's hand or another willed bodily movement?" A reality that is outside us would have to rise into consciousness instead of stopping short of it. It would require the kind of process that takes place in our own body without entering consciousness—a process just as external but intimately connected with us in the same way that one's hand movement is for consciousness. Thus, we would have to have something that belongs intimately to us and yet plays into us as though from outside, something that we would experience in our soul and yet be experienced in the soul as an outer element. It would have to be as artfully constructed as a device for picking up a piece of chalk and be similarly based on firm external laws in our consciousness. Something would have to enter our consciousness that would then work lawfully within it. Its nature would be such that we would not think as we do with other kinds of willed activities, such as when we say, "On the one hand there is a thought of picking up the chalk, and on the other, firmly separated from it, something beyond my knowledge—a process that, at best, I can view as a perception of something outer." In fact, these two things would have to coincide, to become exactly the same thing. The event would have to be directly connected with soul awareness, coinciding as though all the aspects of the motion of the hand took place not outside consciousness but within it. It is this process that takes place in *intuition*.

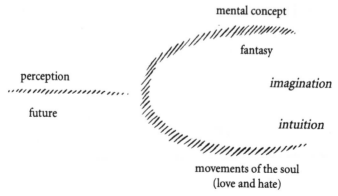

mental concept

fantasy

perception

imagination

future

intuition

movements of the soul
(love and hate)

We can, therefore, say that when we grasp with our own consciousness something that lives entirely within it, not as mere knowledge but as a process, we are dealing with *intuition, intuition* in the higher sense described in *How to Know Higher Worlds*. Thus, within *intuition* we are dealing with the wielding will. That extremely intelligent psychologist Brentano finds only emotions among the ordinary aspects of the soul and not a trace of will, because it is not present there, since the will lies outside normal consciousness. Only the consciousness rising into the higher regions finds in itself something that at the same time is a process. That is where the world enters into consciousness. That is *intuition.*

Here, too, there is another transition, only it is not as easily noticed as the transition from mental picturing through fantasy to *imagination*. This transition occurs when we learn to observe ourselves such that we are not able merely to will something and then carry out an action, simply having thought and action separated by a gap. It is when we begin to extend our emotions over the quality of our acts. That, in many cases, is quite difficult to do, but it does happen in life that we can have a kind of pleasure or revulsion at our own actions. I do not believe that an unprejudiced observer of life can deny that it is possible to extend the emotions to allow the characteristics of our own state of being to stream into our actions to the point that we have what can be described as sympathy or antipathy for an action in our emotions. This experiencing of our own actions in our emotions can be heightened. When it is intensified to the point where it becomes what it should be, the transition between emotion and *intuition* is what we can call human conscience, the stirrings of conscience. If we try to locate conscience, we find it in this transition. We can, therefore, say that our soul is open on two sides—to *imagination* on the one side and to *intuition* on the other. It is closed on the side where, through perception, we come up against our physical bodies. Our soul experiences fulfillment on entering the imaginative realm and again, coupled with an event, on entering the realm of *intuition.*

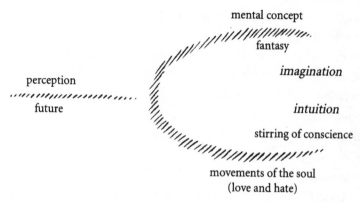

mental concept
fantasy
imagination
intuition
stirring of conscience
movements of the soul
(love and hate)
perception
future

Since both *intuition* and *imagination* have to occupy a single soul, how can some sort of mediation, a kind of connection, come about between them? We have in *imagination* a picture, a filled image, of the spiritual world, and in *intuition* an event that the spiritual world precipitates. An event that approaches us in the ordinary physical world disturbs our peace. We try to find out about it and discover its underlying essence. That is also true of that event that is in the spiritual world and penetrates our consciousness. Let us examine that more closely. How does *intuition* enter our awareness? We must first seek it in the direction of the emotions. It penetrates into our consciousness, into our soul, but from the side of the emotions rather than from that of mental picturing. That is how things stand with *intuition*; it can penetrate our consciousness, our soul, without our being able to make a mental image of it. We said of *imaginations*, too, that we can have them without being aware of them. They come into fantasy because they work directly within mental picturing, but we must put *intuition* on the other side, on the side of emotions. In the whole of human life, *intuition* lies completely on the side of emotions. At this point I would like to give an example that I recently spoke of, a well-known dream.

It is about a couple who had a son. He was taken ill quite suddenly, and though he received all possible medical help, he died the same day. His parents were deeply affected by his death. They became totally absorbed in thinking about him, that is, their memories were completely occupied with him. One day it became apparent that during the night both parents had had the same dream. They told each other about it. You can find this dream referred to by a more or less materialistic investigator of dreams, who goes through all kinds of contortions to explain the dream but cannot deny its existence. The parents reported that in the dream, their son appeared to them and besought them to have his grave opened, for he had been buried alive. The parents made every possible effort to find out whether that had actually happened, but they lived in a country where the authorities would not allow the grave to be examined after the passing of so much time.

Now what will enable us to understand this dream, which I have brought up only to throw light on the relationship of *intuition* to the emotions? You can assume at once that, because the parents' memories were so constantly occupied with their son, who was present in the spiritual world as a spiritual being after dying, their thoughts built a bridge to him. The directing of their thoughts created a bridge that connected them with the continuing individuality of the son. You certainly will not be able to accept that there was nothing more than a subjective element in the revelations of the dead son that must have been present after all the veils separating the living and the dead had been penetrated, because both parents had the same dream. Or it might be so-called chance that both dreamed alike, but then everything imaginable could be explained away in that way. In reality, however, there was a connection that night between the son and his parents, and he did tell them something or, rather, instilled something into their souls. Since the parents were quite unable to raise to consciousness what he had communicated to them, it was only the dream image that contained familiar mental images that stood like a shield in front of the real occurrence. The son wanted to communicate something of an entirely different nature, but the parents had to clothe it in a mental image that they took from the material of their usual conceptual life. This presented itself as a dream that obscured the nature of the actual event.

Let us take another dream. A farmer's wife dreams that she goes to church in the city. She dreams every phase of the experience: how she enters the church; how the minister stands there with his hands uplifted, preaching with extraordinary ardor; and the enthusiasm this engenders in her. Now a strange transformation comes about. The preacher's shape changes; he receives wings and feathers and a different voice that more and more resembles a crowing. Finally, he changes completely into a crowing rooster. The woman awakens to hear a rooster really crowing outside the house. As you can well imagine, it was the crowing of the rooster that caused the whole dream. You will also have to admit that this crowing could have been the cause of many other dreams. Some young rascal could have dreamed that he was startled by the crowing of the rooster and had then perhaps dreamed that he had thought about something for a long time, for instance, how he could open a lock. Then another, more clever rascal gave him a suggestion that turned into a rooster's crowing. You see from this that the mental image that obscures the reality need have nothing to do with what the soul actually experiences. What did the parents experience, for example? They experienced a connection with, a revelation from, the son that flowed straight into their souls. In the other case, the farmer's wife was a very devout woman, reveling completely in an atmosphere permeated with piety. She had really experienced that. As she was wrenched from sleep, she still had the sense of having been somewhere else, but her entire consciousness was claimed by the rooster's crowing, which obscured the experience by appearing to be the preacher in the church. Soul experience thus becomes what is dreamed.

When individuals become practiced in relating dreams to reality, it appears that before they come to the inner reality, they must pass through a soul state of being uplifted or of grief, in short, of some tension or release of the feelings. The mental images related to the experiences in the spiritual world usually dissolve into a kind of nothingness. One has to form very different mental images of the actual events. In other words, spiritual events are closer to the emotions than to mental picturing, since the mental images are not all relevant to the soul-spiritual events. The events that project into our emotions during sleep are in the spiritual world, but we are unable to reach far enough with our capacity for mental picturing to discern and identify them.

Thus, it is possible to show that *intuition* also stands in a particular relationship to the emotions. That is why mystics have a kind of vague, dim experience of the higher worlds before forming clear mental images of them. Many such mystics are satisfied with that and many with even less. Those who truly meditate in the higher worlds, however, all describe in the same way the soul conditions of devotion, their frame of mind in directly experiencing the spiritual world.

If we wanted to progress further through this *intuition* that plays into our feelings, we would not succeed very well, for that is better undertaken from the other side. In order to avoid a general wallowing in emotions and to come instead to a concrete seeing of the spiritual world, we must try to develop *imaginations* and turn our attention to them regarding that world. Then a connection is gradually established in our lives between *intuition*, which is still more merely sensed rather than understood, and *imagination*, which consists of images only and is still more or less afloat in unreality. We discover the connection when we finally approach the thought that we have now come to the beings that can carry out the spiritual deed. Our arrival at those beings, we call *inspiration*.

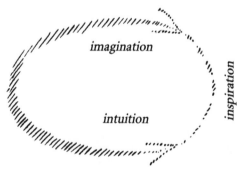

We have here, in a sense, the reverse of the processes that we find in the external, corporeal world. Here we have the thoughts we form about things, whereas there, the things simply exist, confronting us, and we form thoughts about them. Here, the thing or event that first appears in *intuition* for the emotions is completely indistinct, and the *imagination* as such would hang in the air. It is only when the two come together and *imagination* works via *inspiration* into *intuition*, when, in other words, our mental imaging leads further to *imagination* and we sense the *imagination* as coming to us from beings, that the essence of these beings streams into us as a process. *Imagination* provides us with something that streams in from *intuition*, and we perceive in the event a content that may be likened to the content of the mental image. We perceive these thoughts, for which we have prepared ourselves by means of *imagination*, to be contained in the event that *intuition* has given us.

I have described to you today how, on the other side of our soul life, we human beings grow into the spiritual world. I have, of course, anticipated a few matters that spiritual science alone is able to contribute from spiritual research, but it was necessary to do so in order to be able more easily to understand the main topic of tomorrow's lecture, a description of the uniqueness, the essential and unique nature of the spiritual world itself.

4.

Nature, the Evolution of Consciousness, and Reincarnation

S INCE THERE was time for only four lectures at this general meeting, it is certainly understandable that only a very short and, in a sense, superficial sketch of what pneumatosophy might be can be given. It is natural that much has been so lightly touched upon in such scanty indications that a good deal more elucidation and detail are awaited. It may even be difficult in some places to see what the connection is between the subject and what we have been calling pneumatosophy. Yesterday, for example, it was shown how we advance from the soul realm, or mental images, on the one hand, and from our emotional life, on the other, to regions whose whole nature requires that they be considered a part of the supersensible world. It was seen that this is what they are from the simple fact that the soul realm stops prematurely at a certain boundary line in relation to such matters. Even intelligent psychologists have had to halt at that point in their investigations of the soul. The kinds of concerns we encounter in *imagination, inspiration,* and *intuition* are, of course, familiar to theosophists from other perspectives.[1] Thus, we can assume that the subject that has grown familiar from completely other viewpoints, such as in my book *How to Know Higher Worlds,* is seen as justified when all the threads are followed that lead from the everyday life of the soul—from mental picturing, the emotions, and judging—to *imagination, inspiration,* and *intuition.*

---

1. Steiner's early articles on *imagination, inspiration,* and *intuition* are collected in *The Stages of Higher Knowledge.*

It is very natural that, in order to advance from matters of soul to those of spirit, people pay closest attention to the aspect of soul most familiar from their own soul and spiritual life in attempting to gain self-knowledge of a soul-spiritual nature. It has been pointed out in these lectures that within Western development up to the nineteenth century and even until our own time, humankind has found it difficult to recognize a fact that seems basic to us. The fact we are speaking of is that our human spirit passes through more than one earthly life. At the end of the second lecture, we familiarized ourselves with the typical struggles exemplified by the psychologist Frohschammer, whose scientific honesty led him to ask how it could be that our eternal spirit could be thought to descend again and again into a physical body that resembles a kind of purgatory or a kind of dungeon or prison. Must we, he asked, regard everything that has to do with love relationships and the contrast between the sexes only as devices for imprisoning people's souls for the period between birth and death?

In view of such sincere objection to the doctrine of reincarnation, it is necessary to ask whether Frohschammer is taking one standpoint—that is nothing more than that, one standpoint—and whether still some other viewpoint isn't possible. We will have to grant Frohschammer his sincere enthusiasm for all the beautiful and glorious aspects of life. For it is from the spiritual life of the West that he drew the enthusiasm he felt for the external world and for everything that is great and beautiful in it. It seemed to him that the reincarnation doctrine was attempting to say that there is an eternal spirit in the human individual that is capable of leading a good and blissful life in the spiritual world and that is being thrust into and imprisoned in a world not in the least suited to its lofty nature. If that were asserted, people who are rightly enthusiastic about the beauty and grandeur of God-given nature, of historical evolution, and the ennobling passions and drives of which the soul is capable, might well rise up and rebel with Frohschammer. They might object against souls being subjected to reincarnation and thereby doomed to repeated imprisonment.

Is that the only possible view of the matter? We have to admit that there are indeed people among the supporters of the reincarnation doctrine who share Frohschammer's idea that the human spirit descends from lofty heights to what amounts to imprisonment in the body. Views like this, however, are just a collection of vague ideas about repeated earthly lives, not what spiritual science is in a position to offer as the fruit of spiritual research. We must ask whether it cannot be acknowledged that the situation into which we are born upon entering life between birth and death is marvelously beautiful and grand and that the human being as encountered in the physical form is indeed a kind of image of the godhead, as the Bible says. That would suffice to make us enthusiastic about it. Then, too, it would have to be admitted that we are not transferred to a prison but set down, on being reincarnated, in a wonderfully beautiful place, into a glorious dwelling. Does it actually depend on the house and its size and beauty whether we feel that we belong there and can be at home in it, or, rather, does it depend more upon whether we have traits that imprison us there? Does what we feel really depend on the house at all, or does the fact that we, as individuals inhabiting it, feel it imprisons us because, despite its beauty and grandeur, we do not know how to use it and feel chained there? The fact that the house we live in is beautiful and that the bad part is at worst that it is just we ourselves who are lifelong prisoners in it, is demonstrated by the spiritual observation that rises, by way of *imagination* to *inspiration* and *intuition*, to true insight into the element in the human being that passes through different earthly lives.

The first experience that we have as we go in reverse sequence from the life of mental picturing into the imaginative world is a world of pictures. Into this world, in every time, the most different kinds of people have entered. If we take this imaginative world that can be revealed on the basis of careful concentration, meditation, and so forth, or upon the basis of special capacities of the soul, purely according to its manifestation, then it presents itself at first as the rudiments and remains of the yet external sense-perceptible world. The human being sees all kinds of things in that imaginative world, such as houses, animals, people, and this or that event, that really play out pictorially. We have before us scenes and beings in a very living world of pictures. On the other hand, that imaginative world has the characteristic of belonging to the supersensible, in a certain sense, in that people cannot simply arbitrarily determine the symbols or pictures. They underlie an inner lawfulness that leaves its imprint upon them. Particular supersensible relationships are expressed in particular symbols and pictures. Where the imaginative world is concerned, we can be quite sure that in all circumstances, we will find that a specific stage of our soul development, a specific capacity, lives in certain regions of the supersensible world, characterized in pictorial imaginative form as being handed a chalice, or being led through a river, or being baptized, and so on. It can also happen that we have unpleasant experiences, like seeing our various characteristics approach us symbolized in animal forms, either as huge terrifying beasts or small scrabbling, crawling ones. Of course, it is impossible, since we find ourselves dealing with a world far richer than our sense world, to give an adequate description of this first level of the imaginative world that the human being can reach.

It must be said that on the whole this world, even when it presents itself in its most unpleasant and horrible aspects—and we have to admit that such unpleasantness is symbolic of our own nature—is still something that the beholders find fairly pleasing. Its usual aspect is such that those beholding it overlook the quality of the experience and are quite happy that they are in the spiritual world at all. That is perfectly understandable. For even when it is distinctly horrid, the spiritual world entered is not hard to bear, being basically a world of pictures. Only if we lack sufficient strength and are thereby overwhelmed or weighed down by this world does it destroy our healthy soul life.

A sense of moral responsibility or a feeling of responsibility toward all creation does not necessarily follow such viewing of the imaginative world. Indeed, the exact opposite can be the case. It can happen, for example, that individuals who have reached a high degree of perfection in their perceiving of this world become morally loose in regard to their feeling for truth and untruth. There, the clairvoyant is sorely tempted to take the truth pertaining to the physical world lightly and then not to develop a special sense of responsibility with regard to truth. It is, in a sense, a calamity that with imaginative clairvoyance something like an incapacity to distinguish between the objectively true and the false can occur. Standing firmly in that world and having the capacity to give it its proper meaning is a question of development. We can actually be quite undeveloped as human beings and still have the imaginative world before us. We can have many, many vision-like *imaginations* of the higher world, but we do not need to stand particularly high as human beings. As I said, it is a question of development.

With time, development helps us to learn the difference between various *imaginations*, just as we learn to differentiate in the physical world. Differentiating in the physical world, however, occurs at such an early age that we normally do not give it any consideration. In the physical world we do not confuse a tree frog with an elephant. We learn to differentiate among various phenomena. We learn to separate and to arrange them to make the physical world appear orderly. People initially confront the world of *imagination* as though they were in the physical world and were about to confuse a frog with an elephant, unable to differentiate between them. The world of *imagination* seems homogeneous and it all appears to have a uniform level of importance. We must first learn to be able to give one thing more weight and another less. A peculiarity of that world is that it does not appear large or small to us because of its own nature but because of *our own*.

Suppose, for example, that a man is very arrogant. His arrogance is pleasant to him. But if the world of *imagination* now opens to him, the feeling of pleasure in his arrogance carries over to become the size of the beings he sees there. Everything in the world of *imagination* that represents arrogance or pride appears gigantic. To him, it appears to have tremendous importance. On the other hand, something that would seem large to a humble person appears to him to be small, like a tiny frog. The perspective that world presents all depends on the characteristics of the viewer. It is a question of human development that the proper relationships, intensities, and qualities of that world be accurately recognized. Everything there is quite objective, but people can distort it and then see caricatures. The important thing is that along with this knowledge of the supersensible, people must, in a certain way, experience what they themselves are. That means that people must learn to know themselves in an imaginative way. That is, of course, fatal, because the perspective for what is in the imaginative world is completely determined by the person's own qualities of soul; it can be directed in a false or a proper sense.

What does it really mean to say that we have to learn to understand ourselves through *imagination?* It means that we have to confront the self in the world of *imagination* as an objective image among all the *imaginations* and images there. Just as we confront a bell or any other object in the physical world, we must confront ourselves in the world of *imagination* in objective reality, as we truly are. This can be achieved appropriately only through ascending (by means of meditation and the like) from perception of the external world to the life in our mental images. This can be accomplished by imagining very specific symbols as already mentioned, in order to free ourselves from the external world and learn to live in the purely inner life of mental picturing long enough to experience that life as something natural. We then notice something in the nature of a splitting of our being, of our personality. Often we have to pull ourselves together to avoid letting a particular condition develop too much. When this condition develops, we gradually come to experience a mental image in which we live and become wholly absorbed, so that we no longer say, "I am what my body is." Instead, we have before us an *imagination*: "That is you! That is how you are." Then it happens that we occasionally notice how the other part of our being, which had not freed itself, acts as though it were an automaton, that we are living above and beyond it but that it nevertheless has a desire to talk automatically, gesticulate, and so on. Unschooled individuals sometimes discover themselves making all sorts of grimaces, because they have pulled something out of themselves with the *imagination*, and the leftover part of them engages in all sorts of automatic behavior. That is something that should not be allowed to go beyond the point of experimentation; it must be kept under control. We must always bring ourselves to the point of having our own being outside us, as we do material objects..

Regarding the *imagination* that we are to develop, it is of tremendous importance that we should already have developed certain qualities of soul, for all sorts of illusions crop up at this point in imaginative self-knowledge. All that is human conceit and all that comes from the human capacity for illusion, which may arise from the most varied characteristics, lurk in the background. We can see all kinds of things in the imaginative world. Among the variety of things experienced there, we naturally discover a feeling for ourselves, and it is typical to consider oneself the cream of the crop. When people see themselves in the imaginative world and want to draw a conclusion about what they were earlier, such that they could now be such an extraordinary child of humanity, they arrive at the conclusion that, at the very least, they must have been historically a person of very high rank—a king, for example. It happens repeatedly that clairvoyant novices become convinced that they were Charlemagne, Napoleon, Julius Caesar, Marie Antoinette, or some other great historical figure in a previous incarnation. The reason is that these people, imprisoned in a body though they are, seem to themselves in self-perception as so significant that they must have been extraordinary individuals in a past earthly life (they can even mistake themselves for a saint or someone equally exalted). At one point, the Marquise de Pompadour, Marie Antoinette, Frederick the Great, the Duke of Reichstadt, and various other most impressive personalities were all gathered around the same table. You may laugh, but such things are in fact very serious. Such matters make us see that the way individual souls appear to themselves depends completely on their own imaginative experience.

We learn to know our own being when we really free ourselves completely from ourselves, when we proceed with every bit of our energy to rid ourselves of the characteristics that we ordinarily recognize to be intolerable, that are bound to affect others as objectionable, that we carry around with us constantly, and, if we think about it objectively, that we should not have. We should take these matters to heart, for it is not a case of saying things that will please everybody but of saying things that are true and that are meant completely objectively. You can be sure that if we set about it objectively enough, we have a full-time job criticizing ourselves, and only in an instance of most extreme necessity, compelled by outer circumstances, should we engage in the commonplace human activity of criticizing and complaining about others. Those who spend much time judging others or criticizing them may be certain that they are losing the time needed to discover in themselves what they must discover and to rid themselves of what they must rid themselves to attain true imaginative self-knowledge. If, after occupying themselves with spiritual science a long time, people ask why they have not advanced or achieved sight in the spiritual world, the answer that they could give themselves may be quite obvious. It might be that they should take care to abstain from all criticism of others except when extreme necessity requires it and, above all, to learn what such abstention really means. For many people forget, as they begin their day, what that means. It means occasionally to accept from others treatment that can be unpleasant and unfortunate in life. We must be able to accept it, for we know, if we take karma seriously, that what others do to us is something that we have inflicted upon ourselves. Karma requires that it be done to us.

It takes endless effort to arrive at imaginative knowledge of ourselves. Then one begins to see why Frohschammer's picture of imprisonment does not fit the facts. You notice that your life is actually such as to compel you to say that being incarnated, having the life you are living on the Earth, could be beautiful, wholly wonderful and glorious, but you aren't in tune with it. You cannot seem to undertake everything you could with the body you have and in the place you have been set down with it. You come to realize that you are living at a particular time and place in a beautiful world teeming with grandeur, that you have bodily organs responsive to it and to all that is glorious and impressive. An unprejudiced feeling has to say that the world we live in is a paradise. We ought to say this even when things are going very badly indeed. It is not a question of how we are getting along but of whether the world is glorious and beautiful, for if we are having a hard time, our karma could account for it. How the world is depends only on the world itself and may not be judged according to our personal standpoint. Our bodies and organs have been given to us for full reception of what the world has to offer, for the greatest satisfaction and delight.

There is a vast difference between what we could be drawing from our life in this paradise, in our existence between birth and death, if we were to take all it has to offer, and what we actually take. Why do we take so little? That is because something is embodied in our corporeality that is small in comparison with the universe and that allows only the smallest portion to be taken. Just compare what your eyes see in the course of a day with what they really could see, and you have the ratio between what you might take in and what you truly absorb.

Through such knowledge we experience our extraordinary relationship with spirit. When we come to know ourselves in spirit, we sense that we are not as well suited to it as we might be if we were to put our entire organization to use. Now we discover that something else in the cosmos must counteract what imaginative self-knowledge shows us to be. We come here to an interesting situation. And we must allow it to have complete effect in our souls if we are determined to have self-knowledge. Once we become truly familiar with ourselves in the world of *imagination*, it is impossible to think of ourselves—compared with the surrounding world—as beings of great and noble nature, as though we were from a higher world and set down in an earthly prison. Indeed, we find that we fail instead to measure up to this earthly prison. How infinitely more we could do with our bodies if we could use them completely. This is the way it actually is and why the universe (which corrects our inadequacies that result from our failure to fully use our physicality) confronts what we are in the world of *imagination*. It would be tempting to compare the two spheres in full detail. The whole cultural evolution of humankind, from the beginning of Earth to its finish, confronts what we are in the imaginative world. Why does the world of cultural development from the beginning of Earth to its end stand over against what we appear to be in our own *imagination* in an incarnation, in our existence between birth and death?

If we want to answer this question, we come to understand that what we cannot become in a single incarnation has to be achieved in a series of many lives in the course of Earth's evolution. We have to keep coming back. We long for new incarnations so that we can gradually become what we cannot become in a single life. It is just when we develop insight and a feeling for what we could be in a single incarnation, but cannot be because of our inner nature, that we know what our predominating feeling must be as we pass through the gates of death. It must be to come again in order to become in the next and all following earthly lives what we cannot be in a single life. This must be the strongest driving force, this longing of ours for ever further incarnations during Earth evolution.

This thought can only be suggested. If you think it out further, you'll be able to see that the strongest confirmation of reincarnation results. That this statement can be made rests upon still another consideration. We can continue our efforts to enter the spiritual world. I've said that we come purely technically to imaginative self-knowledge by withdrawing our attention from all external perception and devoting ourselves as described to the life of mental picturing. There is another possibility of giving meditation and inner concentration a certain turn. It consists of trying in uttermost faithfulness and conscientiousness to let what we call memory run its course. We need to do so for a few hours only, but the effort must be a truly earnest one. What are we really in ordinary life? We discover through our contemplation, as well as through logic and the theory of knowledge, that we are individually an I. In ordinary life, however, we are this I in a very questionable sense. In ordinary life, it is very questionable what fills this I. Our impressions of everyday life are what make us what we are at any given moment. People playing cards are what the impressions of card playing make them. They are not the I then; they are, but not in the sense of being conscious of it. For what we genuinely have in our consciousness are the impressions of ordinary life. We can certainly try to reach our I, but it is something highly variable, flighty, and fluctuating. We get behind what we are in reality only when we give ourselves up to memories and view them in such a way that, whereas they are normally behind us, they are now in front of us. That is an extraordinarily important process.

Essentially, we are always the results of past experiences living in our memory. You can see in small matters that we are products of our memory. Imagine, for example, that you've had a day full of unpleasant events. Now imagine the way you feel in the evening and how the day has affected you. You are irritable and negative; you turn up your nose at things and so on. Compare this with a day full of satisfying experiences, and what are you? You are joyous, smiling, pleasant to be around, maybe even enjoyable. You are no more real on one occasion than on the other, since you are essentially the product of past experiences.

When we review the experiences behind us, going backward through them, then we set them in front of us and we are ourselves behind them. If you do that seriously, not in a routine, mechanical way, but if you really live further into them in a very vivid way, even if for only a few hours, then something enters your soul, if it is sufficiently able to pay attention to itself, that one might call a fundamental tone that you yourself seem to be. We can sometimes experience that we appear to ourselves to be a bitter, acid-bitter fundamental tone. If you then go to work on yourself thoroughly, which again really depends on your development, that process will rarely show you to yourself as a sweet being. Rather, you will, as a rule, find yourself to be a bitter being; you will find a bitter fundamental tone in yourself.

That is the truth. Someone who is capable of applying the requisite attention to him- or herself will in this way gradually arrive at what may be called an inspired self-cognition. The path leads through bitter experiences, but then one truly appears to oneself to be like an instrument badly out of tune. In the world of the harmony of the spheres, we usually cause a discord at first.

As our self-knowledge increases, we realize more fully how incapable we are of making the most of this glorious, divine nature from which we could derive so much if we were only equal to it. If we do such an exercise often and repeatedly, we are forced, as the decline of our life approaches—after one has passed the age of thirty-five—to recognize from the peculiar sounding of our basic tone that it can be interpreted only as a sign that we have much, very much, to do in the way of improving the efforts begun in our present incarnation. It can only be interpreted to mean that we must long with all our power to be clothed again in such a physical body so that we might correct what we neglected in this present life. The desire to be reincarnated is one of the most important consequences of attaining self-knowledge. People who are repelled by the thought are simply revealing how far all that they have garnered of the glorious divinity of the nature they were born into falls short of what is possible.

The second thing achieved is, therefore, the inspired human being, when individuals recognize themselves in the spiritual world of tone as they come there in the previously characterized way. What we experience there on learning to recognize our own tone is how little we measure up to what surrounds us in the great world outside. At this point, we can go from the merely moral aspect to that of destiny and take note of how little we are able to achieve the inner serenity and harmony in life that we so desire. Individuals empowered by self-knowledge will, if they adhere to it, often have to admit how little they can find that peace and certainty in themselves that they most crave. To characterize this, we may be reminded here of a beautiful passage in one of Goethe's writings, in which he describes sitting on a mountain peak that exemplified the peaceful order of nature and seeing spread out before him that "oldest son of nature," granite. He senses the inner consistency, the grandeur of nature's lawfulness, its tranquillity, which is in such contrast to the inward movement and the alternating between pleasure and suffering, between ecstasy and despair, that are the basic inner tone of human nature.

When we begin with such a mood and look at the laws of nature that existed when human beings lived under quite different cultural conditions long ago and that still govern nature today, we will realize something that it would take ten or twenty lectures to deal with adequately. Just as cultural development is the counter-image of the imaginative picture of the human being, the world of the true, natural laws is the counter-image of the inspired human being. Despite the element of maya, natural laws reveal to us the world of spiritual activity with the calmness and consistency that human error turns into restlessness and disharmony. And we identify them as such when we recognize the inspired human being within us. Now, the thought may arise that, if we recognize the laws of nature in their true essence, we will realize that earthly evolution transforms from one manifestation to another, from stage to stage. We also know that something inherent in those laws allows us to know that, as we pass through our various incarnations, we receive what we must during Earth's ongoing evolution, since the possibility for it already exists within the scope of a single incarnation. We will find at the end of Earth's existence the conditions in the outer world that, because of the inherent steadfastness and dependability of natural lawfulness, will compensate for what we spoil as a result of insufficient development as inspired human beings.

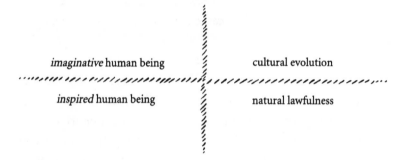

Thus we see a deep connection between what lies spread out as laws of nature, as the deeds of the spirit in the natural world, and what appears to us as a kind of counter-picture when we discover the deeper human being in us through *inspiration*. For this reason, the inner serenity and harmony of the lawfulness of nature were always featured in esoteric life and in the mysteries of all ages as the model for our own inner order. It was not for nothing that those who attained the sixth degree of initiation were called "sun heroes," to indicate that their own inner being had achieved such order and that they could just as little err from that appointed path because of their inner regularity and their inner certainty than the sun could stray from its course through the cosmos. If it were to do so for a single moment, indescribable chaos and destruction would have to take place in the cosmos.

There is, of course, a further stage of self-knowledge. We could progress to an intuitive knowledge of the human being. That means an ascent into heights so lofty that it would be difficult to characterize it or what appears in the external world as a counter-picture of the intuitive human being. Keep in mind the situation that is pictured in the preceding diagram. We have the possibility of looking at what we are inherently capable of being in that glorious creation, the external world in which we are "imprisoned"—not imprisoned because it is a bad world but because we fail so drastically to measure up to it.

We see here that very important matters depend on correctly assessing all the cosmic relationships; they depend on realizing the basis of the spiritual knowledge of human nature that contemporary humankind can receive through spiritual science. Any objections to it are usually based on complete misinterpretations of cosmic circumstances.

Finally, we must ask why it became necessary for us to be embodied. To further illustrate the answer, I will remind you of lectures by Dr. Unger on the position of the I—the "I am"—in terms of our whole inner life. I will also remind you of what I presented on this subject in *Intuitive Thinking as a Spiritual Path* and in *Truth and Science.* A slight effort in thinking is certainly enough to show us that important beings exist behind the I, the "I am." But what we first experience, we experience only in our consciousness, precisely in our I-consciousness or self-awareness. This is interrupted every night in sleep. If we were only to sleep and never awaken, then, in spite of the fact that we could be an I, we would never, of ourselves, notice that we are. Upon what, then, does becoming aware of the I depend? It depends upon our experiencing ourselves as we are while we are awake, using our physical bodies and organs and confronting the entire physical world. We must experience our I-being in our body.

If we never descended to Earth to make use of a body, we would eternally sense ourselves as just a part of an angel, say, or of an archangel, in the way a hand feels itself to be part of our organism. We would never be able to come to an awareness of our independent being; that would be absolutely impossible. We could develop all sorts of contents of consciousness, experience all the great aspects of the universe, but never could we develop an I-consciousness without entering a body. It is from the body that we have to derive our I-consciousness. When you study the sleep state and what dreams reveal, you see that there is something working in them that is independent of the I. Imprisonment in a body and making use of our senses and our brain is essential to I-consciousness. When, as we have seen, we make very incomplete use in a single

incarnation of all we've been given to use, we should find it quite understandable, rather than surprising, that clairvoyant consciousness says
that to the extent we truly investigate a human I-being, to the extent
that we see it in its true form, we will discover within it as its primary
force a desire to return again and again to the Earth in a new body in
order to develop the consciousness of the I continually further and to
make it ever richer and richer.

In this respect, we duplicate in our own individuality what the theosophists of the eighteenth century so often said, something that, when we
transform it into spirit-knowledge or pneumatosophy, can be extraordinarily helpful to us. How did theosophists of the eighteenth century,
such as Oetinger, Bengel, and Volker, whose writings appear so primitive to us in comparison with the spiritual science of today, express the
meaning of the spiritual activity of the gods (or, as they put it from their
monotheistic standpoint, of God himself)? They had a very beautiful
formula for expressing the basic attribute of the divine spirit. They said,
"Bodily nature, the world of matter, is the end of the paths of God."
That is a wonderful saying. It meant that the impulses inherent in the
godhead had prompted it to traverse many worlds of the spirit and
descend in order to come to a kind of end, an end from which it turns
around in order to rise again. This end is the shaping, the crystallizing,
of divine beings in the bodily form.

Translated into terms more expressive of inner reality, what the theosophists of the eighteenth century were saying was that, looked at from
the standpoint of higher worlds, the spirit is seen to be thirsting for
embodiment and that this longing is stilled only when embodiment is
achieved, when the end of the paths of God is reached in the corporeal
and the return journey begins. This saying was a beautiful one, more
illuminating and revelatory of the occurrences in the being of the
human than much that the philosophy of the nineteenth century had to
offer. Although there was absolutely no theosophical work or activity
going on in the first half of the nineteenth century particularly, and
none in its second third, theosophists of the older sort were still to be
found in the first half of the eighteenth century. What was missing in
their insight was something that was lacking due to suppression by the

development of Christianity in the West: the knowledge of repeated earthly lives. The early theosophists knew that material embodiment was the goal of the spirit-path of the godhead, but they did not recognize it as applying to human beings also. In human beings they would have had to see that human nature is such that at every further incarnation, the longing must arise for still further embodiment, until our incarnations have rendered us mature enough to be able to go on to other forms of existence.

With the ending of these lectures on pneumatosophy, I feel more keenly than ever how sketchy and merely indicative a picture could be given in these four hours. And the same thing holds true for the lectures on pneumatosophy as for the two previous series on anthroposophy and psychosophy: they were meant to serve as indications only. You will find, if you pursue them, that they contain rich material that can be worked with in a great variety of ways. To do so, you will need to look about you in the world and draw on many resources to corroborate what could be offered here in a brief and cursory form only, in a sort of "charcoal sketch," instead of giving it the stretch of time it would have taken to form a complete picture. Because spiritual science is so comprehensive, if we were to proceed in the systematic way in which other sciences work, we would not have arrived, after ten years' work in our section, at the point where we now stand. We would perhaps be only at the point where we were at the end of the first quarter of the year. Let me say, as we end this cycle, that we count on individuals in our community having the serious will and the independent impulse to go on working on what was given here as indications. Much will surface in such independent work from those regions that could not even be mentioned, and everyone will be able to find, in his or her way, the starting point for the work. Each of you will be able to convince yourself, when you proceed in an independent way, that our community will best stand the test if the feeling for inner independence becomes greater and greater. It is the feeling that you receive something that motivates you in such a way that your inner being comes more and more to experience the world that can be opened to humanity through that spiritual stream we refer to as "theosophical."

Further Reading

Works by Rudolf Steiner:

Anthroposophical Leading Thoughts. London: Rudolf Steiner Press, 1998.

The Anthroposophic Movement. London: Rudolf Steiner Press, 1993.

Anthroposophy (A Fragment): A New Foundation for the Study of Human Nature. Hudson, NY: Anthroposophic Press, 1996.

Christianity as Mystical Fact, trans. Andrew Welburn. Hudson, NY: Anthroposophic Press, 1997.

Cosmic Memory. Blauvelt, NY: Garber Communications, 1990.

Cosmosophy, vol. 1, Hudson, NY: Anthroposophic Press, 1985.

The Effects of Esoteric Development. Hudson, NY: Anthroposophic Press, 1997.

The Foundations of Human Experience. Hudson, NY: Anthroposophic Press, 1996 (previous translation titled *Study of Man*).

How to Know Higher Worlds: A Modern Path of Initiation, trans. Christopher Bamford. Hudson, NY: Anthroposophic Press, 1994.

The Human Being in Body, Soul, and Spirit. Hudson, NY: Anthroposophic Press, 1989.

Intuitive Thinking as a Spiritual Path: A Philosophy of Freedom, trans. Michael Lipson. Hudson, NY: Anthroposophic Press, 1995; also, The Philosophy of Spiritual Activity: A Philosophy of Freedom, trans. Rita Stebbing. London: Rudolf Steiner Press, 1992.

An Outline of Esoteric Science, trans. Catherine Creeger. Hudson, NY: Anthroposophic Press, 1998.

Psychoanalysis and Spiritual Psychology. Hudson, NY: Anthroposophic Press, 1990.

The Riddles of Philosophy. Anthroposophic Press, Hudson, NY, 1973.

Rudolf Steiner, An Autobiography. Blauvelt, NY: Garber Communications, 1977.

Spiritual Beings in the Heavenly Bodies and in the Kingdoms of Nature. Hudson, NY: Anthroposophic Press, 1992.

The Spiritual Guidance of the Individual and Humanity. Hudson, NY: Anthroposophic Press, 1992.

The Spiritual Hierarchies and the Physical World: Reality and Illusion. Hudson, NY: Anthroposophic Press, 1996.

The Stages of Higher Knowledge. Hudson, NY: Anthroposophic Press, 1967.

Theosophy: An Introduction to the Spiritual Processes in Human Life and in the Cosmos, trans. Catherine Creeger. Hudson, NY: Anthroposophic Press, 1994.

Toward Imagination: Culture and the Individual. Hudson, NY: Anthroposophic Press, 1990.

Truth and Knowledge. Blauvelt, NY: Rudolf Steiner Publications, 1981 (also *Truth and Science.* Spring Valley, NY: Mercury Press, 1993).

A Way of Self-Knowledge, trans. Christopher Bamford. Hudson, NY: Anthroposophic Press, 1999.

Works by Other Authors:

van Emmichoven, F. W. Zeylmans. *The Anthroposophical Understanding of the Soul.* Hudson, NY: Anthroposophic Press.

Kühlewind, Georg. *From Normal to Healthy: Paths to the Liberation of Consciousness.* Hudson, NY: Lindisfarne Press, 1988.

—— *The Life of the Soul between Subconsciousness and Supraconsciousness: Elements of a Spiritual Psychology.* Hudson, NY: Lindisfarne Press, 1990.

—— *Stages of Consciousness: Meditations on the Boundaries of the Soul.* Hudson, NY: Lindisfarne Press, 1984.

Sardello, Robert. *Facing the World with Soul: The Reimagination of Modern Life.* Hudson, NY: Lindisfarne Press, 1992.

—— *Love and the Soul: Creating a Future for the Earth.* New York: Harper Collins, 1995.

Soesman, Albert. *Our Twelve Senses: Wellsprings of the Soul.* Stroud, UK: Hawthorn Press, 1998.

Treichler, Rudolf. *Soulways: The Developing Soul-Life Phases, Thresholds, and Biography.* Stroud, UK: Hawthorn Press, 1989.

Index

A

action, and emotion, xxix
aesthetics, 72–73, 123–26
Aham ("I"), 32
Angeloi (angelic beings), 30
angels, xxxv, 30, 31, 220
animals, 24, 25, 60, 61, 69, 189
  are never bored, 101
  physiology, 51–52
  soul experience, 65, 101–2
anthropology, 6–7, 49
anthroposophical work, soul element
  in, x
anthroposophists
  dysfunctional, ix–x
  errors made by, xxiv
anthroposophy, vii, xxxi–xxxiii, 9–
  10, 13–14, 68. *See also spe-*
  cific topics
  groundwork for, 17–18
  initiatory path of, as psychospiri-
    tual endeavor, x
  meaning, 4
  psychology and, ix–xi
  vs. theosophy, 4–5
  as the wisdom that humans
    speak, 5
Anthroposophy (A Fragment), xxii
Aquinas, Thomas, 184
archai, 30n
archangels, xxxv, 30, 31, 220
archetypes, xiii

Aristotle, 164–69, 171, 173, 176, 181–
  83
arrogance, 211
art, 73, 123–24. *See also* aesthetics
artistic endeavors, x
associations, healing effect of eliciting, xx
astral body, xx, xxxi–xxxvi, 10–11,
  22–23, 26, 27, 43, 45–46, 51,
  66, 147–48
  definition, 136
  origin, 55
astral substance, 30–31
astrality, 28, 31
Atma, xxxi–xxxiii
Atman, 22
attention, 115–16. *See also* concentration
aversion, 80

B

balance, sense of, 15, 23–26
beauty, 124–26. *See also* aesthetics
behavior, trying to explain based on
  past, xix–xx
believers *vs.* scientists, 172–73
Bergson, Henri-Louis, 91
blood, 52
  circulation, 65
  as ruled by spiritual beings, 52
  as changing, xxxvi
  as closed *vs.* open system, xxxii

expressions, xxxvii
feeling for well-being of, xxxiii
living human, xxxii
psychology, xxxi, xxxii, xxxiv,
    xxxv
wholeness, xxxiii–xxxiv, 11
border phenomena. *See* soul life,
    boundaries
boredom, 100–103
cure for, 103
brain, 48, 84
Brentano, Franz Clemmens, xv, 151–
    52, 158–65, 169, 171, 189,
    201
phenomenological method, xv–
    xvi
Buddhi, xxxi, xxxii, xxxiv, 22n, 23.
    See also life spirit
Buddhists, 183

C
Catholic Church, spirit prohibited
    by, 157–58
chakra, 38n
Christ Being, xxxv
Christianity, 157–58, 164, 222
clairvoyance, xxxi, xxxiii, 51, 59,
    136–37, 150, 177, 210–11
dim, 59
color. *See* perception; sight
comprehension soul. *See* intellectual
    soul
concentration, xxv, 180, 193. *See also*
    attention
concept, sense of, 18, 34, 36–38, 64.
    See also visualization
concepts, self-movement of, 175
conscience, xxv–xxvi, xxviii, 210
as transition between emotion
    and intuition, 201–2
consciousness, xiii, xxxi, xxxiii, 132,

133, 197, 201. *See also* clair-
    voyance
consciousness soul, 27, 28, 44, 45, 71
cosmic development, 10n
cosmic events, 4
cosmology. *See* planets
countenance, human, 63
creativity, xxviii, 185. *See also* imagi-
    nation
criticizing others, 211, 213–14
currents, 66–67, 70–72, 122. *See also*
    astral body; etheric body;
    physical body; sentient
    body; time

D
death, 167, 216. *See also* reincarna-
    tion
decision making, 117–19, 121–22.
    See also judgment
desire, xi–xii, 80, 92, 114–19, 128. *See*
    also under judgment
origin, xi
satisfaction, 120–21, 134–35
devil, 181–83
discomfort, 99–100
distinguish, failure to properly, 104
divinity, 183–84, 194
doubt, 119
dreaming, 197, 202–4

E
Earth, 66–68
ego, *vs.* "I," xxiv
ego-consciousness, xxiii–xxiv
ego-personality, xiii, xvi–xviii, xxiii
egotism, xxvi
Eleusis (Hegel), 109–12, 130, 131
embodiment, xxxi–xxxvii, 220, 221.
    See also body
embryonic development, 60–61

emotion, 161–62, 192. *See also* feelings; *specific emotions*
    action and, xxix
    will and, xxix
Ephesus, 8
error, 179–81, 192–93
    originates in spiritual world, xxv
    spiritual element, 192
    transforming into truth, 177–79
ether body, 10n, 21, 30
etheric body, xxxi–xxxvi, 21–23, 28,
    43, 46, 51, 54, 66, 138, 140,
    144
    inner fulfillment, 142–43
    meaning, 136, 139, 149
    origin, 55
Eucken, Rudolf, 174
evolution, 60–61, 64–65
    cosmology and, 10–12, 55
    cultural, 219
experience, essential qualities of, xvi

F
fantasy, xxvii, 197–98, 201
    as universal creative principle,
    185
"feeler," 27
feeling soul, 43
feelings, 113, 117. *See also* emotion
    based on satisfaction *vs.* frustra-
    tion, 121
    related to past *vs.* future, 134
Feuerbach, Ludwig Andreas, 176
flower. *See* lotus flower
folk spirits, 30n, 31, 37
form, language and meaning of, xiii
Frederick the Great, 49
Freudian approach, 150
    sexuality and, 150
Frohschammer, Jakob, 184–87, 208–
    9, 214

frustration, 120–21
future, 190, 191
    moving toward *vs.* being pushed
    from behind, xx
    teleological imagination of, xx
future time, xx–xxi

G
God, 181–82
Goethe, 37, 72–73, 77, 94–96, 130,
    131, 148, 192, 218
group souls, 65–67
Günther, Anton, 157

H
harmony, 34–36
hate, 80–83, 87, 113, 135, 161–62
    origin, 82–83
hearing, sense of, 17–19, 30, 34–35
heart, 12–13
    evolution of, 12
Hegel, 109–12, 130, 131, 148, 173–
    75, 185
Heraclitus, 8–9
Huber, 188–89

I
I-being, xxiii, 43, 92, 140–41, 147
I-consciousness, xxiii–xxiv, 90–94,
    128, 142, 146, 220
    cannot exist at night, 145
    development, 139–40
    interplay between soul life and,
    xxiv
"I," group
    of animals, 65
"I," the, xxii–xxiv, 32, 51, 65. *See also*
    spirit
    bias against, xxiv
    vs. ego, xxiv
    forgetting, 99

illness, 103
imagery, autonomous, xxviii, xxix
images, xv, 83, 91, 97–99, 107–8,
    126–27, 160–64, 190–92. *See
    also* concept, sense of; imag-
    ination
    autonomous, xxviii
    contemplation of, xxv
    as response outward from within,
        133
    "stream of," 133–35, 138, 149
    symbolic *vs.* real, xxv, 90, 180,
        193, 194
imagination, xxvi–xxviii, 7, 195–98,
    201–2, 205–6, 211–12, 215
    creative, xxvii
    spiritual, xxvii, xxix
    development of healthy, xxvii
    true *vs.* illusory, xxvii
imaginative sense, 38–39
imaginative world, 209–13
impatience, 118
incarnation, 6, 166–68, 215–21. *See
    also* reincarnation
initiation
    secrets of human, 109–12
    work of, xvii
inspiration, xxvii, xxix–xxx, 7, 38–40,
    205, 209, 219
    recognizing the qualities of, xxx
intellectual soul, 27, 28, 44, 46, 58,
    61, 71, 72
intellectuality, mode of, xvii–xviii
introspection, xvi
intuition, xxvii, xxix, 7, 38–40, 200–
    206, 209, 219

J
judgment/judging, xiv, xv, 46, 79–84,
    97, 104–6, 141, 146, 195.
    See also criticizing others

aesthetic. *See* aesthetics
    as attempt to reach final conclu-
        sion, xiv
    desiring and, 87–89, 92, 116–19,
        122–24, 127
    as fusing concepts, 160–61
    vs. interest, 137
    as "mulling over," xiv–xv, 119
    perceptual, 82–83, 116, 145–46
Jungian psychology, xxvii

K
Kant, 115
karma, 152
knowledge, 4. *See also* "not-knowing"

L
language, 32–33, 104–7, 128–29. *See
    also* speech
life body. *See* ether body
life-feeling. *See* life sense
life force, 10n
life sense, xxxii–xxxiii, 14–15, 21, 22
    experience of, xxxiii
life spirit, xxxiv, 22n, 23. *See also
    Buddhi*
Lipps, Theodor, 152
listening, 99
lotus flower, 38–40
love, 36, 80–83, 87, 113, 135, 161–62
    origin, 82–83
love-hate tension, xiii
Lucifer, 181–83

M
Manas, xxxiv, 22, 23
materialists, 174–76
meditation, xxv, xxxiv, 180, 193
melody, 34–36
memory, xxiii, 69–71, 128, 133, 143–
    45, 149, 150, 216

mental illness, xxvi, xxx
mental images. *See* images
Minotaur, 14
mirrors and mirroring, 138–40, 142,
    143, 175, 177
Moon, 11, 12, 55
moral responsibility, 210
moral sensibility, xxv–xxvi, xxviii,
    201–2
moral soul force, importance of, xxvi
motor nerves, 84
mousetraps, 25
musical tones, 34–36
Mysteries, 130

N
narcissism, xviii
natural lawfulness, 219
nervous system, 48, 84–85
"not-knowing," xxi
    capacity to live consciously in, xxi
"not-yet," xx, xxi

O
Occident, 182, 183
organs. *See* physical body, anatomy;
    specific organs
otoliths, 24
outer world, 78–80, 87–89, 97
overtones, 38

P
past, aspects of
    autonomous existence in soul life,
    xx
past lives, 58. *See also* reincarnation
perception, 39–41, 59, 85–86, 90, 93,
    114, 116, 133, 191, 194
    vs. apperception, xix
perceptual judgment, 82–83, 116,
    145–46

philosophers, 8–9, 158, 173. *See also*
    specific philosophers
philosophy, 8–9, 158
physical body, 10, 43, 46, 54, 66, 147
    anatomy, 11–13, 45–48, 54, 56,
    58, 84–85, 113–14
    as denial of the divine, 183
    organ symmetry, 54
    origin, 55
    outer world revealed to soul
        through, 78–80
    soul life and, 78
planets, 10–12, 55, 55n, 56
plant world, 24–25
pneumatosophy, vii, viii, xxiv–xxv,
    xxx, 171–72, 184, 187, 207,
    222
"possibilizer," xxi
present, living in the
    creating one's responses to each
        moment, xxi
pride, 211
primal beings. *See archai*
projection, 211
psychoanalysis. *See* Freudian
    approach
psychological imbalance, xxvi–xxix
psychological mode of thought, xvii–
    xviii
psychological thinking, xv–xix
    art of, xviii
psychologists, 98. *See also specific*
    psychologists
psychology, xv–xix, 171. *See also*
    spiritual psychology; *specific*
    topics
    categories, xviii
    function, xiv
    intellectual training, xvii
    method, xvi–xvii
    misuse, xvii

new foundation, ix
pop culture, xii
scope, xii
psychopathology, xxvi, xxx
psychosophy, vii, viii, xi, xvii–xix,
    xxxviii, 158, 171
    as deliberation on soul, xv, 77

R
reason, 173, 176
reasoning capacity, 131
reflection, 119
reincarnation, 58, 166, 168, 184–85,
    208–9, 213, 216–18. See also
    incarnation
reliving life, while living it, xv
remembering. See memory
responsibility, sense of moral, 210
Rose Cross, xxv

S
satisfaction, 120
Saturn, 55, 56
Schopenhauer, Arthur, 27, 114, 185
science, 4, 26, 172–73
self
    forgetting one's, 99
    habitual, xvii
    higher, 5
self-absorption, xxvi
self-awareness. See I-consciousness
self-interest, freedom from, xxv
self-movement, 174, 175
self-movement sense, 15, 22–23
self-perception, 41–42
sensation, 39–40, 86, 89, 116–17
    vs. feeling, 120
sensation body, 43, 45
sense of life. See life sense
sense organs. See physical body, anat-
    omy

sense-perceptible human being, 42
senses, xxxi–xxxv, 13–14, 113–14. See
    also intuition; perception;
    visualization; specific senses
    cannot err, 192
    of comprehension, 19
    definition, 17
    higher vs. lower, xxxv, 17, 19–20,
    40, 69
sensing, xxxi, xxxvi
    and the body, xxxi, xxxii
sentient body, 28–29, 41–45, 51, 56–
    57, 63
sexuality, xx, 150
shadow sides of soul, importance of
    facing, xxvii
sight, sense of, xxxv, 16–17, 28
    vs. hearing, 20
sleep, 92, 145
smell, sense of, xxxiv–xxxv, 15, 19,
    20, 25, 27, 28
Soesman, Albert, xxxiv
Solger, 7, 9, 10
soul, xi, xiii, 37n, 43. See also con-
    sciousness soul; intellectual
    soul
    activity of, lies beyond soul, 122–
    23
    apperception of, xix
    cannot be homogeneous, 95
    capacities, 189–91. See also spe-
    cific capacities
    denial of, 171–72
    as medium for spiritual experi-
    ence, xxvi, xxvii
    movements of. See hate; love
    perception of spiritual world,
    xxii, xxiv–xxv
    picture/image of, 63
    from the place of soul, xii–xiii
    relation to outer world, 79–80

sentient, 28, 29, 41–42, 56–57, 63
shadow sides, importance of facing, xxvii
speaking within, xvi–xvii
wisdom of. See psychosophy
soul body. See astral body
soul development, xxiv
soul experience
to develop capacities for experiencing spiritual worlds, xxx
as I-experience, 90
inner and essential characteristics, 80
life of desire as origin of, xi
as reintensifying of what we encounter, xv
soul life, x, xv, xviii, 78. See also psychosophy; spiritual psychology
ability to control, xi
boundaries with body and spirit, xxii, xxvii–xxxi, 42–43, 80, 85, 87–89, 117, 120, 122, 123, 126, 147–48
consciously standing within, xvi
contradictions in, 97
gives interiority to experience, xv
lack of control over, 99
qualities, x–xi. See also hate; judgment; love
phenomena that derive from, xxi–xxii
study of, 126–27
as subject matter of psychology, xi–xv
understanding, xxviii
soul pathologies vs. soul-spirit pathologies, xxx
soul-spirit, xxxvi–xxxvii, 162
soul time, xix–xxi

soul world, 87
speech
pronunciation, 32–33, 67
sense of, 18–19, 64
tones of, 31, 34–36, 67–68
speech development, 64–65
spirit. See also "I"
Aristotle's view of, 164–69, 173
autonomous nature of, xxii
bias against, xxiv
self-movement of, 174
Spirit Body. See Atman
spirit human being. See Atman
spirit self. See Manas
spirit-soul. See soul-spirit
spiritual beings. See angels
high. See folk spirits
spiritual capacities
developing, without moral balance, xxvi
spiritual experience, foundation of, xxv
spiritual hierarchies, 30n
spiritual perception. See also intuition
development, 38
spiritual practice(s)
destructive, xxvi–xxvii
without soul life, x
spiritual psychology, xxi–xxx
all psychology must be, xxiv
as psychology of future human beings, xxvi
spiritual research, 60
spiritual science, 10n, 50, 52, 57, 61, 63–64, 169
future mission, 72
spiritual truths, verification of, 52
spiritual worlds
developing capacities for experiencing, xxx

entry/intrusion into soul life,
xxviii, xxix
perception of, xxii, xxiv–xxv,
xxvii–xxviii
between world of nature and, 5
static sense. *See* balance
Steiner, Rudolf, vii, x–xi, xx, xxvii,
xxxvi, 151n
An Outline of Esoteric Science,
xxv, xxxii, xxxv, 10n, 179
Anthroposophy (A Fragment),
xxii
How to Know Higher Worlds,
xxii, xxvi, 4, 179, 201,
207
methods of, xv–xvii
psychological mode of thinking,
xviii
speaks from soul, xvii
Theosophy, xxxii, xxxv, 10n
Sun, 10–12, 55
"sun heroes," 219
supersensibility, 166, 176, 178, 180–
82, 188, 192, 194, 198, 210
symbolic images, xxv, 90, 180, 193,
194
symmetry *vs.* asymmetry, 54–56

T
taste, sense of, xxxv, 16, 19, 27, 28
temperature, sensing of, xxxv, 19n,
29–30. *See also* warmth
theology, anthropology and, 7–8
theosophical path, 5
theosophical *vs.* anthropological
view of humans, 11
theosophy, 3–5, 9, 10, 13, 50, 174,
221, 222
Theosophy (Steiner), xxxii, xxxv, 10n
therapy, goals and purpose of, xxxvii
thinking, xviii, 40, 48, 131–32

dead, xviii
thought(s)
purely logical, 40
speaking and perception of, 64
time, xx–xxi, xxiii, xxxvii, 101–3,
132–35, 140, 147
time beings. *See archai*
time body, xxxvii
tone, 18n, 39–40
sense of, 31. *See also* speech
touch, sense of, xxxv, 18–19, 26
science's disastrous views of, 26
truth, 173–78, 182, 198. *See also*
error
capacity to discern, 131
truth seeking, 125

U
Unger, Carl, 50, 59, 91, 181
Universal Being. *See* Christ Being

V
visualization, 65, 97. *See also* concept, sense of
origin and development, 67–68
vital force, 10n, 21. *See also* life force

W
Wachsmuth, Guenther, 3
warmth, sense of, 17, 19, 29. *See also*
temperature
will, xix, xxix, 28, 128–29, 162, 163,
198–200
words
going beyond, xiii
sense of, 31. *See also* speech
Wundt, Wilhelm, 152

Z
Zimmerman, Robert, 9

During the last two decades of the nineteenth century the Austrian-born Rudolf Steiner (1861–1925) became a respected and well-published scientific, literary, and philosophical scholar, particularly known for his work on Goethe's scientific writings. After the turn of the century he began to develop his earlier philosophical principles into an approach to methodical research of psychological and spiritual phenomena.

His multifaceted genius has led to innovative and holistic approaches in medicine, philosophy, religion, education (Waldorf schools), special education, economics, agriculture (Biodynamic method), science, architecture, drama, the new arts of speech and eurythmy, and other fields of activity. In 1924 he founded the General Anthroposophical Society, which today has branches throughout the world.

Freud, Jung & Spiritual Psychology

5 lectures, Nov. 1917; Feb. 1912; July 1921
(CWs 178, 143, 205)

Rudolf Steiner
Introduction by Robert Sardello

ISBN: 978-0-88010-492-0
Paperback, 144 pages

"Imagine, just for a moment, how many people in the world practice psychotherapy, how many are patients of one therapy or another, and how many are now involved in the growing numbers of therapeutic groups focused on various addictions. One might think that a great deal of 'soul work' goes on here. But, due to the fundamental errors at the very founding of the discipline, it may well be that psychotherapy is oriented toward conquering soul rather than entering into soul wisdom....

These lectures on psychoanalysis and spiritual psychology, given at the very time when the 'talking cure' was in its beginnings, force us to confront the inadequate knowledge used in founding psychoanalysis and psychotherapy as a method of soul work.... A truly spiritual psychology leads to wisdom of the soul [and] not only takes us out of the limited domain of psychology as concerned with subjective states and into the broader culture, it also takes us into an understanding of the body as the necessary organ through which spiritual perception must find its orientation."

—from the introduction by Robert Sardello

In these five talks, Rudolf Steiner laid out the foundations for a truly spiritual psychology. The first two lectures take a critical look at the principles of Freud and Jung's early work. The last three lectures describe the threefold structure of human consciousness and then outline a psychological approach that considers both the soul's hidden powers and the complex connections between psychological and organic, bodily processes.

Robert Sardello, codirector of The School of Spiritual Psychology, contributes an important and provocative introduction from the perspective of a practicing psychotherapist.

www.steinerbooks.org

Jung and Steiner
The Birth of a New Psychology

Gerhard Wehr, Foreword by Robert Sardello, Afterword by Hans Erhard Lauer

Translated by Magdalene Jaeckel

ISBN: 978-0-88010-496-8

Paperback, 340 pages

A series of extraordinary questions begin to hover when we consider C.G. Jung and Rudolf Steiner together.

What is the relationship between their views of psychology? How can we compare their views on evil, East and West, life after death, technology, clairvoyance, the Christ, alchemy, spiritual practice? Is Jung's individuation process the same as Steiner's development of individuality? How does the Jung's Self relate to Steiner's "I"?

To answer these questions, Gerhard Wehr—an anthroposophist and C.G. Jung biographer, as well as author of books on the Western spiritual tradition—visualizes Jung and Steiner and the essential elements of their thinking together. This opens us to new insights and forms a basis for a spiritual psychology that integrates both approaches.

Wehr's skilled and articulate understanding of Jung and Steiner takes us into many themes. He clarifies the difference between soul consciousness and spiritual consciousness. He shows how meditation relates to the image work of the soul; and he compares the soul and spiritual views of sexuality.

The author also considers the Grail stream as a way of uniting Jung and Steiner. He discusses the significance of a therapeutic perspective large enough to address the cultural problems of our time. By approaching two such important worldviews with depth, they are enlarged, strengthened, and revitalized. If taken to heart, this work can free both the spiritual science of Steiner and the analytic psychology of Jung from the dangers of dogmatism. This work marks a significant step toward genuine spiritual psychology.

www.steinerbooks.org

CPSIA information can be obtained
at www.ICGtesting.com
Printed in the USA
FFHW02n0707070818
47629177-51202FF